In cooperation with the council of the Center for Economic Studies of the University of Munich

The Economic Ef
of Constitutions

The Economic Effects of Constitutions

Torsten Persson and
Guido Tabellini

The MIT Press
Cambridge, Massachusetts
London, England

This book was set in Palatino on 3B2 by Asco Typesetters, Hong Kong, and was printed and bound in the United States of America.

Library of Congress Cataloging-in-Publication Data

Persson, Torsten.
 The economic effects of constitutions / Torsten Persson and Guido Tabellini.
   p.   cm. — (Munich lectures in economics)
 Includes bibliographical references and index.
 ISBN 0-262-16219-9 (hc. : alk. paper)
 1. Constitutional law—Economic aspects. I. Tabellini, Guido Enrico, 1956– II. Title.
III. Series.
K3165.P474   2003
338.9—dc21   2003046343

10 9 8 7 6 5 4 3 2 1

To our mothers

Contents

Series Foreword

Every year the CES council awards a prize to an internationally renowned and innovative economist for outstanding contributions to economic research. The scholar is honored with the title "Distinguished CES Fellow" and is invited to give the "Munich Lectures in Economics."

The lectures are held at the Center for Economic Studies of the University of Munich. They introduce areas of recent or potential interest to a wide audience in a nontechnical way and combine theoretical depth with policy relevance.

Hans-Werner Sinn
Professor of Economics and Public Finance
Director of CES
University of Munich

Preface

This book is intended for the scholar or graduate student who wants to learn about a new topic of research: the effects of constitutional rules on economic policymaking and performance. We draw on existing knowledge in several fields: economics, political science, and statistics. In particular, the book builds on theoretical work from the last few years, and it forms a natural sequel to our previous book, *Political Economics: Explaining Economic Policy*, published by MIT Press in 2000. Whereas the previous volume focused mainly on theory, the purpose of this new book is uncompromisingly empirical. Taking the existing theoretical work in comparative politics and political economics as a point of departure, we ask which theoretical results are supported and which are contradicted by the data, and we try to identify new empirical patterns for a next round of theory.

The empirical results we present in the book go beyond those in our recent articles and working papers on the same general topic. But there are other reasons why the entire thing is greater than the sum of its parts. We take advantage of the book format to present a more thorough discussion of measurement and methodology than is possible in a single paper. In the end, the empirical picture we offer stands out quite clearly and convincingly when a number of related issues are considered with a similar methodology.

Our decision to embark on the empirical research program that resulted in this book was made when one of us (Tabellini) gave the Munich Lectures, hosted by the Center for Economic Studies (CES), in November 1999. At that point, we had produced several theoretical studies of constitutional rules and economic policy, but we had only started to look at the data, and our empirical results were still preliminary. The comments received from the Munich audience, and in particular from Hans-Werner Sinn and Vito Tanzi, were an essential input and inspiration for the research that followed. The warm hospitality and the outstanding atmosphere of excitement and enthusiasm at CES made those lectures a particularly memorable event.

Another event that helped focus our minds, when this project was further underway, was the Walras-Bowley Lecture, given by one of us (Persson) at the Econometric Society World Congress in Seattle in August 2000. On this occasion, as well, we obtained important feedback that led to major improvements in our research.

Having completed a first full draft, in May 2002, we had the opportunity to present overviews of the manuscript to different audiences in Uppsala, at Princeton, Harvard, the European Science Days in Steyr, Austria, and the Yrjö Jahnsson Foundation in Helsinki. At these presentations, and at numerous seminars on the underlying research papers, many colleagues made insightful comments that improved the quality of our research. Here, we particularly want to thank our colleagues who generously gave up their time to read and comment on the first draft: Jim Alt, Tim Besley, Robin Burgess, Jon Faust, Jeff Frieden, Emanuel Kohlscheen, Per Molander, Olof Petersson, Per Pettersson-Lidbom, Gérard Roland, Ludger Schuknecht, Rolf Strauch, David Strömberg, Jakob Svensson, and three anonymous MIT Press readers. We also owe special gratitude to Andrea Ichino, as well as Richard Blundell, Hide Ichimura, and Costas Meghir, whose comments on our empirical papers were instrumental in directing us toward some of the econometric methodology that figures so prominently in the book.

Putting together the two data sets used in this book involved a great deal of work on data collection, database management, and estimation. We were lucky enough to benefit from expert help with these tasks from a number of research assistants belonging to different cohorts of graduate students: Gani Aldashev, Alessia Amighini, Alessandra Bonfiglioli, Agostino Consolo, Thomas Eisensee, Giovanni Favara, José Mauricio Prado Jr., Andrea Mascotto, Alessandro Riboni, Davide Sala, and Francesco Trebbi (also a coauthor of one of our articles). We benefited greatly from their efforts, as will other researchers with free access to the data sets used in the book.

The last stretch of work on a book manuscript can be an open-ended period of frustration, when every chapter, table, figure, and footnote seems to be in constant flux imposed by authors' desperate last-minute changes, as well as the publisher's rigorous style requirements. Luckily, in this case, as in our previous book project, we could rely on the outstanding assistance of Christina Lönnblad. We are deeply grateful to her for helping us out with editing and style and for cheerfully putting in some long hours, even on days off and weekends. We are also very grateful to Lorenza Negri for her efficient and professional editorial assistance in various stages of the project.

Although the initial agreement with MIT Press to publish this book was made with Terry Vaughn, he left for greener pastures before the book was seriously on its way. We are grateful to our editor, John Covell, for taking over and for being patient with our changing schedule, as we were gradually upgrading our ambitions for the final product.

Finally, we gratefully acknowledge financial support from a number of sources for the research program underlying this book: Bocconi University, London School of Economics, Stockholm University, Ministero dell' Università e della Ricerca Scientifica, and the Italian and Swedish Research Councils.

Stockholm and Milan, January 2003

1 Introduction and Overview

Since the 1990s, constitutional reforms have been the subject of heated debate in many democracies, and such debate has already led to a number of important reforms. Among the industrial countries, Italy abandoned its former reliance on full proportional representation (PR), introducing a first-past-the-post system for 75% of the seats in its national assembly. Similarly, New Zealand introduced a mixed PR-plurality system, but from the opposite point of departure: the traditional British system of appointing all lawmakers by plurality rule in one-member constituencies. Japan also renounced its special form of plurality voting in favor of a mixed system. In Latin America, Bolivia, Ecuador, and Venezuela undertook large-scale electoral reform in the 1990s, as did Fiji and the Philippines elsewhere in the world.

Other reforms are still under debate. In the United Kingdom, discussions about switching to a mixed or proportional electoral system have recently resurfaced. In Italy, key political leaders are considering proposals for injecting elements of presidentialism or semipresidentialism into the current parliamentary regime; in France, some commentators would like to go the other way, toward more parliamentarism. Alternative ideas of how to address inefficient decision making and the "democratic deficit" in the European Union involve constitutional reforms introducing clearer principles of either parliamentary or presidential democracy at the European level.

These debates about constitutional reforms often concern the alleged effects of such reforms on economic policy and economic performance.[1] Is it true that a move toward more majoritarian

---

1. The contributions in Shugart and Wattenberg 2001 discuss the motives behind, and the political consequences of, reform in these and other countries adopting mixed electoral systems in the 1990s.

elections would stifle corruption among politicians, as presumed by the vast majority of Italians who approved the electoral reform? Would it also reduce the propensity of Italian governments to run budget deficits? If the United Kingdom were to abandon its current first-past-the-post system in favor of proportional elections, would this change the size of overall government spending or that of the welfare state? Can we really blame the poor and volatile economic performance of many countries in Latin America on their presidential form of government? More generally, what are the economic effects of constitutional reforms? Knowing the answers to these types of questions is important not only for established democracies contemplating reform, but also for new democracies designing their constitutions from scratch. The goal of this book is to contribute to the body of empirical knowledge about these very difficult, yet fundamental, issues.

1.1 Constitutions and Policy: A Missing Link

Surprising as it may seem, social scientists have not, until very recently, really addressed the question of constitutional effects on economic policy and economic performance. In fact, some observers have even gone as far as deeming it impossible to predict the consequences for a country's economy of constitutional reforms it undertakes (Elster and Slagstad 1988). But this is clearly an extreme position. Analyzing the effects of alternative constitutions has long been a main research topic in political science, as exemplified by the contributions of Sartori (1994), Powell (1982), and Lijphart (1994), to name just a few. Yet despite this long and honored tradition, little is known empirically about the economic effects of alternative constitutions.

To understand why, consider the stylized view of the democratic policymaking process presented in figure 1.1. Citizens and groups in a particular country have conflicting preferences over economic policy. Political institutions aggregate these preferences into specific political outcomes, and these in turn induce public policy decisions in the economic domain (the arrows on the right in the figure). Public policies interact with markets and influence the prices of different goods, employment, and remunerations in different sectors of the economy, and these market outcomes feed back into policy preferences (the arrows on the left). In this view of the interaction between

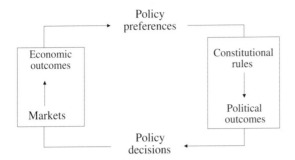

Figure 1.1
The democratic policymaking process.

politics and economics, the formal rules of a country's constitution influence political decisions over its economic policy, given some distribution of (primitive) preferences over economic outcomes in the population. Our goal is to learn more about the effects of these formal constitutional rules on specific economic policies.

The box on the right-hand side of figure 1.1 is the domain of traditional comparative politics. Political scientists in this field of research have spent decades identifying the fundamental features of constitutions and determining their political effects. Apart from a few recent exceptions mentioned below and in chapter 2, however, this research does not extend beyond the assessment of political phenomena: how different electoral systems affect the number of parties or the incidence of coalition governments, how different forms of government affect the frequency of government crises and political instability, and so on. In terms of figure 1.1, the political science research on constitutions has remained within the confines of the box to the right, dealing with the link between constitutional rules and political outcomes. Yet the conclusions reached in this research often point squarely in the direction of this arrow, that is, toward an investigation of systematic policy consequences that result from the application of constitutional rules. For example, the comparative politics literature portrays the choice between majoritarian and proportional elections as a trade-off between accountability and representation.[2] It is plausible that this choice will be reflected in observable economic policy consequences: better accountability might show up in less corruption, and broader representation

2. Powell 2000, for example, makes this point very clearly and thoroughly.

in more comprehensive social insurance programs. A few political scientists have recently asked the empirical "so-what" question of how constitutional rules influence economic policy. Largely based on simple correlations in relatively small data sets of developed democracies, these studies have not come up with clear-cut evidence of a mapping from electoral rules, or forms of government, to policy outcomes.[3]

It is not fair to say, however, that all research in political science has remained inside the box on the right-hand side of the figure. Another substantial political science literature relates economic policy to political outcomes, such as party structure or political instability. But these political outcomes are typically taken as the starting point of the analysis, and they are not explicitly linked to specific constitutional features. This can be conceptualized as a study of the arrow from "Political outcomes" to "Policy decisions" in figure 1.1. Since the political outcomes are indeed systematically related to the constitutional rules we study in this book (electoral rules, e.g., help shape the party structure), this research is also relevant for our main research question, and we discuss it further in chapter 2.

The box on the left-hand side of figure 1.1 is the domain of traditional economics. Economists in the field of political economics have tried to escape from this box, devoting their attention to the other issues illustrated in figure 1.1. They have asked how economic policy interacts with markets to shape the policy preferences of specific individuals and groups and how the distribution of those preferences in turn induces economic policy outcomes and performance. Until very recently, however, this literature portrayed the aggregation of policy preferences in simple games of electoral competition or lobbying, devoid of institutional detail.[4] Thus, the literature on

---

3. Lijphart (1999) asks a so-what question about some macroeconomic outcomes, including budget deficits, in different democracies classified largely by their electoral rules. Using mainly bivariate correlations in a sample of 36 countries, he finds few systematic effects. Castles (1998) studies possible determinants of economic policy, including the size of government and the welfare state, in 21 developed member democracies of the Organisation for Economic Cooperation and Development (OECD). One of the determinants Castles studies is an institutional indicator, mixing five different constitutional provisions, including the rules for elections and the form of government (see chapter 2). Castles finds little effect of this indicator, once again, mostly on the basis of bivariate analysis.

4. Recent textbook treatments of this literature can be found in Drazen 2000a, Grossman and Helpman 2001, and Persson and Tabellini 2000a. We also refer to some of the relevant contributions in chapter 2.

political economics has mainly focused its attention on the remaining parts of figure 1.1, while treating the box on the right-hand side as a black box. As a result, this research as well has generated few predictions about, let alone empirical tests of, how constitutional features influence economic policy outcomes.[5] Once more, asking this so-what question is a logical next step.

To sum up, questions about constitutional effects on economic policy are an example of interesting research topics falling in the cracks between existing disciplines and research traditions. The main motivation for writing this book is precisely to fill the void between the fields of economics and political science.

1.2   Which Constitutional Rules and Policies?

The general topic of constitutional effects on economic policies is still far too wide for a single book. We narrow it down by considering just a few constitutional features and areas of policy and by focusing almost exclusively on empirical evidence rather than theoretical modeling. Thus we limit our attention in this book to two broad aspects of constitutions: the rules for elections and the form of government. On the policy side, we consider different aspects of fiscal policy, political rents taking the form of corruption and abuse of power, and structural policies fostering economic development. Moreover, we focus exclusively on the direct (or reduced-form) link between constitutions and policies, neglecting the intermediate causal effects of the constitution on political outcomes, and from these, on economic policies.

Why have we chosen to focus on these specific constitutional provisions and policies? An obvious reason is that a small recent theoretical literature has dealt precisely with the link between some of them. This literature has generated a number of specific predictions, which suits our empirical purpose. In that sense, we are looking for

---

5. This statement is misleading with respect to constitutional rules regulating the degree of decentralization to lower levels of government and with respect to some specific rules, such as budgetary procedures; both of these types of rules have been the subject of extensive and influential empirical and theoretical work by economists. The traditional literature on public choice has concentrated precisely on issues of constitutional economics (cf. Buchanan and Tullock 1962; Brennan and Buchanan 1980; Mueller 1996). But this literature is mostly normative and has not led to a careful empirical analysis of the economic effects of alternative constitutional features, with the main exception of a few interesting papers on referenda (e.g., Pommerehne and Frey 1978).

the key under the street lamp. But our theoretical street lamp shines on pretty interesting pieces of ground.

First, electoral rules and legislative rules associated with different forms of government are the most fundamental constitutional rules in modern representative democracies. Voters delegate policy choices to political representatives in general elections, but how well their policy preferences get represented and whether they manage to "throw the rascals out" hinge on the rules for election as well as the rules for approving and executing legislation. Politicians make policy choices, but their specific electoral incentives and powers to propose, amend, veto, and enact economic policies hinge on the rules for election, legislation, and execution. Electoral rules and forms of government are also the constitutional features that have attracted the most attention from researchers in comparative politics. We thus have a solid body of work to rely upon when it comes to measuring and identifying the critical aspects of these political institutions in existing democracies.

Second, our chosen areas of policy and performance display a great deal of variation in observed outcomes. If we look across countries in the late 1990s, we observe that total government spending as a fraction of GDP stood around 60% in Sweden and well above 50% in many countries of continental Europe, but around 35% in Japan, Switzerland, and the United States. We also see striking variations among countries in the composition of spending: transfers are high in Europe, but low in Latin America; among the 15 members of the European Union, spending on the unemployed in the 1990s ranged from 2% of total spending (Italy) to 17% (Ireland). Perceptions of corruption and ineffectiveness in the provision of government services are generally higher in Africa and Latin America than in the countries of the Organisation for Economic Cooperation and Development (OECD) but still differ a great deal among countries at comparable levels of economic development. Output per worker and total factor productivity vary enormously across countries, reflecting the wide gaps in living standards not only across the world, but also within the same continents.

Looking instead across time over the last 40 years, we see some common patterns in the data. In a large group of countries, average government spending grew by about 10% of GDP from the early 1960s to the mid-1980s, stabilizing around a new higher level toward the end of the century. Budget deficits in these countries were, on average, below 2% of GDP in the early 1960s and the late 1990s but reached 5% of GDP in the early 1980s. In spite of such common trends, however, we observe substantial differences in the time paths of individual countries.

As we shall see later in the book, considerable policy differences remain among countries, even as we take into account the level of development, population structure, and many other observable country characteristics. Hence, it is interesting and plausible to explore whether some of the variation that remains after taking these characteristics into account can be attributed to different political systems. This is exactly what we do in the rest of the book.

But we are not just interested in finding nice correlations in the data. Our ultimate goal is to draw conclusions about the causal effects of constitutions on specific policy outcomes. We would like to answer questions like the following: If the United Kingdom were to switch its electoral rule from majoritarian to proportional, how would this affect the size of its welfare state or its budget deficit? If Argentina were to abandon its presidential regime in favor of a parliamentary form of government, would this facilitate the adoption of sound policies toward economic development? That is, we would like to answer questions about hypothetical counterfactual experiments of constitutional reform.

It goes without saying that this is a very ambitious goal. Drawing inferences about causal effects from cross-country comparisons is a treacherous exercise, and much of the book revolves around the question of how to draw robust inferences about causation from observed patterns in the data. But we are not groping in the dark. A large and sophisticated econometric literature has dealt with exactly this difficulty, how to use observed correlations to make inferences about causation. So far, the main applications of the econometric techniques developed in this literature have been in applied microeconomics. One of the contributions of this book is to bring these techniques into the field of comparative politics, in an attempt to discover some economic effects of political constitutions.

1.3   Overview of the Book

We finish this brief introductory chapter by sketching the broad plan of our campaign. Chapter 2 provides a starting point by describing a small and recent theoretical literature produced by economists on the link between constitutions and policy outcomes. As the book focuses on empirical evidence, we keep this discussion brief and nonformal, mainly summarizing the testable predictions of the theory. The chapter also comments on other nonformalized, but related, ideas in the political science and economics literatures, as well as some possible extensions of existing theory. It ends with a list of empirical questions, some taking the form of well-defined testable hypotheses, others really amounting to quests for systematic patterns in the data. This list sets the agenda for the empirical work to follow.

The most interesting constitutional variation, in terms of our big-picture questions, is observed at the national, rather than the subnational, level. We have thus assembled two different cross-country data sets for our purposes. One takes the form of a pure cross section, measuring average outcomes in the 1990s for 85 democracies. The other has a panel structure, measuring annual outcomes from 1960 to 1998 for 60 democracies. Chapter 3 presents the bulk of these data. Specifically, it describes our measures of the size and composition of government spending, budget deficits, political rents, structural policies, and productivity—an ultimate measure of economic performance. This chapter also introduces our data on many other cross-country characteristics that we need to hold constant in the empirical work to follow. We show how these characteristics are correlated with policy and performance outcomes across both countries and time.

Chapter 4 describes our empirical measures of electoral rules and forms of government. As the theory in chapter 2 refers to collective decision making in democratic societies, we first describe how we restrict our two data sets to countries and years of democratic governance. We then introduce an overall classification of electoral rules as majoritarian, mixed, or proportional, as well as some continuous measures of the finer details of these rules. Similarly, we provide an empirical means of classifying countries into presidential and parliamentary forms of government. Examining the history of current constitutional rules, we find deep constitutional reforms to be a very rare phenomenon among democracies. We also uncover a systematic, nonrandom selection of countries into different constitutional rules, based on observable historical, geographical, and cultural characteristics.

The rarity of deep constitutional reforms implies that any direct constitutional effect on policy must be estimated from cross-sectional variation in the data. But the nonrandom selection means that we risk confounding the causal effects of constitutions with other, fixed country characteristics. Chapter 5 discusses the potential statistical pitfalls in estimating the causal effect of constitutional reforms from cross-country data under these circumstances and introduces a number of econometric methods that might help us circumvent them. Although the discussion is cast in the context of our particular problem, this is mainly a methodological chapter. Some of the traditional methods we discuss (such as linear regression, instrumental variables, and adjustment for selection bias) are probably well known to many of our readers. Other, quasi-experimental methods (such as propensity score matching) are newer and may thus be less familiar.

Chapter 6 presents a first set of empirical results. We apply the econometric methods from the previous chapter and estimate constitutional effects on fiscal policy, exploiting the cross-sectional variation in the data. For most of our policy measures, we obtain constitutional effects robust to the specification and estimation method. Presidential regimes have smaller governments than parliamentary regimes. Majoritarian elections induce smaller governments, less welfare state spending, and smaller deficits than do proportional elections. Many of the effects expected from theory also appear to exist in reality. Moreover, some of them are not only statistically significant but quantitatively very important.

Chapter 7 presents another set of results, on constitutional effects on political rents, growth-promoting policies, and productivity, once more estimated from the cross-sectional variation in the data. Lower barriers to entry for new candidates or parties (measured by the number of legislators elected in each district) and more direct individual accountability of political candidates to voters both lead to less corruption and greater effectiveness in the provision of government services; the crude classifications of electoral rules and forms of government are less important for outcomes. Lower barriers to entry and individual accountability also promote better growth-promoting policies and higher productivity. Finally, parliamentary forms of government and older democracies seem to have better growth-promoting policies, but we also uncover some subtle interactions between forms of government and the overall qualities of democratic institutions. As in chapter 6, these effects are both statistically and economically significant.

Chapter 8 exploits the time variation in our panel data on fiscal policy. Because constitutional features exhibit a high degree of inertia, we cannot use institutional reforms to estimate direct constitutional effects on fiscal policy. We thus pose a somewhat different question, focusing on the interaction between (mainly fixed) constitutions and time-varying policies. Are different constitutional rules systematically associated with different responses to important economic and political events? We discover that cyclical adjustment of spending and taxes differs crucially depending on the form of government. Presidential democracies exhibit a slower rate of growth of government spending than parliamentary democracies until the early 1980s, with less inertia and less response of spending to economic fluctuations. Proportional and parliamentary democracies alone display a ratchet effect in spending, with government outlays as a percentage of GDP rising in recessions, but not reverting in booms. Regardless of their political system, countries cut taxes in election years, but other aspects of electoral cycles are highly dependent on the constitution. Presidential regimes postpone fiscal contractions until after elections, whereas parliamentary regimes do not; welfare state programs are expanded in the proximity of elections, but only in democracies with proportional elections.

Finally, chapter 9 takes stock of our findings. Although most of the results we obtain are clearly consistent with theory, others are not, and we speculate on the reasons for the successes and failures. Several of our estimates uncover new (and sometimes unexpected) patterns in the data. These results suggest further extensions of existing theory, as well as additional measurement to create new data sets. Based on our discoveries, we argue that the next round of work in the comparative politics of policymaking should be both theoretical and empirical. In that endeavor, it should attempt to integrate the policymaking incentives emphasized by economists with the political mechanisms emphasized by political scientists regarding party structure and government formation.

2   What Does Theory Say?

2.1   Introduction

Economic policymaking generates conflicts in different dimensions: among different groups of voters, among different groups of politicians, and between voters and politicians. The basic idea in the literature discussed in this chapter is that the resolution of these conflicts—and therefore the policy outcomes we observe—hinges on the political institutions in place.

At a general level, this idea is familiar to economists and has an analogy in microeconomic theory. Markets generate conflicts of interest between consumers and producers over price and product quality and among different producers over profit. How these are then resolved depends on market institutions. Equilibrium prices, qualities, and profits hinge on regulations determining the barriers to entry and the scope for competition among producers. They also hinge on legislation determining how easily consumers can hold producers accountable for bad product quality or collusive pricing behavior. The literature on political institutions and economic policy offers a similar idea.

"Political institutions" is a label that has been attached to a wide range of different phenomena: from written constitutions, through organizations like political parties or trade unions, all the way to existing social norms. In this book, we investigate only formal rules, as laid down by explicit provisions in constitutions (or other laws). Moreover, as anticipated in chapter 1, we concentrate on two fundamental aspects of constitutions: electoral rules and forms of government. The former determine how the voters' preferences are aggregated and how the powers to make decisions over economic policy are acquired by political representatives; the latter determine

how these powers can be exercised once in office and how conflicts
among elected representatives can be resolved.

Three distinct, but related, lines of research have compared alternative electoral rules and forms of government and their consequences. The oldest and most established tradition is comparative
politics, one of the main fields in political science. Researchers in
comparative politics have focused on the *political* consequences of
alternative constitutions (for instance, the number of parties, the
emergence of political extremism, and the frequency of political
crisis). A basic insight of this line of research is that alternative constitutional features entail different combinations of two desirable
attributes of a political system: accountability and representativeness. If a political system is said to have accountability, this means
that it is possible under that system for the voters to identify who is
responsible for policy decisions and to oust officeholders whose performance they find deficient. If a political system is said to have
representativeness, this means that policy decisions under that system reflect the preferences of a large spectrum of voters. The trade-
off between accountability and representativeness is very stark in the
case of electoral rules: plurality rule is geared toward holding politicians accountable, and PR toward representing different voters in the
legislative process. But a similar trade-off also emerges in the evaluation of alternative forms of government, even though the distinctions are then more subtle. A presidential regime leans toward
accountability, because it concentrates the executive powers in a
single office directly accountable to voters and provides checks and
balances through a clear separation of executive and legislative pre-
rogatives. A parliamentary regime instead leans toward representativeness, since the government represents and must hold together a
possibly heterogeneous coalition in the legislature. Research in comparative politics is so extensive and well known that we do not
attempt in this brief discussion to summarize its main contributions.[1]

A second, very recent line of research has exploited the insights of
the comparative politics tradition to ask how electoral rules and
forms of government shape *economic policy outcomes*. If alternative

---

1. Classics within the political science literature on comparative politics from the last
two decades include Powell 1982 and 2000, Lijphart 1984a and 1999, Taagepera and
Shugart 1989, Shugart and Carey 1992, and Cox 1997; see Myerson 1999 for a discussion of the theoretical literature on the consequences of different electoral rules.

constitutional features have relevant implications for accountability and representativeness, this is likely to be reflected in economic policy decisions emanating from the political process (for instance, in the extent of political corruption and abuse of power, or in the size and scope of redistributive programs). This line of research uses the analytical tools of economics and formally models the political process as a delegation game between voters and politicians. It asks how alternative rules of the game embedded in alternative constitutional features shape the incentives of rational players and ultimately the equilibrium policy outcome. This theoretical research generates strong predictions regarding the causal effect of the constitution on economic policy but typically neglects its effect on the political phenomena studied by political scientists. The primary goal of this chapter is to summarize the main predictions of this theoretical line of research. In section 2.2, we begin by describing its general approach. Next, we describe the specific predictions of the theory, first regarding alternative electoral rules (section 2.3), then regarding alternative forms of government (section 2.4).

Finally, a third group of related studies in political science and economics has taken an intermediate approach, linking economic policy outcomes not to a country's constitution, but to other political phenomena such as the number and type of political parties and the incidence of minority, coalition, or divided governments. This line of research is mainly empirical and does not attempt to study the whole chain of causation from the constitution to political phenomena to economic policy outcomes, focusing instead on the latter link. But since the party structure and the types of governing coalitions in a country are known to be influenced by its constitution, these studies are also relevant for our task. Section 2.5 briefly mentions some of the relevant contributions, with no pretence of completeness. The results of this line of research provide additional motivation for some specific hypotheses we wish to test and suggest a number of more exploratory empirical questions.

In section 2.6, we take stock of the main ideas presented in the chapter and set the agenda for the empirical work in the book by listing the specific hypotheses we wish to test, as well as the open questions we wish to confront with the data. Section 2.7 briefly describes how the remaining chapters of the book try to make progress on this agenda.

2.2 A Common Approach

Political institutions aggregate conflicting interests into public policies. As we are interested in conflicts with an economic origin, we focus in this overview on economic policy in general, though most of the specific applications in the literature deal with government spending. It is useful to distinguish among three types of economic policy on the basis of the beneficiary. Economic policy can provide benefits to (1) *many citizens*, (2) *a narrow group of citizens*, or (3) *virtually no citizens, but a specific group of politicians*.

Each of these types of policy induces a specific kind of economic conflict. Broad programs in the form of general public goods like defense or broad redistributive programs like social insurance or pensions are examples of type (1) policies, which provide benefits to many individuals. Because of their broad nature and universalistic design, these programs cannot easily be tailored to the specific demands of well-defined groups of citizens. Hence, large groups of beneficiaries evaluate them similarly. Many of the entitlement programs typical of the modern welfare state belong to this category. Local public goods or specific redistributive programs, like agricultural support or transfers to government enterprises, are examples of type (2) policies, benefiting only narrow groups of citizens. The spending involved in these kinds of programs is referred to as "pork barrel" and often, though not always, reflects discretionary policy decisions. Such narrow programs can much more easily be targeted to groups in specific geographic areas than the broader type (1) programs.[2]

The third type of economic policy generates *rents* to politicians. These rents can take various forms: literally, they are salaries for public officials or the financing of political parties. Less literally, one can consider various forms of corruption and waste as ultimately providing rents for politicians. Whereas broadly or narrowly targeted programs induce conflicts among voters, rents for politicians are at the core of the political agency problem, pitting voters at large against politicians (or other government officials). Voters are unani-

---

2. Naturally, the theoretical distinction is not as crystal clear in reality. For example, social security programs may include early retirement provisions that could be targeted to workers in occupations or sectors predominating in specific geographic areas.

mous in their desire to limit the rents extracted by politicians but
may lack the necessary means to achieve this goal. The amount of
resources appropriated as rents is probably small in most modern
democracies, compared to the overall size of tax revenues. But since
they directly benefit the agents in charge of policy decisions, the
political struggle to appropriate such "crumbs" can nevertheless
strongly influence other policy decisions. Moreover, in developing
democracies, particularly those at lower levels of development, the
direct extraction of resources by powerful political leaders can be
quantitatively significant, as revealed by well-publicized examples
in Africa, Asia, and Latin America.

The discussion presented here suggests a general approach to
modeling the outcome of policymaking. How the three types of
conflict are resolved and thus what economic policy we observe in a
particular country hinges on its constitutional rules. In the approach
pursued in the recent economics literature, economic policy is the
equilibrium outcome of a delegation game in which the interaction
between rational voters and politicians is formally modeled as a
game on extensive form. The voters (the multiple principals) elect
political representatives (the agents) who, in turn, set a policy to
further their own objectives. The principals have some leeway over
their agents because they can offer them the rewards of election or
reelection. But these rewards are mostly implicit, not explicit, so that
the constitution becomes an "incomplete contract," leaving the politicians with some power in the form of residual control rights. The
crucial aspects of constitutions are those setting the rules of this
delegation game, namely, electoral rules and rules for government
formation and dissolution.

This approach to the politics of policymaking forces the theorist to
be precise about the rules of the game. It is then quite natural to ask
what the effects are of changing these rules, letting alternative rules
of the game represent alternative constitutional provisions. Thus,
comparative politics becomes a natural, almost inevitable item in
this research program.

We now survey a number of recent theoretical studies that apply
a comparative politics approach of the type discussed above, with
the purpose of extracting the testable predictions made by these
studies. As the focus of the book is decidedly empirical, we keep
the description of theory brief, emphasize the main ideas and the

intuition behind the results, and do not attempt to reproduce any of the formal arguments.[3]

2.3 Electoral Rules

We begin with recent studies of alternative rules for electing a legislature. All of these studies focus on different aspects of fiscal policy (and in particular, on government spending), but the main idea generalizes to other economic policies. Legislative elections around the world differ on several dimensions. The political science literature discusses these dimensions in great detail but commonly emphasizes three of them: *district magnitude, electoral formula,* and *ballot structure.* District magnitude simply determines the number of legislators (given the size of the legislature) acquiring a seat in a typical voting district. One polar case is that all legislators are elected in districts with a single seat; the other is that they are all elected in a single, all-encompassing district. The electoral formula determines how votes are translated into seats. Under plurality rule, only those who win the highest vote shares get seats in a given district, whereas PR awards seats in proportion to the vote share obtained. The ballot structure, finally, determines how citizens cast their vote, choosing among different individual candidates or different party lists. As discussed further later in the chapter (and in chapter 4), these three dimensions are strongly correlated among real-world electoral systems.[4]

2.3.1 District Magnitude

A series of related papers compares two-party electoral competition under plurality rule in single-member districts versus a single national district. The winner sets policy (the so-called winner-takes-all assumption). All these papers predict that district magnitude influences the *composition and allocation of spending* promised during the electoral campaign.[5]

---

3. Many of the ideas are described in greater detail in Persson and Tabellini 2000a (chaps. 8–10).

4. Cox 1997, Blais and Massicotte 1996, and Grofman and Lijphart 1986 give recent overviews of the electoral systems across the world's democracies.

5. Given the simple framework of two-party competition and the assumption that the winner takes it all, the distinction between district magnitude and electoral formula is hard to draw. In a single national district, plurality rule and a strictly proportional electoral formula are equivalent. Thus, these papers can also be considered as comparing strictly majoritarian to strictly proportional elections in a simple framework.

Persson and Tabellini (1999, 2000a, chap. 8) use a probabilistic-voting model with two parties in which the outcome of an election is uncertain ahead of the elections, when the two parties design their electoral platforms. Economic policy outcomes are determined by the parties' commitments to these platforms. Larger districts diffuse electoral competition, inducing parties to seek support from broad coalitions in the population (and from the whole population in the extreme case when the whole legislature is elected in a single district). Smaller districts instead steer electoral competition toward narrower, geographic constituencies, which are thus the primary beneficiaries of the electoral promises of both candidates. Specifically, when districts are small and not altogether homogeneous in the composition of their voters, each party is typically a certain winner in some "safe" districts, and electoral competition becomes concentrated in the remaining pivotal districts. Both candidates thus have strong incentives to target their policies toward voters in these districts. Clearly, broad programs are more effective in seeking broad support and targeted programs in seeking narrow support. Elections involving larger districts should thus be more biased toward nontargeted programs, such as general public goods or broad transfer programs. In an examination of the U.S. electoral college, Strömberg (2002) studies a more general version of the same kind of model. Focusing on the allocation of electoral campaign spending, he predicts that both candidates in a presidential election should spend more in pivotal electoral districts, which is consistent with data from recent U.S. presidential elections.

Under the winner-takes-all assumption and plurality rule, district magnitude has a second effect that reinforces the previous prediction. Votes for a party not obtaining plurality are completely lost, and small district magnitude reduces the minimal coalition of voters needed to win the election. With single-member districts and plurality, for example, a party needs only 25% of the national vote to win (50% in 50% of the districts). With a single national district, by contrast, it needs 50% of the national vote. Politicians are thus induced to internalize the policy benefits for a larger segment of the population, which gives them stronger incentives under PR than under plurality rule to select policy programs with broad-based benefits. Lizzeri and Persico (2001) make this point in a general model of electoral competition in which voters are forward looking and two political candidates commit to electoral promises of how to split a given budget between national public goods and transfers that can be targeted to any coalition of voters. The equilibrium has more public-goods provision under a single national district than under several single-member districts. Persson and Tabellini (2000a, chap. 9) reach the same conclusion in a model in which policy choices, rather than being committed to before the election, as in Lizzeri and Persico's model, are instead made by an incumbent once in office. Voters follow a retrospective strategy, reelecting incumbents whose policy choices give them sufficiently high utility to surpass a reservation level. Once more, the equilibrium has more public-goods provision with a single national district.[6]

Milesi-Ferretti, Perotti, and Rostagno (2002) obtain a similar result in a model in which the policy is instead decided upon after elections in bargaining among the politicians elected to the legislature. Voters understand the working of the postelection legislative bargaining and elect their representatives strategically. As a result, legislators mainly represent socioeconomic groups when districts are large, whereas they mainly represent groups in specific geographic locations when districts are small. Smaller districts again become associated with the targeting of narrow geographic groups, whereas larger districts become associated with broad programs benefiting voters across many districts. Milesi-Ferretti, Perotti, and Rostagno also obtain the result that larger districts are associated with larger *overall spending*, whereas Persson and Tabellini (2000a, chap. 8) find the effect of district size on overall spending to be ambiguous.

District magnitude is also likely to influence *rent extraction*, with larger districts reducing the rents extracted by politicians. One mechanism through which this may occur is analyzed by Myerson (1993). In his model, parties (or equivalently, candidates) differ along two dimensions: their intrinsic honesty and their ideology. Voters prefer honest candidates but disagree on ideology. Dishonest incumbents may still cling to power if voters sharing the same ideological preferences cannot find an honest substitute candidate. With large districts, an honest candidate is available for all ideological positions, and in equilibrium, dishonest candidates have no chance

---

6. As discussed in the previous note, the papers under discussion can also be thought of as considering a reform from a strictly majoritarian with a strictly proportional electoral system, where both district magnitude and the electoral formula are changed at the same time. Thus, the effect on the composition of spending can also be seen as resulting from the electoral formula.

of being elected. With single-member districts, the equilibrium can be very different. Even if honest candidates of all possible ideological types run for office, only one candidate can win the election. Voters may strategically vote for a dishonest, but ideologically preferred, candidate: if voters on one side of the ideological scale expect others with the same ideology to vote in the same way as themselves, switching to the honest candidate entails a risk of giving the victory to a candidate on the other side of the ideological scale. Small districts and strategic voting thus raise the barriers to entry into the electoral system and make it more difficult to oust dishonest incumbents from office.

In Myerson's model, voting behavior is endogenous to the electoral rule, whereas dishonesty is an exogenous feature of candidates. Ferejohn (1986) instead endogenizes the behavior of incumbents, by letting them choose a level of effort, given that voters hold incumbents accountable for their performance through a retrospective-voting rule. But Ferejohn's model can easily be reformulated such that rent extraction is equivalent to exerting little effort (see Persson, Roland, and Tabellini 2000). In Ferejohn's model, electoral defeat becomes progressively less fearsome as the probability that an ousted incumbent will return to office in the future increases. Although Ferejohn treats this probability as an exogenous parameter, he points out that it is likely to be negatively related to the number of parties or the number of candidates. Given the strong empirical relation between district magnitude and the number of candidates, we obtain the same prediction as above: larger districts should be associated with less extraction of rents.

2.3.2 Electoral Formula

Lizzeri and Persico (2001) also contrast how alternative electoral formulas influence the *composition of government spending*. They interpret a proportional electoral rule as one in which both candidates maximize their vote share (since the spoils of office are divided among candidates in proportion to the share of the vote they receive). Plurality rule is instead associated with the winner-takes-all assumption (since the spoils go entirely to the winner). This model's prediction turns out to be ambiguous: proportionality is associated with more public goods and less targeted redistribution, compared to plurality rule, only if the public good is very desirable for the voters; otherwise the opposite may occur. The intuition is that if the public good is very desirable, reducing it implies a large drop in the vote share of the nonpivotal voters. Under plurality rule, candidates disregard this cost. But if they also care about vote shares, they internalize the cost, which leads them to provide more public goods at the expense of targeted redistribution.

Austen-Smith (2000) suggests another mechanism whereby the electoral formula may shape the *overall level of taxation and spending*. His model takes the party structure as exogenous but makes the empirically plausible assumption that fewer parties are represented under plurality rule (two parties) than under PR (three parties). Policy, in the form of redistributive taxation, is decided in postelection legislative bargaining. Under plurality rule, the winner-takes-all assumption results in the party commanding a majority making single-handed policy decisions, but under PR, no party commands a majority, and more than one party must form a coalition to set policy. The interaction among elections, redistributive taxation, and the endogenous formation of economic groups typically produces, under PR, politico-economic equilibria with higher taxation than under plurality.

2.3.3 Ballot Structure

Whereas voters typically cast their ballot among individual candidates under plurality rule, they cast it among party lists under PR. Such lists may dilute the incentives for individual incumbents to perform well. Persson and Tabellini (2000a, chap. 9) examine the policy consequences of this difference between plurality rule and PR in a model where individual politicians can extract personal rents in the policy process. Politicians in this model also have career concerns, however, and they can enhance their careers (i.e., improve their chances for reelection) by building a reputation for competency among imperfectly informed voters. Politicians thus face countervailing incentives: current rent extraction has a direct benefit, at the cost of a diminished reputation. In this model, voting on party lists is associated with more rent extraction than voting on individuals, because the career concern (reelection) motive becomes a weaker counterweight to the rent extraction motive for politicians when they are collectively, rather than individually, accountable.

Specifically, when voters choose among party lists, politicians' incentives are diluted by two effects. First, there is a free-rider problem among the politicians on the same list. The reason is that under

PR the number of seats depends on the votes collected by the whole list, rather than on the votes for each individual candidate of the party. Second, if the list is closed and voters cannot choose their preferred candidate, individual chances of re-election depend on their ranking in the list, not on their individual performance. If lists are drawn up by party leaders (as is commonly the case), the ranking is likely to reflect criteria unrelated to competence in providing benefits to voters, such as party loyalty or effort within the party (rather than in office). Then, individual incentives to perform well are much weaker. This model thus predicts that political rents and corruption are higher the lower the proportion of representatives elected via individually assigned seats rather than party lists. Moreover, rents ought to be higher if the list is closed (i.e., voters have no choice on the ranking of individual candidates in the list) than if it is open.

Earlier nonformalized work in political science expressed related ideas, even though it was only implicitly or tangentially concerned with economic policy outcomes. One good example is Carey and Shugart 1995, which discusses the incentives in different electoral systems for politicians to act so as to cultivate a "personal vote." Carey and Shugart use this criterion to classify real-world systems on the basis of ballot structure and other features (including district magnitude and distinctions between open and closed lists in PR systems; see chapter 4). However, their work emphasizes the distinction between inter-party competition (which is deemed good for voters) and intra-party competition (which may be bad for voters).

2.3.4 Empirical Predictions

The discussion above entails a number of predictions for policy outcomes. On the composition of spending, large districts and PR both pull in the direction of broad programs, whereas small districts and plurality pull in the direction of programs narrowly targeted at small constituencies. These reinforcing effects are important when taking the predictions to the data, because of the strong correlation between district size and electoral formulas across real-world electoral systems. Some systems can be described as majoritarian, combining small voting districts with plurality rule (cf. elections to the U.K. parliament or the U.S. Congress, in which whoever collects most votes in a district obtains the *single* seat). As we have seen, both small districts and plurality rule favor narrow programs. Other electoral rules are instead decidedly proportional, combining large electoral districts with PR (cf. Dutch or Israeli elections, in which parties obtain seats in proportion to their shares of the vote in a single national voting district), both of which favor broad programs. Although we find some intermediate systems, most countries fall quite unambiguously into one category or the other in this crude classification (see further the discussion in chapter 4).

Some models (albeit not all) predict that majoritarian systems will overall be associated with smaller government spending and taxes. In Milesi-Ferretti, Perotti, and Rostagno 2002, the reason for this association is a smaller district size, whereas in Austen-Smith 2000, the reason is plurality rule.

When it comes to rents for politicians, our predictions are more subtle. Because of their smaller districts, majoritarian systems present higher barriers to entry than proportional systems, which should permit more rent extraction. But they also have more direct accountability because voters choose among individuals (under plurality rule) rather than among parties, which should restrict rent extraction. The overall effect is ambiguous, depending on which of these two features is quantitatively more important. Ideally, empirical work should identify the separate consequences of these different features of electoral rules.

Finally, some of the ideas discussed above might have relevant implications for electoral cycles in spending and taxes. As noted in section 2.1, and as emphasized by political scientists, accountability is greater in systems with majoritarian elections, in particular, under plurality rule. Thus, elected officials might have stronger incentives to please their voters (or at least to appear to do so) in the imminence of elections under majoritarian than under proportional electoral rule. A reasonable conjecture is thus that electoral cycles in spending or taxes are more pronounced in majoritarian (plurality and individual-centered) systems.[7]

2.4 Forms of Government

Recent theory has devoted less effort to studying the rules for legislation than those for elections. But it has clarified the consequences of two aspects of the legislative regime inherent in different forms

---

7. Indeed, commenting on the career concern model discussed above, Persson and Tabellini (2000a) formulate this conjecture with regard to the effect of the ballot structure.

of government. These concern the powers over legislation: to make, amend, or veto policy proposals. One is the allocation of these powers to different offices: is there an effective separation of powers across different politicians and offices, or is there a single office vested with several different powers? The other aspect is how these powers are maintained over time: in particular, is the executive subject to a *confidence requirement* of continued support from a majority in the legislative assembly? With some provisos as noted below and further discussed in chapter 4, these two aspects of legislative rules can be associated with the two predominant forms of government, namely, presidential and parliamentary democracies.[8]

2.4.1 Separation of Powers

Many presidential regimes have a stronger separation of powers—between the president and the legislature, and also among legislative committees holding important proposal (agenda-setting) powers in different spheres of policy (think about the United States)—than many parliamentary regimes, in which the proposal powers over legislation are instead concentrated in the hands of the government. This statement is a stark simplification, as the separation of legislative powers also differs a great deal within each of these forms of government, depending on more detailed constitutional arrangements (see further chapter 4). Still, it is a useful starting point for contrasting the two types of regimes.

Why should separation of powers be of importance for economic policy? A classical argument, formulated in a clear fashion by James Madison more than 200 years ago, holds that checks and balances among different offices constrain politicians from abusing their powers. Persson, Roland, and Tabellini (1997, 2000) formally demonstrate this venerable point. In the setting of both papers, incumbent politicians set policy under alternative assumptions about legislative bargaining designed to capture some basic distinctions between different forms of government. The incumbents are held accountable by retrospective voters. Because of the greater concentration of powers in parliamentary regimes, it is easier for politicians to collude with each other at the voters' expense; in equilibrium,

---

8. Lijphart 1984a presents a useful discussion of different forms of government. Shugart and Carey 1992 provides an exhaustive treatment of presidential regimes in the world, with a thorough discussion of separation of powers as well as executive survival.

weaker electoral accountability results in higher rents and higher taxes than in presidential regimes, in which more pronounced checks and balances help the voters hold the politicians more accountable for abusing their powers by diverting tax money for private gain.

2.4.2 Confidence Requirement

A second crucial distinction between presidential and parliamentary democracies (indeed, one of the defining distinctions between these forms of government) is the presence or absence of a confidence requirement.[9] Presidential regimes lack such a requirement: once appointed (typically in a direct election), the executive can hold on to her powers without the support of a majority in the legislature. According to the main principle of parliamentarism, cabinets in parliamentary regimes instead need the continuous confidence of a majority in the legislature to maintain their powers throughout an entire election period. (How to make this classification in practice is discussed in chapter 4.)

The presence or absence of a confidence requirement is important in terms of how the legislative process works. Parties supporting a parliamentary executive hold valuable powers that they risk losing in a government crisis. Therefore, a confidence requirement creates strong incentives to maintain party discipline, as noted by, among others, Shugart and Carey (1992) and as formally modeled by Huber (1996). But as analyzed in detail by Diermeier and Feddersen (1998), the incentives to hold legislative cum executive majorities together extend from members of the same party to coalitions of parties. To use the jargon of the literature, the confidence requirement creates "legislative cohesion," namely, stable majorities supporting the cabinet and voting together on policy proposals. The absence of a confidence requirement, by contrast, fosters unstable coalitions and less discipline within the majority.

Building on this idea of legislative cohesion, Persson, Roland, and Tabellini (2000) make two predictions about fiscal policy in their model, where incumbent legislators elected by retrospective voters in different districts set policy in alternative arrangements for legislative bargaining. In arrangements modeled on parliamentary regimes, a stable majority of legislators tends to pursue the joint

---

9. Another distinction is often made on the basis of the executive, presidential regimes having an individual executive and parliamentary regimes a collective executive.

interest of its voters. Spending thus optimally becomes directed toward broad programs benefiting a majority of voters, such as broad social transfer programs or general public goods. In presidential regimes, the (relative) lack of such a majority instead tends to pit the interests of different minorities against each other with respect to different issues on the legislative agenda. As a result, the model predicts the allocation of spending to target powerful minorities among the constituencies of powerful officeholders (e.g., heads of congressional committees in the United States).

Moreover, in parliamentary regimes, the stable majority of incumbent legislators, as well as the majority of voters backing them, become "residual claimants" on additional revenue; they can keep the benefits of spending within the majority, putting part of the costs on the excluded minority. Both majorities thus favor high taxes and high spending. In presidential regimes, on the other hand, no such residual claimants on revenue exist, and the majority of taxpayers and legislators therefore resist high spending. On the basis of this mechanism and the other mechanisms described above, Persson, Roland, and Tabellini (2000) unambiguously predict larger governments (higher taxes and overall spending) in parliamentary regimes than in presidential regimes.

2.4.3 Empirical Predictions

In summary, several predictions result from the theoretical research on how policy outcomes are affected by the legislative rules enshrined in different forms of government. According to the separation-of-powers argument, presidential regimes should be associated with less rent extraction and lower taxation than parliamentary regimes. According to the confidence requirement argument, they should also be associated with more targeted programs at the expense of broad spending programs. Overall, we should find parliamentary regimes to have larger governments than presidential regimes.

2.5 Related Ideas

The research surveyed in the previous sections tries to model the direct effects of constitutional rules on policy outcomes through the policymaking incentives of political candidates or incumbents, leaving out prospective indirect effects through intervening political outcomes. This may be an important omission, as we have very good reasons to expect such indirect effects to exist.

Specifically, many contributions by political scientists stress the implications of electoral rules and government regimes for party structure and type of government. As mentioned above, proportional elections entail lower barriers to entry for political parties, and we do observe that larger districts and a proportional electoral formula go hand in hand with a larger number of parties (see Rae 1967; Taagepera and Shugart 1989; Lijphart 1990 and 1994). Related to this, parliamentary regimes with majoritarian electoral rules are much more likely to produce single-party majority governments, whereas coalition and minority governments are more likely under PR (Taagepera and Shugart 1989; Strom 1990; Powell 2000). Moreover, presidential regimes are sometimes associated with a divided government, with presidents and congressional majorities coming from different parties, whereas this is ruled out in parliamentary regimes (Shugart and Carey 1992).

The political outcomes described in the previous paragraph may, in turn, have systematic effects on economic policymaking, thus creating an indirect link between constitutional rules and economic policy outcomes of interest. Indeed, the general idea that party structures and types of government shape economic policy reappears in many studies. All of the specific ideas may not have been fleshed out with the same analytical rigor as in the recent theoretical literature, and some conclusions are derived from observed empirical correlations, rather than coherent theoretical models, but some of these studies suggest the same reduced-form predictions as the hypotheses presented above.

In particular, some studies of the so-called common-pool problem in fiscal policy suggest that this problem is more pervasive under coalition governments. The common-pool problem refers to a situation where the benefits of government spending are concentrated among relatively narrow groups of beneficiaries, whereas the costs involved in raising revenues are shared among all taxpayers. In this situation, all groups have an incentive to push for more of the spending from which they benefit, since they internalize only part of the cost. An equilibrium in such a situation is likely to result in aggregate overspending. Since the distortion in the incentives increases as the number of groups increases (or equivalently, as the group size decreases), Kontopoulos and Perotti (1999) argue that government spending might increase in the number of coalition parties, and they provide evidence consistent with this hypothesis. Scartascini and Crain (2001) produce similar empirical results. Because coalition governments are more common under proportional than majoritarian electoral rules, we obtain an indirect positive association between the size of government and proportional electoral rules (i.e., the same ultimate conclusion as was arrived at in the studies cited in section 2.3).

Scholars in political sociology have investigated determinants of welfare state programs and spending, including constitutional determinants. The broad study by Huber, Ragin, and Stephens (1993) is of particular interest. Huber and her colleagues argue that presidentialism, as well as majoritarian elections, produces dispersed political power and multiple points of influence on policy and that this will hamper welfare state expansion, an argument similar to that in the formal models discussed above. Moreover, they show that a constitutional index including these and other features has a strong negative influence on welfare state expenditures, when a number of other economic and social variables are held constant, in a data set encompassing 17 developed democracies over 30 or more years.[10] More recently, similar arguments have appeared in Swank 2002 and the contributions in Pierson 2001.

Related studies suggest further questions that can be posed to the data. In their review of the extensive work on government budget deficits, Alesina and Perotti (1995), drawing on work by Velasco (1999), argue that coalition governments face a severe dynamic common-pool problem that makes them prone to run deficits. Hallerberg and von Hagen (1998, 1999) explicitly link the severity of the common-pool problem to electoral systems and forms of governments and argue that the appropriate reforms of the budget process differ across constitutional rules. These arguments are supported by empirical evidence from European and Latin American data sets.

As coalition governments have more veto players, such governments could be subject to a more serious status quo bias in the face of adverse shocks (Roubini and Sachs 1989; Alesina and Drazen 1991). Government crises are a priori more likely and empirically more frequent under proportional elections (because of the greater incidence of minority and coalition governments in systems with

---

10. More precisely, their index has five parts: indicators for federalism, bicameralism, referenda, presidentialism, and majoritarian elections.

proportional elections). Such crises could lead to greater policy myopia and larger budget deficits (Alesina and Tabellini 1990; Grilli, Masciandaro, and Tabellini 1991). These ideas are related to those in Tsebelis's (1995, 1999, 2002) studies, in which a larger number of veto players (and a larger ideological distance between them) tends to "lock in" economic policy and its ability to handle outside shocks. In Tsebelis's conception, proportional elections often lead to multiple partisan veto players in government and thus to more policy myopia, even though the electoral rule is not the primitive in his analysis.

Finally, large swings in the ideological preferences of governments as a result of elections are less likely in systems where coalition governments are the norm. Alesina, Roubini, and Cohen (1997) suggest that coalition governments (and thus, proportional elections) correlate with less pronounced "partisan" cycles after elections, and Franzese (2002) provides further evidence on this correlation.

These studies suggest that we should expect to find greater budget deficits under proportional than under majoritarian elections (at least among parliamentary regimes). They also suggest another question: are adjustments of spending or taxes to economic shocks conditional on electoral rules? Finally, they put forward an additional argument, beyond that presented in section 2.3, as to why electoral cycles might depend on the electoral rule.

Similar empirical questions could be posed about policy outcomes under different forms of government. No formal analysis of which we are aware has tried to compare the size of the budget deficit or the reaction of policy to economic shocks in presidential and parliamentary regimes. A priori, the comparison could go either of two ways. On the one hand, the more effective separation of powers under presidential regimes might, to the extent that it increases the number of veto players above that in parliamentary regimes, imply a greater status quo bias in policymaking. Indeed, some authors have tried to explain the occurrence of budget deficits and the adjustment to shocks in U.S. states as the result of a divided government in which governors and majorities in state congresses are controlled by different parties (Alt and Lowry 1994). The common criticism among political scientists of Latin American presidential regimes as being commonly deadlocked and ineffective can be read in the same way. On the other hand, the fixed term of office and the greater durability of the executive in presidential regimes could reduce policy myopia relative to parliamentary regimes.

Moreover, we do not know of any formal analysis that tries to predict the relative size of electoral budget cycles under different forms of government. But if the strength of electoral cycles depends on electoral accountability, the more pronounced separation of powers, and the individual nature of the executive in presidential regimes, the strength and nature of such cycles may well be systematically associated with the form of government.

The above discussion has centered on fiscal policy, broadly defined to include rents for politicians, which certainly reflects the orientation of the literature. But it is not difficult to think of plausible extensions into other areas of economic policymaking, such as regulatory policy or trade policy. The same mechanisms within presidential regimes and under majoritarian elections that bias policy decisions toward spending programs targeted at narrow groups may bias policy decisions toward boosting the incomes of geographically concentrated special interests through, say, tariff protectionism or regulation of entry. Thus it is plausible to conjecture that such structural policies also differ systematically across political systems, though demonstrating this is still an open research agenda for both theoretical and empirical analysis.

Whether we are economists or not, at the end of the day, we are interested not only in government policies per se, but also in their overall effect on more fundamental economic and social performance measures. Asking precise questions about how different political systems perform in these final dimensions is certainly much too difficult to undertake at our present state of knowledge. Even if we knew the precise effects of specific constitutional forms on different policy outcomes, these policies interact with one another in complicated ways and most probably affect economic performance in different directions. For instance, the greater accountability of majoritarian elections might discourage the corruption of elected officials, but at the same time, less representativeness and the associated weaker incentives for public-goods provision might result in an ambiguous net effect on economic development or private investment. Moreover, separating the influence of the political system from that of other features of society is a Sisyphean task. Thus existing theoretical research or background empirical and historical knowledge does not enable us to entertain any precise prior hypothesis about the likely causal effects of alternative constitutional features on measures of economic performance, such as labor productivity or economic growth.[11] Nevertheless, it is tempting to take a look at the relation between political systems and economic performance and try to clarify at least some of the policy links whereby political systems shape economic performance. Once more, such an exercise should not be seen as the testing of specific theories, but it could serve as a suggestive exploration of the data.

2.6   What Questions Do We Pose to the Data?

Given the discussion in this chapter to this point, some of the empirical questions we will pose take the form of specific hypotheses, whereas others really amount to a search for systematic patterns in the data. We also confine ourselves to posing questions on reduced form—is there a link from constitutional rules to policy outcomes?—without trying to discern whether any effects we might find are direct or indirect, running through political outcomes such as party structures. As discussed in chapter 9, identifying the precise channels of constitutional influence on policy is certainly a very important task. But we have to start somewhere and thus leave this task for future work, including a substantial investment in new data.

With this qualification, let us summarize the main empirical questions we would like to address with the help of table 2.1. In the first rows of the table, we encounter the theoretical predictions from sections 2.3 and 2.4. According to theory, presidential regimes should have smaller governments than parliamentary regimes and also less spending on broad government programs versus targeted programs (these predicted spending differences between presidential and parliamentary regimes are indicated by minus signs in the two upper entries of the right-hand column). Presidential regimes are also predicted to have less rent extraction than parliamentary regimes. Under majoritarian elections, we should observe less spending on broad programs than under proportional elections (this spending difference between majoritarian and proportional elections is indicated by the minus sign in the second row of the left-hand column). Several, but not all, models predict that the electoral rules also shape the size of government, with proportional elections associated with larger governments (thus, we enter a minus sign and a question

---

11. Roll and Talbott (2002), however, provide interesting and convincing evidence of democracy's being unambiguously good for economic performance. See also Barro 1996 and Alesina et al. 1996.

Table 2.1
Constitutions and economic policy: Theoretical predictions and open questions

Policy outcome	Electoral rules Majoritarian vs. proportional	Form of government Presidential vs. parliamentary
Overall size of government	$-/?$	$-$
Composition: Broad versus narrow programs	$-$	$-$
Rent extraction	$+/-$	$-$
Government deficits	$-/?$	?
Structural policies / Economic performance	?	?
Adjustment to shocks	?	?
Electoral cycles	$+/?$	?

Note: A plus (minus) sign in a column indicates that the constitutional feature on the left at the top of the column will induce a greater (smaller) degree or a higher (lower) level of the policy outcome for that row than the constitutional feature on the right. A question mark indicates no strong prior regarding the sign of the constitutional effect. See the discussion of this table in section 2.6 for more specific interpretations of the symbols.

mark (to indicate theoretical ambiguity) in the first row of the column for majoritarian versus proportional policy outcomes). Given the correlation between district size and electoral formula discussed earlier in the chapter, the different predictions concerning electoral rules and spending in the literature typically reinforce one another. In the case of rent extraction, however, the district size and ballot structure commonly encountered in majoritarian elections pull in opposite directions: whereas smaller districts imply larger rents, voting on individuals implies smaller rents (hence, the plus and minus signs in the electoral rules column). All of these predictions are cross-sectional in that they have been explicitly derived by comparing equilibria in static game-theoretic models.

Moving down the table, we reach the more open-ended, cross-sectional questions formulated in section 2.5. We are interested in the effect of the two constitutional provisions listed at the top of the table on budget balance (surplus or deficit). Although several theories suggest that majoritarian elections should be associated with smaller deficits, the prospective impact of forms of government on budget balances is more uncertain. In light of the discussion in section 2.5, we would also like to know whether structural policies promoting economic growth and efficiency differ systematically under alternative electoral rules or forms of government. We also want to explore whether different political systems entail systematic differences in economic performance, but once more, we have no precise prior hypothesis to guide the exploration.

Farther down the table, we find some predictions and questions that are squarely in the time series domain. One plausible conjecture has been made above: stronger incentives for politicians to perform should generate more pronounced electoral cycles under majoritarian elections than under proportional elections. We have no theoretical prior as to the strength of electoral cycles under different forms of government. Similarly, we would like to investigate empirically whether the reaction of fiscal policy to economic shocks differs across political systems, but we have few strong theoretical priors of what to expect.

2.7   The Empirical Agenda

The empirical questions summarized in table 2.1 set the agenda for the remainder of the book. A first task is to make operational the different aspects of policy and performance discussed in the table. How do we measure the composition of government programs, the amount of rent extraction, or economic performance in practice? What shocks should we consider and over what period? And so on. We have collected data for a large number of countries, both for the most recent decade and for a longer period going back to 1960. In chapter 3, we describe the measures of observed policy outcomes we have developed for use in the book. Because the existing theoretical models deliver—at best—ceteris paribus predictions about the effect of constitutional features on policy outcomes, we must also take into account a number of other country characteristics that may shape the outcomes we seek to explain. We therefore introduce these other variables in chapter 3 and show how they influence policy outcomes.

Chapter 4 tackles another crucial question: how should we classify and measure real-world constitutional features? As the theory underlying the predictions deals with democratic decision making, the chapter starts by defining what we mean by a democracy in practice. It then moves on to classify electoral rules and forms of government into the broad categories of table 2.1 and also to develop continuous measures of some detailed features of electoral rules.

Ideally, we would like our measures to be consistent with the distinctions among different electoral and legislative rules made in the game-theoretic models generating the predictions we want to test. Because of the rich variation among actual constitutions, however, achieving this consistency requires making a number of specific decisions. In chapter 4, we show that constitutional rules have a great deal of inertia: the broad features of electoral and legislative rules (as we measure them) are very rarely reformed. This is both a blessing and a curse in terms of our inference. It implies that we cannot hope to draw conclusions about direct constitutional effects by observing the consequences of reform. Instead, we must rely on cross-country comparisons. But it also means that the chain of causation is likely to go from institutions to policies and not vice versa. We take a first look at the data by constitutional group and find strong evidence that the selection of different constitutional rules is certainly not random, relative to geography, history, and other country characteristics. Gaining a better understanding of these non-random patterns of constitution selection is also one of the important goals of chapter 4.

Chapter 5 is devoted to some nontrivial methodological issues. How exactly do we define a causal "constitutional effect"? And how can we estimate it in a reliable way, given the aforementioned non-random selection and inertia of constitutional rules? We propose a number of econometric methods designed to address different statistical pitfalls but requiring different assumptions to identify a constitutional effect. These assumptions are scrutinized in the context of our data. The methodological discussion in this chapter takes us into statistical territory, parts of which may be familiar to many readers, and other parts of which may not.

In chapter 6, we apply the battery of methods resulting from our statistical exploration in chapter 5 to draw inferences from cross-country variation in fiscal policies and institutions. The theoretical predictions summarized in the rows of table 2.1 regarding the constitutional effect on size of government, composition of government, and budget deficits are applied to the data and tested with a variety of alternative statistical methods. Despite the different estimation methods used, many of the results are surprisingly stable.

In chapter 7, we turn to the table's predictions regarding the constitutional effects on rent extraction and the open questions regarding structural policies and economic performance, once again relying on the cross-sectional variation in the data. In this chapter, as in the prior one, we find robust results partly in line with theory. Here, however, the finer measures of district magnitude and the ballot structure play a more important role than the crude classification into majoritarian and proportional electoral rules.

Chapter 8 returns to fiscal policy but exploits its variation over time. We explore the open issues with question marks in the lower part of table 2.1. How do countries with different types of constitutions adjust when hit by common or idiosyncratic economic shocks? Does fiscal policy behave in a particular way immediately before or after elections? If so, are these electoral cycles different when conditioned on electoral rule or form of government? We find the answer to all these questions to be in the affirmative and, in the process, we uncover a number of new stylized facts.

Finally, chapter 9 starts with a brief discussion of what we have learned from the empirical evidence presented in the preceding chapters with regard to each row in the table. It ends by asking where research in this area should go next.

3   Policy Measures and Their Determinants

3.1 Introduction

Now that we know what questions to explore regarding constitutional effects on different policies, it is time to turn to the data. In this chapter, we describe the measures of performance we use and the economic policies we seek to explain on the basis of alternative constitutional features. (Data on the constitutional rules of interest are discussed in the next chapter.) We start the chapter with fiscal policy: size of government, composition of government spending, and budget deficit, measuring these outcomes in alternative ways. Then we proceed to proxies for rent extraction by politicians: perceptions of the incidence of corruption and of (in)effectiveness in government services. Finally, we turn to composite measures of growth-promoting policies, such as the protection of property rights, and the impact of these policies on long-run indicators of economic performance, namely, labor productivity and total factor productivity.

Because it is hard to find interesting variations in electoral rules or forms of government at the subnational level, we focus on comparisons among nation-states. We are interested in the policy variation across both time and place. It is therefore convenient to separate our data into two different data sets corresponding to the two dimensions of policy variation. Since the theory underlying the predictions outlined in chapter 2 refers to democratic decision making, these data sets are restricted to democracies. The next chapter explains in detail our (sometimes quite generous) criteria for determining whether to include particular countries in the two sets of democracies.

To study cross-sectional variation in policy, we design a data set that includes 85 countries that can be considered democracies in the 1990s. For these countries and a large number of variables, we take an average of the yearly outcomes over the 1990–1998 period, referring to the resulting data set as "the 1990s cross section" or "the 85-country cross section." This data set then forms the main basis for our empirical work on constitutional rules and policy outcomes across countries in chapters 6 and 7. It is used to analyze all of our measures of performance and policy outcomes: fiscal policy, rent extraction, growth-promoting policies, and productivity.

To study time variation in policy, we design an alternative data set with 60 countries in which data are available for a sufficiently long period. Annual observations are kept in panel format for each of the years 1960–1998, although data are missing for many variables and countries for some of these years. We refer to this data set as "the 1960–1998 panel" or "the 60-country panel." We use it mainly in our empirical work on constitutional rules and policy outcomes across time in chapter 8. This work focuses on time variation in fiscal policy, since data on the other policy variables are not available for a long enough time interval to meaningfully study the variation of policy over time.

Naturally, the policy and performance outcomes we investigate reflect many other economic, social, cultural, geographical, and historical factors besides any influence we may find of constitutional rules. Both data sets therefore include a variety of such auxiliary determinants of policies and performance. In this chapter, we also describe these determinants (control variables). Rather than merely listing the variables, however, we introduce them in their context as explanatory variables for specific policies. Thus we show how each of our main policy measures correlates with a number of prospective determinants across countries and time that are suggested by theory or—more often—earlier empirical work. This provides us with an opportunity to review briefly some of the main findings of earlier related empirical studies, with no pretense of completeness. In the course of this discussion, we present estimates of linear regressions relating each policy measure to alternative sets of specific determinants. The constitutional variables of interest are omitted; they are defined in chapter 4, and their effect on policy and performance is studied in chapters 6 through 8. Our statistical analysis in this chapter is very simple: the regression results are displayed not for the purpose of statistical inference or hypothesis testing, but as an economical way of describing the patterns in the data.

We begin with fiscal policy (section 3.2), turning to rent extraction (section 3.3) and finishing with productivity and productivity-enhancing policies (section 3.4). The text provides only a broad summary discussion of our empirical measures and their sources. More precise descriptions of these measures are relegated to the data appendix.

3.2 Fiscal Policy

3.2.1 Size of Government

Two alternative measures of the size of government appear in both our data sets. Our primary measure is central government spending (inclusive of social security) as a percentage of GDP ($CGEXP$), but we also consider central government revenues as a percentage of GDP ($CGREV$). For most OECD countries and many countries in Latin America, data on central government spending and revenues are available for all years in our 1960–1998 panel. For many developing countries, however, the availability is limited to the period from the 1970s and onward. The statistical source for all these variables is the International Monetary Fund (IMF) (the International Financial Statistics (IFS) database).

The size of government varies a great deal, across both time and place. In the 1990s cross section, the mean value of central government spending is 29.8% of GDP, with a standard deviation of 10.4%. The range is more than 40% of GDP, from 9.7% (in Guatemala) to 51.2% (in the Netherlands). Figure 3.1 shows the size of government for the entire 1960–1998 panel (about 2,000 observations in total). Once more, government expenditure in a typical year ranges from below 10% of GDP to well above 50%.[1] The distribution drifts upward over time, reflecting growth in the average size of government (the curve in the figure) by about 8% of GDP from the 1960s to the late 1990s. Most of this growth takes place in the 1970s and 1980s.

A natural question is, why do we examine central, rather than general, governments (the latter also include local and regional gov-

---

1. To obtain clearer graphics, in drawing the figure, we have censored the observations where $CGEXP$ exceeds 60% of GDP. The censored observations apply to years of war or unrest in Israel and Nicaragua.

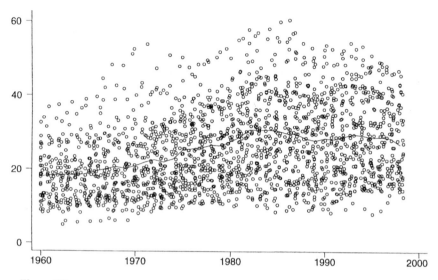

Figure 3.1
Size of government in 60 countries, 1960–1998

ernments)? The main reason is data availability and comparability.[2] Data on general government spending are available in the Government Financial Statistics (GFS) database of the IMF from the early 1970s onwards, but only for 41 of the democracies in our sample. Moreover, even for these countries, the definition of the relevant government entities or the precise definition of government outlays and revenues is often not comparable across countries or time. Central government data, however, are more reliable. For countries where data on general governments are available, the correlation coefficient between the size of central and general governments is very high (about 0.9). Moreover, centralization of spending (measured as the ratio between central and general government spending) is not correlated with the constitutional variables of interest (electoral rule and form of government) defined in the next chapter. Thus, we are quite confident that focusing on central rather than general governments does not bias our inferences. Nevertheless, we always include an indicator variable for federal political structures (called *FEDERAL*) in our cross-country analysis. The source of this

2. Strictly speaking, the theory reviewed in chapter 2 concerns decisions made by central government politicians. These are likely to control all levels of government more easily in unitary than in federal states.

variable is Adserà, Boix, and Payne 2001, which in turn, relied on data from Downes 2000.

Several other basic country characteristics are likely to correlate systematically with size of government. One idea originating in Wagner's law (Wagner 1893) is that government spending goes up with income. To measure differences in level of development, we use (the log of) each country's real per capita income (LYP), taken from the Penn World Tables and the World Bank. We also use a binary indicator variable for OECD membership in the early 1990s ($OECD$).[3]

Another relevant characteristic, particularly given our interest in constitutional effects, is quality of democratic institutions. We measure this feature using an index produced by Freedom House ($GASTIL$) for the 85-country cross section and a similar variable compiled by Eckstein and Gurr (1975) ($POLITY\_GT$), rescaled by us and expressed in the same units as the Freedom House index for the 60-country panel. Both variables run on a scale from 1 to 7, with higher values indicating weaker democratic institutions. They are described in detail in the next chapter.

Most empirical work on the size of government finds strong correlations between the demographic composition of the population and government spending, older populations being associated with higher spending. To measure these aspects, we use two variables: the percentages of the population between 15 and 64 years of age ($PROP1564$) and over 65 ($PROP65$). Earlier empirical work, starting with Cameron 1978, has found more open economies to have larger governments. This might reflect increased demand for social insurance in more open (and hence, more risky) economies, as suggested by Rodrik (1998), but it might also reflect readily available tax bases resulting from taxes on exports and imports, often exploited in developing countries (cf. Goode 1984). Here, we use a measure of a country's openness ($TRADE$), defined as exports plus imports over GDP. These three variables are all extracted from the *World Development Indicators* of the World Bank (2000).

Variation across Countries How do these variables correlate with the size of government across countries? Column 1 of table 3.1

---

3. As we treat OECD membership mainly as a (binary) indicator of development, we include all OECD members in the early 1990s except Turkey, which had a considerably lower GDP per capita than other OECD member states.

Table 3.1
Size of government and its determinants: Cross-sectional estimates

	(1)	(2)	(3)	(4)	(5)	(6)
Dependent variable	CGEXP	CGEXP	CGREV	CGEXP	CGEXP	CGEXP
GASTIL	−2.08 (1.24)*	−2.27 (1.18)*	−1.82 (1.29)	−1.19 (1.14)	−1.68 (1.16)	−0.49 (1.02)
LYP	−1.64 (2.15)	0.05 (2.10)	2.75 (1.80)	−0.50 (2.14)	−1.10 (2.23)	1.15 (2.10)
TRADE	0.05 (0.02)**	0.03 (0.02)	0.06 (0.02)***		0.04 (0.02)	0.03 (0.02)
PROP1564	−0.32 (0.34)	−0.30 (0.36)	−0.34 (0.32)	−0.14 (0.34)	−0.18 (0.38)	−0.74 (0.36)**
PROP65	1.65 (0.43)***	1.10 (0.42)**	1.06 (0.41)**	1.66 (0.43)***	1.24 (0.45)***	2.39 (0.57)***
FEDERAL	−4.56 (2.25)**	−4.78 (2.54)*	−4.76 (2.50)*	−4.79 (2.75)*	−4.07 (2.82)	−3.54 (2.95)
OECD	−0.21 (3.67)	−3.71 (3.99)	−4.07 (4.19)	−0.97 (3.88)	−1.98 (3.88)	−10.21 (4.20)**
AFRICA		−2.83 (4.57)	4.26 (5.19)		−3.81 (4.24)	−5.49 (4.89)
ASIAE		−7.05 (3.16)**	−2.56 (3.27)		−7.08 (3.03)**	−8.47 (3.49)**
LAAM		−9.01 (3.13)***	−4.66 (3.96)		−8.06 (2.81)***	−12.22 (3.60)***
COL_ESPA		0.53 (5.55)	0.87 (4.90)		0.36 (4.76)	6.89 (5.05)
COL_UKA		2.59 (3.13)	0.22 (2.68)		1.90 (3.03)	2.29 (2.37)
COL_OTHA		−1.11 (3.03)	−0.55 (3.08)		−2.22 (2.89)	−5.11 (3.15)
LPOP				−0.88 (0.59)		
AVELF				3.96 (4.15)		
MINING_GDP					0.28 (0.09)***	0.17 (0.12)
GINI_8090						0.15 (0.16)
Number of observations	80	80	76	80	75	63
Adjusted R^2	0.59	0.65	0.64	0.57	0.68	0.75

Note: Robust standard errors in parentheses.
*significant at 10%; **significant at 5%; ***significant at 1%.

shows the results of a multiple linear regression of central government expenditures on the seven country features described above.
The sample consists of the 80 countries in the 1990s cross section for
which all variables are available. These seven variables explain
about 60% of the variation in the dependent variable. As expected, a
large share of old people is strongly associated with government
spending: the elasticity is even above unity, so that an additional 1%
of inhabitants age 65 or older (at the expense of 1% fewer 15-year-
olds in the population) raises spending by more than 1% of GDP.
As expected, central government spending is also lower in federal
states, almost 5% of GDP. More open countries seem to have larger
governments; the effect is statistically significant but relatively small:
it takes a 20% increase in trade share to raise government spending
by 1% of GDP. Similarly, better democracies have larger governments: moving from the status of "semifree" (a *GASTIL* score of 3.5;
see chapter 4) to "free" (a score of 1.5) is associated with a 4% higher
spending share. In this specification, neither level of income nor
OECD membership significantly affects size of government, ceteris
paribus.

There are strong reasons to believe that geography and history
might also correlate systematically with government spending. To
capture geography, we use four dummy variables for continental
location. They refer to countries in Africa (*AFRICA*), eastern and
southern Asia (*ASIAE*) (other than Japan, which is included in the
OECD group), and South and Central America, including the Caribbean (*LAAM*). Taking into account the OECD group (*OECD*), the
default group of countries thus consists of non-OECD countries in
Europe and the Middle East. Among historical aspects, colonial history may be particularly important. We partition all former colonies
in our sample into three groups: British, Spanish-Portuguese, and
other colonial origin. We then define three binary $(0, 1)$ indicator
variables for these groups (*COL_UK, COL_ESP, COL_OTH*). Since
the influence of colonial heritage is likely to fade with time, we
weight these $(0, 1)$ indicators by the amount of time that has elapsed
since their independence as a fraction of the last 250 years, giving
more weight to colonial history in young independent states. (Colonial history dating back more than 250 years receives no weight at
all.)[4] The result of this weighting is three truncated, but continuous,

---

4. Thus, for instance, the variable *COL_UKA* is defined as: $COL\_UK * [(250 - \text{years of independence})/250]$.

measures of colonial origin, adjusted for the amount of time that has elapsed since independence: respectively, COL_UKA, COL_ESPA, and COL_OTHA.

Column 2 of the table adds these continental and colonial variables to the specification in column 1. As expected, the auxiliary variables add explanatory power; the regression now explains 65% of the cross-country variation in the data. We see that Latin American and Asian countries have smaller governments, ceteris paribus. None of the colonial variables significantly affects the size of government. As concerns the covariates discussed earlier, share of old people, federalism, and quality of democracy retain their significant influence. Column 3 of the table reports the results from the same specification with government revenue (CGREV) replacing government expenditure (CGEXP) as the dependent variable. The results are quite similar, except that the positive effect of openness is more precisely estimated.

The controls included in columns 1 and 2 (together with the constitutional variables discussed in the next chapter) constitute the core specifications we use in chapter 6 when estimating the constitutional effect on fiscal policy from cross-country data. These variables are selected either on a priori grounds (for instance, level of per capita income) or because they are found to have a strong and robust correlation with size of government. Nevertheless, we also tried to expand the specification with a number of other covariates. The results of some of these alternative specifications are reported in columns 4–6, in which the dependent variable is the size of government spending.

Alesina and Wacziarg (1998) have suggested that government spending is perhaps influenced by country size (which determines the scope of economies of scale or the heterogeneity of voters' preferences) and not by openness to international trade per se. Naturally, country size and openness are strongly negatively correlated, and when both variables are included in our regressions, neither turns out to be statistically significant. In column 4 of the table, we replace openness with the logarithm of population (LPOP) and a measure of ethnic and linguistic fractionalization (AVELF) that takes on higher values for more fractionalized countries. (This variable is described below with reference to the determinants of corruption.) Both estimated coefficients have the expected sign (negative and positive, respectively), but neither is statistically significant.

For countries at low levels of development, the administrative and deadweight costs of taxation might limit the size of government. But a large mining sector can provide a cheap source of government revenues, either directly, or indirectly through the income of the corporations operating in that sector (Goode 1984). Data on the output of the mining sector are available from the UN national accounts statistics for 75 countries in our sample, although these data are not always comparable across countries or time. When mining as a ratio of GDP (*MINING_GDP*) is added to the regression (column 5), its estimated coefficient is positive and statistically significant, a finding generally robust to alternative specifications and estimation methods. Nevertheless, to avoid shrinking the sample size and given the low reliability of these data, we do not include this variable in our default specification. Mining is not systematically correlated with the constitutional variables of interest, and its omission or inclusion has no impact on the results reported in chapter 6 on the influence of constitution on size of government.

Finally, several median-voter models (starting with Meltzer and Richard 1981) suggest that higher levels of income inequality raise government spending. To capture this aspect, we use the Gini coefficient (*GINI_8090*) sampled around 1980 and 1990 and available for about 60 countries in our sample (the source is Deininger and Squire 1996). Its estimated coefficient in column 6 is not statistically significant, a result that is very robust. Note that in this specification, mining loses its explanatory power.

Comparing these alternative specifications, a few results stand out as the most robust. A federal structure (*FEDERAL*) and location in Latin America (*LAAM*) or Asia (*ASIAE*) are associated with a smaller central government, whereas an older population (*PROP65*) is always associated with a larger government. The other control variables included in our default specification, such as per capita income, openness, quality of democracy, or being an OECD country, do not have a stable estimated coefficient as we vary the specification. This might reflect collinearity with some of the other included regressors. In light of our strong priors and the findings of earlier empirical work, however, we always include them in our default specification.

Variation across Time Next we turn to variation in the size of government over time. In this case, we rely on the 1960–1998 panel, and the results are displayed in table 3.2. In column 1, we report on

Table 3.2
Size of government and its determinants: Panel estimates

	(1)	(2)	(3)
Dependent variable	CGEXP	CGEXP	CGEXP
POLITY_GT	−0.26	0.35	
	(0.10)**	(0.34)	
LYP	3.52	5.94	1.14
	(0.79)***	(0.90)***	(0.93)
TRADE	0.05	0.05	0.06
	(0.01)***	(0.01)***	(0.01)***
PROP1564	−0.12	−0.18	−0.38
	(0.06)*	(0.07)***	(0.08)***
PROP65	2.36	1.99	1.45
	(0.14)***	(0.15)***	(0.18)***
LCGEXP			
OIL_EX			
OIL_IM			
YGAP			
LCGREV			
Country effects	Yes	Yes	Yes
Year effects	No	No	Yes
Sample	Full	Democratic	Democratic
Number of observations	1,941	1,609	1,594
Number of countries	60	60	60
R^2	0.35	0.39	0.49

Note: Standard errors in parentheses. R^2 refers to within-R^2.
*significant at 10%; **significant at 5%; ***significant at 1%.

a regression including "country fixed effects." This means that we add a dummy variable for each country to the right-hand side of the regression. Another way of understanding this specification is to consider the dependent variable as the deviation of each country's government expenditure in a given year from its mean over the entire sample period. In this formulation, country-specific variables remaining constant over time can contribute only to explaining mean expenditures. Thus we must exclude from the regression the indicator variables for federalism, OECD membership, continental

Table 3.2
(continued)

	(4)	(5)	(6)
Dependent variable	CGEXP	CGEXP	CGREV
POLITY_GT			
LYP	0.57	0.86	0.55
	(0.57)	(0.53)	(0.48)
TRADE	−0.00	0.00	0.01
	(0.01)	(0.01)	(0.01)*
PROP1564	−0.04	−0.12	−0.04
	(0.05)	(0.04)***	(0.03)
PROP65	0.21	0.19	0.17
	(0.11)*	(0.09)**	(0.08)**
LCGEXP	0.80	0.79	
	(0.02)***	(0.01)***	
OIL_EX		0.05	0.04
		(0.02)**	(0.02)**
OIL_IM		0.07	0.03
		(0.01)***	(0.01)***
YGAP		−0.11	−0.04
		(0.04)***	(0.03)
LCGREV			0.83
			(0.01)***
Country effects	Yes	Yes	Yes
Year effects	Yes	No	No
Sample	Democratic	Democratic, $|YGAP| < 5$	Democratic, $|YGAP| < 5$
Number of observations	1,550	1,452	1,405
Number of countries	60	60	59
R^2	0.82	0.83	0.83

location, and colonial history that were used above in studying cross-country variation. A fixed-effect specification has the advantage of holding constant any *unobserved* (omitted) country-specific (time-invariant) determinants of size of government. Put differently, the effect of any regressor on size of government is fully identified from its variation over time and not at all from its variation over countries, the sole basis for identification in table 3.1. Note that unlike in the cross-sectional regressions, the quality of democracy is measured by the variable POLITY_GT, which is available over the entire 1960–1998 period (and also comparable over time). Higher (lower) values of this variable, as noted earlier, denote worse (better) democracies.

The results show that the share of old people, openness, and a better democracy continue to be positively related to spending, confirming the results from the cross-sectional regressions of table 3.1. Level of income now has a positive estimated coefficient, as expected from Wagner's law.

The sample of nearly 2,000 observations used in table 3.2 includes all the available data in our 1960–1998 panel. For some countries and years in the sample, the political system cannot be described as democratic, however, because of the rule of military juntas or other restrictions of democratic rights. This may be of little importance here, but it will be important in chapter 8, in which we test for the predicted effect of constitutional form in well-functioning democracies. As further discussed in chapter 4, we therefore restrict the sample to years of democratic rule, which involves dropping about 350 observations. Column 2 of table 3.2 shows the same specification as column 1 under this restriction. Most country panels are still quite long: their average length is 26.2 years (out of the 39 from 1960 to 1998). Income, openness, and demographics retain their earlier sign and significance pattern, but quality of democracy now exerts a positive and nonsignificant influence on size of government. This change in the sign of and the lower precision of the coefficient strongly suggest that the estimate in column 1 captures a threshold effect (of about 1% of GDP, according to the parameter estimate), namely, growth of government in connection with transitions from dictatorship to democracy. But marginal changes in quality of democracy among established democracies have no significant effect on spending.

Although this finding is thought-provoking, our interest in this book is not the effect of democracy, but that of different democratic constitutions. Since a number of observations are missing for the variable POLITY_GT, which plays only a small role in the sample of democracies, the remainder of the table shows the results when this variable is not included among the regressors. The specifications reported in columns 3–6 (and the corresponding samples) are those used in the detailed analyses of chapter 8.

When interpreting the results in columns 1 and 2, it is important to keep in mind that income has a strong upward trend in most countries over this time period, as does share of old people and openness. As we saw above, there is also an upward trend in average size of government, so that the estimated effect of these variables might well be spurious. To rule out this possibility, we use the specification in column 3, which is identical to column 2 with one important difference (besides the omission of quality of democracy). We now also add "year fixed effects" (i.e., a set of year dummies) to the right-hand side of the regression. In the same way as country dummies pick up country averages over all years, these year dummies pick up year averages over all countries. Including year dummies, we clean the estimates of the impact of jointly trending variables. The demographic variables and openness retain their expected signs, but the estimate of income becomes much smaller and turns statistically insignificant. The likely explanation for this result is that the strong effects in columns 1 and 2 at least partly reflect upward trends in both income and spending (including or omitting POLITY_GT makes no difference).

A measure of the cumulative growth of government over a certain period can be obtained by finding the difference between the estimated coefficients on the last and the first year dummy of the period (which is preferable to using the simple year averages plotted in figure 3.1, as the country fixed effects take care of the potential problem of countries with different [average] sizes of governments entering and exiting the panel at different times). This measure suggests a cumulative rise in government spending of about 12% of GDP in the 25-year period from the early 1960s to the early 1980s, when government spending peaks, and a subsequent decline of about 3% of GDP from that peak until the late 1990s.

The size of the government in a particular country is likely to change relatively slowly over time and thus to exhibit a great deal of inertia. This has, so far, not been taken into account in the estimates. A simple way of capturing these dynamics is to add the lagged (one-year) size of government (LCGEXP) to the right-hand side of the regression, which we do in column 4.[5] As the estimates show, there is indeed a strong positive inertia in expenditures: a coefficient of 0.8

---

5. The addition of a lagged dependent variable to a panel regression can create statistical problems with biased estimates, particularly when the panel is short. As stated above, we have more than 26 years for the average country panel, so this problem is likely to be relatively small in our case. Chapter 8 includes a more extensive discussion of the prospective methodological problems in dynamic panels and possible ways around them.

means that 80% of the change in spending in a given year remains in the next year. The other right-hand-side variables generally retain their earlier signs but some, particularly income and openness, lose statistical significance. Furthermore, the point estimates are smaller in absolute value, which is natural, as the specification now allows the adjustment to a shock to spread out over time. The fit of the regression increases considerably, so that in column 4 we explain more than 80% of the variation in the dependent variable, as opposed to 50% in the previous columns.

The year dummies we employ capture the total effects of *common* unobserved economic and political shocks to the countries in our panel. But a few of the most salient common shocks over this period may also be observable. An obvious example is the oil shocks that hit the world's economies in the 1970s and 1980s. To gauge these common shocks, we use the price of oil in U.S. dollars. Because this variable is common for all countries in the sample, we remove the year fixed effects to avoid perfect colinearity. As the effect of an increase in oil prices is likely to be quite different for oil-exporting countries than for oil-importing countries, we interact oil prices with dummy variables for oil exporters and importers (which allow a country's net export status to shift over time), thus creating the variables *OIL_IM* and *OIL_EX*.

We also add to the regression idiosyncratic economic shocks in the form of a country-specific business cycle. Specifically, we take the (log) difference between real GDP in a particular country and its trend (as computed with the so-called Hodrick-Prescott filter). With that definition, we can interpret the resulting variable (*YGAP*) as the deviation of aggregate output from its trend value in percent, a measure sometimes called the output gap. Figure 3.2 displays the frequency distribution of these output gaps, pooling together all observations in our default sample (in the figure, each data point has been approximated with its closest integer). Quite a few output gaps take on extremely large positive and negative values. To avoid drawing inferences from such extreme outliers, we drop all output gaps exceeding 5% in absolute value from the sample.

Column 5 of table 3.2 shows the results when these additional variables, *OIL_IM*, *OIL_EX*, and *YGAP*, are added to the previous specification. All of these variables are strongly significant with the expected sign. For oil importers, a rise in oil price and a negative output gap raises spending as a fraction of GDP. Thus, the ratio of

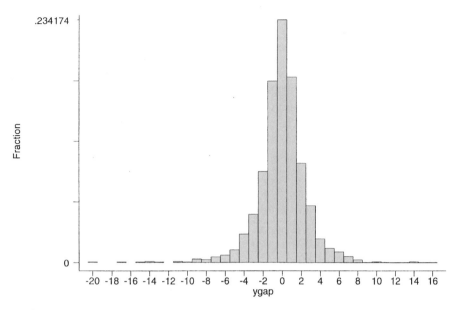

Figure 3.2
Distribution of output gaps in the 1960–1998 panel.

government spending to GDP is countercyclical (meaning that government spending does not move in proportion to income during the business cycle or may even move in the opposite direction). A negative output gap on the order of 3% of GDP is associated with a higher spending level of about a third of 1% of GDP, whereas an oil price hike of $10 raises the ratio of government spending to GDP by about half a percentage point. Oil exporters raise their spending by almost as much as oil importers, suggesting a direct effect of the oil price on spending via government income. Demographics now regain some of their explanatory power (perhaps because oil price does not purge the effects of common trends as effectively as the year dummies).

Finally, column 6 of table 3.2 relies on the same specification, but with government revenue rather than expenditures as the dependent variable. The results are essentially the same for most variables, except that output gaps are no longer statistically significant and the estimated coefficients on oil prices are smaller. This makes intuitive sense (at least for oil importers): tax revenue in a given country in nominal terms is likely to be more sensitive than government spending to the state of the economy, implying a smaller reaction when both measures are scaled to GDP.

3.2.2 Composition of Government

When discussing the composition of government spending, we focus on welfare state programs as a percentage of GDP. We measure the size of these programs in a country using the level of social security and welfare spending by central government (SSW), which includes spending within programs such as pensions and unemployment insurance. The source of this variable is the GFS database of the IMF. Data on SSW are available for 72 countries out of 85 in the 1990s cross section. The 1960–1998 panel is missing data on SSW for only a few countries.

We use this variable to test the predictions sketched in chapter 2 concerning (geographically) targeted versus nontargeted spending under different constitutional rules. In advanced industrial countries, broad social transfer programs like pensions and unemployment insurance certainly cannot be finely targeted toward narrow geographical constituencies, whereas spending on goods and services can. Hence, SSW measures the size of broad redistributive programs likely to benefit large groups in the population, as opposed to narrow geographical constituencies. Whether the interpretation of this variable also applies to developing countries is less evident: in such countries, the size of social welfare spending is generally very small and often directed toward urban residents.

Like size of government, welfare state spending varies a great deal over time and place. The mean value of SSW in the 1990s cross section is 8.1% of GDP and its standard deviation 6.6%. The maximum value is 22.4% (for Sweden) and the minimum 0.1% (for Bangladesh). The distribution in a given year of the 1960–1998 panel has a similar range. Over the period from the early 1970s to the 1990s, the average level of welfare spending across countries rose by about 2.5% of GDP.

The basic determinants of social transfers are likely to coincide with those of overall spending. Column 1 of table 3.3 thus shows the result from the same basic regression in the 85-country cross section as column 1 of table 3.1, but now with SSW rather than $CGEXP$ as the dependent variable. The seven left-hand side variables in the basic specification presented in column 1 explain almost 80% of the cross-country variation in social transfers. As the table shows,

Table 3.3
Welfare spending and its determinants: Cross-sectional and panel estimates

	(1)	(2)	(3)	(4)
Dependent variable	SSW	SSW	SSW	SSW
GASTIL/POLITY_GT	−0.67	−0.62	−0.07	
	(0.46)	(0.56)	(0.03)***	
LYP	0.18	0.33	0.18	0.34
	(0.76)	(0.95)	(0.24)	(0.28)
TRADE	0.01	0.01	−0.01	−0.01
	(0.01)	(0.01)	(0.00)***	(0.00)***
PROP1564	−0.16	−0.12	−0.02	−0.02
	(0.13)	(0.14)	(0.02)	(0.02)
PROP65	1.34	1.29	0.09	0.05
	(0.15)***	(0.27)***	(0.04)**	(0.04)
FEDERAL	−0.15	−0.58		
	(1.19)	(1.23)		
OECD	−1.78	−2.05		
	(1.81)	(2.11)		
AFRICA		0.66		
		(2.00)		
ASIAE		−0.99		
		(1.87)		
LAAM		−0.47		
		(2.23)		
COL_ESPA		3.39		
		(3.16)		
COL_UKA		−1.43		
		(1.73)		
COL_OTHA		−1.72		
		(1.30)		
LSSW			0.80	0.80
			(0.02)***	(0.02)***
OIL_EX			0.01	0.01
			(0.00)	(0.01)
OIL_IM			0.01	0.00
			(0.00)*	(0.00)
YGAP			−0.03	−0.08
			(0.01)***	(0.01)***
Country effects			Yes	Yes
Year effects			No	No
Sample			Full	Democratic, |YGAP| < 5
Number of observations	69	69	1,092	890
Number of countries			58	56
Adjusted R^2	0.79	0.80	0.75	0.77

Note: Robust standard errors in parentheses. "Adjusted R^2" in panel regressions (columns 3–4) refers to within-R^2.
*significant at 10%; **significant at 5%; ***significant at 1%.

the coefficients have the same sign as in the size regression, but only one of them is significantly different from zero. Although the share of old people still exerts a strong influence, openness and federalism no longer appear as important determinants when it comes to social transfers. Column 2 reports the results when geography and history are added in the form of continental and colonial indicator variables; these variables once more are not statistically different from zero. There are few changes in the other coefficients.

For overall size of government, we experimented with a few alternative specifications, but we do not report the results in table 3.3. Not surprisingly, the size of the mining sector has no explanatory power in this case, nor do income inequality, population size, or degree of heterogeneity. Basically, we can explain about 80% of the cross-country variation in social security and welfare spending on the basis of just a few variables, but the only one to systematically have a statistically significant effect is the share of old people in the population.

The two remaining columns in table 3.3 show estimation results from the 60-country panel. We first rely on a specification with the basic time-varying regressors, country fixed effects, lagged welfare spending ($LSSW$), oil prices (separately for oil exporters and importers) and country-specific output gaps. In column 3, the sample is restricted only by data availability. Column 4 adds restrictions to years of democratic governance and output gaps less than 5% in absolute value and drops the quality-of-democracy variable (which overlaps with the sample and the specification used in chapter 8). As in the case of overall spending, we find strong inertia in welfare spending. A higher share of old people is correlated with higher spending, as expected. More trade is now associated with less welfare spending, in contrast to what might be expected from the argument in Rodrik 1998, although the point estimate of the coefficient on trade is small. Output gaps, but not oil shocks, have a significant and negative effect on welfare spending, particularly in the restricted sample excluding the exceptional output gaps. According to the estimates in column 4, an income fall of 3% below the trend in the average country is associated with higher transfers by about 0.25% of GDP in the same year, followed by further increases in subsequent years (due to the high positive coefficient on lagged transfers). Quality of democracy is estimated to raise spending only when the data include significant democratic transitions (column 3) (in the sample of better democracies, the variable POLITY_GT is never significant even if included). Furthermore, the share of old people has a less pronounced effect in the more restrictive sample (column 4).

3.2.3 Budget Surplus

The final fiscal policy outcome we examine here is the government budget balance, which we measure using the size of the budget surplus of the central government (SPL), once more in percentage of GDP. The source is the IFS database of the IMF. Data are available for 75 countries in our 1990s cross section. The countries in this sample on average run a deficit amounting to 2.2% of GDP (i.e., the mean for SPL is negative). Although the standard deviation is only 3.5%, the range in the sample runs from whopping deficits (the highest being 11.4% of GDP, in Greece) to surpluses (the highest being 12.4% of GDP, in Singapore). In the first decade of the 1960–1998 panel, there is less variation across time. But the 1970s and 1980s see the average country going more heavily into deficit, and the degree of dispersion grows across countries. In the 1990s, there is instead a general trend toward fiscal consolidation. When we take averages over the whole 1960–1998 period for the 60 countries for which data are available, the mean deficit is 2.9% of GDP, with a standard deviation of 2.4%. Israel is the country with the largest average deficit (about 11% of GDP), and Botswana has the largest average surplus (about 4% of GDP) throughout this period.

Table 3.4 presents the results of a set of cross-sectional and panel regressions with surplus as the dependent variable. The specification is the same as for the fiscal policy regressions presented in the previous tables in this chapter. This table explains only a small part of the cross-country or time variation, however, suggesting that relevant variables may be omitted. In particular, our specification neglects variables measuring the availability of funds to specific sovereign borrowers. Some governments may be more risky borrowers than others and may face borrowing constraints, but none of our included variables controls for that.

The cross-sectional estimates in columns 1, 2, and 3 of the table suggest that richer countries have better fiscal balances than poor ones. The same is true for countries more dependent on international trade. But these results appear only in the 1990s data and not in the longer sample. African and Latin American countries appear to have smaller deficits than countries belonging to the OECD, though

Table 3.4
Government surpluses and their determinants: Cross-sectional and panel estimates

	(1)	(2)	(3)	(4)	(5)
Dependent variable	SPL	SPL	SPL	SPL	SPL
GASTIL/POLITY_GT	−0.01	0.06	−1.67	0.10	
	(0.68)	(0.70)	(0.96)*	(0.05)**	
LYP	1.69	1.66	0.03	−0.50	−0.37
	(0.80)**	(0.75)**	(0.92)	(0.39)	(0.49)
TRADE	0.03	0.03	0.01	0.02	0.01
	(0.01)**	(0.01)***	(0.02)	(0.00)***	(0.01)**
PROP1564	−0.11	−0.08	0.01	0.11	0.12
	(0.14)	(0.14)	(0.10)	(0.03)***	(0.04)***
PROP65	−0.16	−0.12	−0.14	0.05	0.05
	(0.14)	(0.18)	(0.13)	(0.06)	(0.08)
FEDERAL	−0.02	0.18	0.41		
	(0.86)	(0.87)	(0.70)		
OECD	−2.02	−1.31	−0.57		
	(1.46)	(1.69)	(1.58)		
AFRICA		2.69	4.32		
		(2.27)	(2.58)		
ASIAE		1.06	2.50		
		(1.59)	(1.56)		
LAAM		1.83	1.37		
		(1.79)	(1.27)		
COL_ESPA		1.19	−1.18		
		(2.49)	(2.24)		
COL_UKA		−2.27	−4.35		
		(1.71)	(1.41)***		
COL_OTHA		0.75	−1.53		
		(1.47)	(1.76)		
LSPL				0.71	0.71
				(0.02)***	(0.02)***
OIL_EX				−0.00	0.01
				(0.02)	(0.02)
OIL_IM				−0.05	−0.04
				(0.01)***	(0.01)***
YGAP				−0.00	0.06
				(0.02)	(0.03)*
Country effects				Yes	Yes
Year effects				No	No
Sample	1990s, broad	1990s, broad	1960–1990s, broad	Full	Democratic, $\lvert YGAP \rvert < 5$
Number of observations	72	72	60	1,832	1,427
Number of countries	72	72	60	60	60
Adjusted R^2	0.30	0.38	0.32	0.57	0.54

Note: Robust standard errors in parentheses. "Adjusted R^2" in panel regressions (columns 3–4) refers to within-R^2.
*significant at 10%; **significant at 5%; ***significant at 1%.

the estimated coefficients are not statistically different from zero. This might reflect borrowing constraints in international financial markets, rather than a lower propensity to borrow. But here it is important to add the following ceteris paribus qualifier: an income difference of two standard deviations corresponds to a larger average deficit of 3% of GDP, according to the point estimates in columns 1 and 2. Former British colonies have worse budget outcomes than noncolonialized countries, but the difference is statistically significant only in the longer time average.

A country cannot keep running large budget deficits forever without becoming insolvent. If a theory makes predictions about tendencies to run budget deficits under specific political systems, these predictions apply to the stock of government debt in the steady state, not to the budget deficit itself. This suggests that, in studying the determinants of budget deficits in a cross section of countries, we must avoid focusing on too short a time period (particularly if it is a period of budgetary consolidation, like the 1990s). For this reason, when we estimate the constitutional effect on the budget balance from cross-country variation in chapter 6, we report only results from data averaged over the whole period 1960–1998 (corresponding to column 3 in table 3.4). (The results for the 1990s are quite similar, though.)

Columns 4 and 5 of table 3.4 display the panel estimates. Column 4 refers to the full sample, whereas column 5 is restricted to that used in chapter 8 (democracies only, extreme output gaps dropped) with the same specification (the quality of democracy variable omitted). Country fixed effects are always included, whereas year fixed effects are not. Deficits, like other fiscal instruments, have a strong positive inertia: the lagged deficit has a precisely estimated positive coefficient that takes on the same value in these and other specifications. Openness to trade retains its positive influence from the cross-sectional regressions in all specifications. For demographics, we obtain a more plausible result than in the cross-sectional estimates, namely, a larger number of working-age people and a smaller number of old people improve the surplus (although the latter not significantly so). The effects of oil prices are also sizeable among oil importers, though not among oil exporters: an oil price hike of $17 (the change in *OIL* in the second oil crisis in 1979) reduces the surplus-to-GDP ratio by almost one percentage point (0.05×17) in the same year as the price increase. These differences in the deficit response between oil exporters and importers are consistent with the results for overall spending and revenues reported above (cf. table 3.2). Positive output gaps do increase the budget surplus, as expected, but only when extreme gaps are dropped (column 5).

3.3   Rent Extraction

3.3.1   Measuring Corruption

An empirical counterpart to rent extraction by politicians is not easily available in a large cross section of countries. Given the theory reviewed in chapter 2, an ideal measure would focus on illegal political rents. Clearly, real-world abuse of a higher political office can take the form of outright corruption and, more generally, misgovernance. We use three different measures in the empirical work to follow, two of which refer to corruption, the third to effectiveness in the provision of government services.

As Tanzi (1998) observes, it is difficult to define corruption in the abstract. Moreover, as corruption is generally illegal, violators try to keep it secret. Cultural and legal differences across countries make it hard to investigate corruption without taking country-specific features into account. Good proxies for political corruption should thus offer reliable information on the unlawful abuse of political power, as well as a strong level of comparability across different countries.

The Corruption Perceptions Index (CPI) goes some way toward meeting these requirements.[6] This index, produced by Transparency International, an organization that disseminates and compiles information about corruption worldwide, measures the "perceptions of the degree of corruption as seen by business people, risk analysts and the general public" (Lambsdorff 1998). Each country's score falls within a range from 0 (perfectly clean) to 10 (highly corrupt). It is computed as the simple average of a given country's score in a given year on number of different surveys that assess the country's performance. The yearly scores thus include information from many sources. The 1998 scores, for example, are based on 12 surveys from seven different institutions, and the 1999 scores on 14 surveys from 10 sources. As discussed at length in Lambsdorff 1998, the results of

---

6. A number of recent empirical studies of corruption have employed this index, including Fisman and Gatti 1999, Treisman 2000, Wei 1997a, and Wei 1997b.

these surveys are highly positively correlated: the pair-wise correlation coefficient among different surveys on average exceeds 0.8, suggesting that the independent surveys really measure some common features. Dispersion across the surveys in the ranking for an individual country is an indicator of measurement error in the average score constituting the CPI. For this reason, we typically weight observations with the (inverse of the) standard deviation among the different surveys available for each country (see chapter 7).

We take the average of these yearly country scores from 1995 to 2000 for the countries in the 1990s cross section. The resulting variable, *CPI9500*, is one of our measures of corruption. It is available for 72 countries and has a mean of 4.8 and a standard deviation of 2.4. The lowest recorded value is 0.3 (for Denmark) and the highest 8.3 (for Honduras and Paraguay).

An alternative corruption measure is based on a similar collection of surveys applying to 1997 and 1998 that are presented and discussed in Kaufmann, Kraay, and Zoido-Lobatón 1999. The observed survey results are combined into different clusters of governance indicators using a statistical, unobserved-components procedure. We use Kaufmann et al.'s sixth cluster, called "Graft." According to these authors, this particular cluster captures the success of a society in developing an environment where fair and predictable rules form the basis of economic and social interactions, with perceptions of corruption playing a central role. The original surveys have scores that range from −2.5 to 2.5, with higher values corresponding to less corruption. We invert and rescale this measure, which we also call *GRAFT*, to the same 0–10 scale as *CPI9500*. As with *CPI9500*, we weight the observations in *GRAFT* by the standard deviation of the original surveys.

Although *GRAFT* is based on a shorter time interval and is less focused on "grand political corruption" than *CPI9500*, it has the advantage of being available for 81 of the countries in our cross section (nine more than *CPI9500*). It has a mean of 4.2, a standard deviation of 1.9, a minimum of 0.7 (for Denmark), and a maximum of 6.9 (for Paraguay). Notwithstanding the a priori differences, it is strongly correlated with *CPI9500* (the simple correlation coefficient is 0.97).

Another cluster of governance indicators presented by Kaufmann, Kraay, and Zoido-Lobatón (1999) instead focuses on surveys of government effectiveness (once more referring to 1997–1998). The purpose of this cluster, "Government Effectiveness," is to combine perceptions of quality of public service provision in a particular country, the quality of its bureaucracy, the competence of civil servants and their independence from political pressures. These scores are also recoded on the same 0–10 scale as the other measures, with higher values meaning lower effectiveness, to produce the variable GOVEF. Like GRAFT, it is available for 81 countries. GOVEF has the same mean as GRAFT (4.2) and a slightly lower standard deviation (1.7) and ranges from 0.8 (for Singapore) to 7.3 (for Zimbabwe). Although it supposedly measures other aspects of government performance than corruption, it is still highly correlated with the earlier corruption measures (the correlation is 0.91 with CPI9500 and 0.95 with GRAFT). (In the next subsection, we refer to a number of empirical studies that have relied on these measures of corruption.)

We have not included panel data on corruption. The only such data available are those produced by the International Country Risk Guide (ICRG) from the mid-1980s onward, a fairly short period for such slowly moving variables as individual perceptions. Moreover, several of the determinants of corruption emphasized in our analysis are either time invariant or not readily available over such a time interval. Nevertheless, Persson, Tabellini, and Trebbi (2003) have also analyzed these panel data, and their results reinforce those of the cross-sectional estimates reported in chapter 7.

3.3.2 Determinants of Corruption

Earlier empirical work based on cross-country data identified a number of economic, social, cultural, historical, and geographic variables associated with the incidence of corruption. We do not attempt an exhaustive review of that literature here, but we refer the reader to the discussion in recent studies by Treisman (2000) and Persson, Tabellini, and Trebbi (2003) and the references in these papers. Based on these studies, we select a number of variables for our basic empirical specification.

Some of these variables appeared in our discussion of fiscal policy above. Thus, a country's economic and political developments are likely to correlate with rent extraction by politicians. As in the case of fiscal policy, we measure these aspects using our democracy index (GASTIL), the level of income per capita (LYP), and the indicator for OECD membership (OECD). Because earlier work has shown openness to trade (see Ades and di Tella 1999) and a decentralized political structure (see Fisman and Gatti 1999) to be negatively correlated with corruption, we include our measure of openness (*TRADE*) and our indicator for federalism (*FEDERAL*) in the basic specification.

Based on the existing literature, we also include some other country characteristics, one of which is population size, measured in millions and expressed in natural logarithms (*LPOP*). Several recent studies have found a higher fractionalization of a country's population with regard to language or ethnicity to be a significant determinant of misgovernance (see, e.g., Mauro 1995 and La Porta et al. 1999). We use one widely available measure for linguistic and ethnic fractionalization (*AVELF*) that is itself composed as an average of five different indexes. Scores on this measure range from 0 to 1, with higher values corresponding to more fractionalization. It is also likely that a more educated population will suffer less from rent extraction by politicians. To allow for this possibility, we use a comprehensive measure of the country's level of education (*EDUGER*), measuring primary and secondary school enrollment as a percentage of the relevant age group in the population (the source for these data is the United Nations Educational, Scientific and Cultural Organisation [UNESCO]). Several authors have also found religious beliefs to be significantly associated with the degree of corruption (see, e.g., Treisman 2000). To allow for this possibility, we use the shares of a country's population with a Protestant or Catholic religious tradition as measured in the 1980s (*PROT80* and *CATHO80*), with scores on these measures varying continuously between 0 and 1, and a dummy variable for Confucian dominance in a country (*CONFU*).

The first three columns of table 3.5 show the results when each of our three measures of rent extraction (*GRAFT*, *CPI9500*, and *GOVEF*) is regressed on the 11 variables discussed above. As mentioned above, the estimation is done by the weighted least-squares method, using the inverse of the standard deviation in the dependent variable as a weight. Together, these basic covariates explain 80–85% of the variation in the dependent variables. Once the effect of these observable determinants has been removed, the unexplained range of variation in corruption (i.e., of the estimated residuals of the regressions) is generally +1 or −1 around the mean, with outlier countries reaching up to +2.5 or −2.5 around the mean. The sign of the estimated coefficient of most right-hand-side variables remains the same across the three columns. Despite a great deal of colinearity among these regressors in our 85-country sample, some of them

Table 3.5
Rent extraction and its determinants: Cross-sectional estimates

	(1)	(2)	(3)	(4)	(5)
Dependent variable	GRAFT	CPI9500	GOVEF	GRAFT	GRAFT
GASTIL	0.12	−0.11	0.17	0.15	0.18
	(0.16)	(0.21)	(0.17)	(0.17)	(0.17)
LYP	−0.87	−1.06	−0.93	−0.97	−0.79
	(0.25)***	(0.30)***	(0.25)***	(0.24)***	(0.27)***
TRADE	−0.01	−0.00	−0.01	−0.01	−0.01
	(0.00)**	(0.00)	(0.00)**	(0.00)*	(0.00)**
FEDERAL	0.05	−0.04	0.28	0.15	0.06
	(0.31)	(0.39)	(0.32)	(0.31)	(0.35)
OECD	−1.41	−2.19	−1.29	−0.92	−0.55
	(0.36)***	(0.51)***	(0.38)***	(0.46)*	(0.58)
LPOP	0.05	0.21	−0.09	0.01	0.01
	(0.11)	(0.15)	(0.11)	(0.12)	(0.12)
EDUGER	−0.01	−0.02	−0.00	−0.01	−0.01
	(0.01)	(0.01)	(0.01)	(0.01)	(0.01)
AVELF	−0.40	−0.94	−0.78	0.71	0.47
	(0.51)	(0.64)	(0.53)	(0.63)	(0.62)
PROT80	−0.01	−0.01	−0.01	−0.01	−0.00
	(0.01)	(0.01)**	(0.01)	(0.01)*	(0.01)
CATHO80	0.01	0.01	−0.00	0.00	0.00
	(0.00)**	(0.00)*	(0.00)	(0.00)	(0.00)
CONFU	0.48	0.18	0.06	0.53	0.67
	(0.47)	(0.71)	(0.51)	(0.52)	(0.60)
AFRICA				−0.39	0.05
				(0.51)	(0.66)
ASIAE				−0.09	0.39
				(0.53)	(0.67)
LAAM				0.77	0.83
				(0.50)	(0.64)
COL_ESPA				−1.36	
				(1.08)	
COL_UKA				−0.75	
				(0.41)*	
COL_OTHA				0.46	
				(0.39)	
LEGOR_UK					−1.37
					(0.60)**
LEGOR_FR					−0.60
					(0.61)
LEGOR_GE					−0.98
					(0.74)
LEGOR_SC					−1.52
					(0.89)*
Number of observations	78	68	78	78	78
Adjusted R^2	0.83	0.87	0.79	0.86	0.86

Note: Standard errors in parentheses. Estimation in all columns by Weighted Least Squares, using [1/std(dep. var.)] as the weight.
*significant at 10%; **significant at 5%; ***significant at 1%.

clearly stand out as more important determinants of rent extraction and as statistically significant. As expected, higher-income countries have less corruption and more effective governments. According to the point estimates, all of them around unity, income must increase by about two standard deviations ($2 \times 0.96 = 1.92$) to reduce corruption or ineffectiveness by one standard deviation (see above). Membership in the OECD has a significant negative effect on rent extraction of roughly the same magnitude. More open economies also seem to have less corruption: the coefficient on *TRADE* may appear small, but the standard deviation of this variable is 47.7. The evidence on religion is more mixed, but with respect to corruption (columns 1 and 2), the estimates suggest that a higher proportion of Protestants and a lower proportion of Catholics in a country's population are helpful in restricting corruption. Finally, and contrary to Treisman 2000, which found federal countries to be more corrupt, federalism does not appear to be a significant determinant of rent extraction.

In column 4 of table 3.5, we add geography and history to the specification, with *GRAFT* as the dependent variable. More precisely, we add the indicators for continental location and the (discounted) indicators for colonial history. Most of the results from column 1 are unaffected, except that Protestant rather than Catholic religion now has a statistically significant influence. Furthermore, the inclusion of the continental indicators makes OECD membership (barely) insignificant. The continental indicators themselves are never statistically significant (recall that the default group is the non-OECD democracies of central and eastern Europe and the Middle East). With respect to colonial history, being a former British colony has a negative effect on corruption.

An alternative aspect of institutional history concerns the history of national legal systems. To measure the influence of legal systems on corruption, we use a set of legal origin indicator variables taken from La Porta et al. 1998. These authors extensively analyzed the impact of these indicator variables on various measures of government efficiency; Treisman (2000) studied their effect on corruption, attempting to separate the legal framework as such from colonial influences on a country's "legal culture" (expectations of the efficiency of the legal system as a whole). The indicator variables classify the origin of legal systems into five different categories: Anglo-Saxon common law, French civil law, German civil law,

Scandinavian law, and socialist law. We use the first four of these categories, creating four dummy variables: LEGOR_UK, LEGOR_FR, LEGOR_GE, and LEGOR_SC. The default is thus the countries with a socialist legal origin.

Column 5 of table 3.5 reports on a regression identical to that in column 4, except that we substitute the legal-origin variables for the colonial-origin variables (the two sets are strongly correlated). As column 5 shows, Anglo-Saxon and Scandinavian legal origins have the strongest negative effects on corruption, relative to the default. Not surprisingly, Anglo-Saxon legal origin seems to pick up the same features as British colonial origin (when both variables are included at the same time, each has a negative sign but neither is significant), but the effect of legal origin seems the more important of the two. Scandinavian legal origin and a large proportion of Protestants in the population apparently capture similar country characteristics (and low perceived corruption levels in Scandinavia), as the proportion of Protestants becomes insignificant once we add the legal-origin dummies. For the rest of the independent variables, the results are not considerably affected.

3.4 Productivity and Policy

The ultimate measure of the lasting success of a country's economic policy is its impact on economic development. As discussed in chapter 2, it is natural to ask whether and how different constitutional rules influence economic development.

When studying economic development, it is useful to distinguish between two different types of questions. One concerns the aggregate accumulation of knowledge that can *potentially* be applied to the production process at any given moment in time. What determines shifts in the knowledge frontier over time? This question is crucial for understanding why the United States and other leading industrial countries keep growing over time and why they are so much richer now than 50 or 100 years ago. But this does not take us very far if our goal is to understand differences in the level of development across countries at the same point in time.

A second type of question concerns how different countries actually apply already available knowledge to their production processes. Why do some countries only apply a fraction of existing technologies to the production of goods and services? And why are other countries so much more efficient in exploiting innovations and incorporating knowledge at the frontier? This second type of question is crucial to understanding international differences in income.

Recent contributions by economists have emphasized that institutions and structural economic policies determine the incentives of firms and individuals to adopt efficient productive techniques, and hence these are the main factors explaining differences in the level of development among countries (see, in particular, Hall and Jones 1997 and Parente and Prescott 2000). In this section, we describe two summary measures of development that we will study more thoroughly in chapter 7. We also introduce some observable features of economic policies and institutions/regulations that seem to promote efficient production techniques. Finally, we discuss additional historical and geographic variables that have been found to explain the adoption of good policies and institutions. As these variables are available only at one point in time, they are included in the 85-country cross section but not in the 60-country panel. An influential paper by Hall and Jones (1999) is the source of these data and the inspiration for our empirical analysis of these issues.[7]

3.4.1 Measuring Productivity and Growth-Promoting Policies

Economic development and economic performance can be measured in many different ways and from many different angles. Hall and Jones (1999) have compiled data on two measures of productivity for a large sample of countries. The more comprehensive measure of the two is labor productivity (i.e., output per worker), which we call *LOGYL*. As a rough correction for differences in the availability of natural resources across countries, this measure is computed by removing the output of the mining sector from total value added. The second measure is total factor productivity (which we call *LOGA*), which is computed as a residual, after imputing a fraction of output per worker to both physical and human capital. Thus, labor productivity measures the amount of aggregate output produced by

---

7. The idea that institutions are the key to understanding economic development has a long and honored tradition among historians, political scientists, and economists; see, for instance, North 1981, Mokyr 1990, and Engerman and Sokoloff 2000. But the contributions by Hall and Jones (1997, 1999) have spurred a recent wave of empirical and theoretical research, including, in particular, Parente and Prescott 2000, Acemoglou, Johnson, and Robinson 2001, Easterly 2002, Easterly and Levine 2002, and Acemoglou, Aghion, and Zilibotti 2002. Reviewing this rapidly growing literature is beyond the scope of this chapter.

an average worker (net of the output produced in the mining sector), whereas total factor productivity measures the average efficiency with which labor is used, taking into account the average education of workers and the average capital per worker. Both variables are measured as logarithms of levels and refer to 1988. Since both measures are expressed in common international prices and refer to the same point in time, they are suitable for cross-country comparisons.

Output per worker is available for 75 countries in our 85-country cross section, whereas total factor productivity is available for 74 countries. Both measures display considerable variation: the output per worker (in logs) varies from 6.95 for Malawi to 10.48 for the United States, meaning that a typical U.S. worker produces about 3.5 times more output than a worker in Malawi. The mean of this variable is 9.23, and its standard deviation is 0.90. Total factor productivity displays about the same range of variation: from 6.28 (in Zambia) to 9.01 (in Italy), with a mean of 8.18 and a standard deviation of 0.61. In fact, these two measures are highly correlated: their correlation coefficient is 0.87. Thus, differences in total factor productivity seem to be a major reason behind cross-country differences in output per worker, with differences in education and capital per worker playing an additional role. Parente and Prescott (2000) stress the crucial role total factor productivity plays in explaining international income differences. But the high correlation between output per worker and total factor productivity could also reflect measurement error in computing total factor productivity.

Hall and Jones (1999) show that the cross-sectional variation in output per worker and total factor productivity can largely be explained by two policy and institutional variables. One (called YRSOPEN here and originally compiled by Sachs and Werner [1995]) measures the number of years a country has been open to international trade during the period 1950–1994. The other (called GADP) measures perceptions of the degree to which economic and institutional environments in a country encourage the production of output rather than its diversion (which can take various forms, such as theft, corruption, litigation, and expropriation). This variable is similar to the perceptions-of-corruption variable described in the previous section; it was compiled by Knack and Keefer (1995) using ICRG data. It is measured over the period 1986–1995 and consists of a simple average of five indicators, two of which (law and order, and bureaucratic quality) relate to the role of the government in protecting property rights against private diversion, the other three (corruption, risk of expropriation, and government repudiation) to the role of the government itself as a source of diversion. Scores on both variables range from 0 to 1, with higher values indicating better policies (more protection of property rights or lower barriers to trade). The mean and standard deviation of our antidiversion policy indicator (*GADP*) are 0.69 and 0.20, respectively; those of openness to trade (*YRSOPEN*) are 0.47 and 0.35, respectively. According to both indicators, Bangladesh has the worst policies and Switzerland the best. Not surprisingly, the indicator of antidiversion policies is highly correlated with the indicator of corruption described in the previous section: the correlation coefficient between *GADP* and *GRAFT* is -0.87 (recall that higher values of *GRAFT* denote more corruption). The correlation coefficient between *GADP* and *YRSOPEN* is smaller, namely 0.64.

Empirical contributions following Hall and Jones (1999) have used similar indicators of how well institutional environments encourage productive economic activities as opposed to rent seeking or appropriation of output produced by others. Acemoglou, Johnson, and Robinson (2001) focus on protection against the risk of expropriation (one of the components of the *GADP* indicator), also originally compiled by Knack and Keefer (1995). Easterly and Levine (2002) rely on the broader indicator estimated by Kaufmann, Kraay, and Zoido-Lobatón (1999). Kaufmann et al.'s variable measuring a "good" institutional environment aggregates over 300 indicators ranging from ratings of country experts to survey results and measuring absence of corruption, protection of property rights and respect for the rule of law, degree of regulatory burden, government effectiveness in the provision of public services, political stability, and freedom.[8] All of these aggregate indicators (or their components) are highly correlated with one another and measure similar features of a country's economic and institutional environment. It is not clear what formal features of political and economic institutions are responsible for the perceptions underlying these measures, which is the main limit of this type of empirical analysis. Yet as we will see,

---

8. The variables *GRAFT* and *GOVEF* discussed in the previous section are components of this broader index by Kaufmann, Kraay, and Zoido-Lobatón (1999).

the underlying features measured by these indicators seem to play an important role in fostering economic development.

3.4.2 Determinants of Productivity and Growth-Promoting Policies

Naturally, neither of these policy measures can be taken as exogenous to economic development: it is likely that they influence as well as are influenced by the level of development. One of Hall and Jones's (1999) main ideas is that some observable historical and geographic features of a country influence productivity exclusively through their impact on the policy and institutional environments in the country, as measured by *GADP* and *YRSOPEN*. That is, Hall and Jones (1999) propose a number of "instruments" that can be used to isolate exogenous variation in these two policy variables and thus estimate their effect on productivity (readers not familiar with instrumental-variables estimation are referred to chapter 5, and the references mentioned therein, for a detailed discussion of such techniques in a cross-sectional setting).

Hall and Jones (1999) propose four instruments. The first two are direct measures of cultural influence: the fractions of the population speaking English as their mother tongue (*ENGFRAC*) or speaking one of the five primary European languages (including English) as their mother tongue (*EURFRAC*). The sources for these variables are Hunter 1992 and Gunnemark 1991. Naturally, the fraction of individuals with English as their mother tongue is much higher among the populations of former British colonies, with a mean of 0.29 versus a mean of 0.04 in the rest of the sample. But contrary to what might be expected, the percentage of English speaking is not just another way of measuring colonial origin: the correlation coefficient between *ENGFRAC* and British colonial origin is only 0.38. Thus, colonial origin and the diffusion of English as a mother tongue measure somewhat different aspects of a country's history.

The third of Hall and Jones's variables measures geographic location: distance from the equator (*LAT01*), measured as the absolute value of latitude and rescaled to lie between 0 and 1. This variable also measures cultural and historical influences. Countries closer to the equator provided a less hospitable environment for the first settlers from western Europe. These regions of the world were thus colonized later and, as argued by Acemoglou, Johnson, and Robinson (2001), were used by the West mainly to exploit their natural resources rather than as settlements for its migrants.[9] Engerman and Sokoloff (2000) also show that in these tropical regions, agricultural production mainly took the form of large plantations, where slave labor was the main factor of production. Whatever the specific argument, the distance from the equator proxies for different patterns and influences of Western colonization.

The fourth and last variable from Hall and Jones (1999) is a composite measure: the (log) predicted trade share of a country's economy based on a gravity model of international trade by Frankel and Romer (1996) (*FRANKROM*) that relies on a country's population and geographic features. The predicted trade share measures the physical endowments and the geographic location of the country.

Some of these variables are also used as instruments for constitutions in our work. We show (in chapter 4) that they are indeed correlated with several of our constitutional measures.

Table 3.6 reproduces some of the findings of Hall and Jones (1999) in our own 85-country cross section. Columns 1–4 present linear regression estimates of a reduced form in which the four instruments, latitude (*LAT01*), fraction of the population whose mother tongue is English or another European language (*ENGFRAC* and *EURFRAC*), and the gravity measure (*FRANKROM*) are used to explain the two productivity measures (*LOGYL* and *LOGA*) and the two policy indicators (*GADP* and *YRSOPEN*). In our data set, these four regressors explain more than 50% of the variation in output per worker (*LOGYL*) and antidiversion policies (*GADP*), but they explain a smaller part of total factor productivity (*LOGA*) and almost no part of the trade policy indicator (*YRSOPEN*).

Latitude is a very important variable in that both productivity and policies improve with the distance from the equator. Acemoglou, Johnson, and Robinson (2001) show that in their data set, this relationship largely reflects the correlation of latitude with settlers' mortality: once the latter is also included in their regressions, latitude tends to become statistically insignificant. The same occurs in our sample of countries: when settlers' mortality is added to the

---

9. Indeed, European soldiers in former colonies in the early 19th century had a much higher mortality rate the closer their colonies were to the equator. The data on settlers' mortality collected by Acemoglou, Johnson, and Robinson (2001) are available for only 36 of the countries in our data set. Among these, the correlation coefficient between the logarithm of settlers' mortality and the variable *LAT01* is −0.48. Countries in our sample with higher settlers' mortality are also much younger democracies.

Table 3.6
Productivity- and growth-promoting policies: Hall and Jones (1999) variables

	(1)	(2)	(3)	(4)	(5)	(6)
Dependent variable	LOGYL	LOGA	GADP	YRSOPEN	LOGYL	LOGA
LAT01	3.08	1.48	0.74	0.53		
	(0.42)***	(0.31)***	(0.09)***	(0.21)**		
ENGFRAC	0.25	−0.02	0.12	0.12		
	(0.24)	(0.19)	(0.05)**	(0.15)		
EURFRAC	0.70	0.59	0.03	0.01		
	(0.17)***	(0.13)***	(0.04)	(0.15)		
FRANKROM	0.11	0.10	0.02	0.07		
	(0.09)	(0.07)	(0.02)	(0.06)		
GADP					3.10	0.79
					(0.88)***	(0.74)
YRSOPEN					1.19	1.40
					(0.89)	(0.80)*
Chi-square: over-id					9.22***	7.69**
Method of estimation	OLS	OLS	OLS	OLS	2SLS	2SLS
Number of observations	74	73	75	75	73	73
Adjusted R^2	0.54	0.35	0.55	0.00	0.59	0.24

Note: Robust standard errors in parentheses. "Chi-square: over-id" refers to the statistic for testing the overidentifying restriction that the instruments included in first-stage regressions in columns 3 and 4 do not enter the second-stage regressions in columns 5 and 6.
* significant at 10%; ** significant at 5%; *** significant at 1%.

regressions reported in columns 1–4 of table 3.6, the effect of latitude vanishes. Since the overlap of our data set with that of Acemoglou, Johnson and Robinson is limited to 36 countries, however, we do not report these results.

Among the language variables, a higher fraction of English speakers in the population is associated with better policies (with a significant effect on antidiversion policies), whereas a higher fraction of speakers of another European language is associated with higher productivity, but not with better policies. Finally, the gravity indicator is almost never statistically significant.

Columns 5 and 6 of the table show estimates of the impact of the two policy and institutional indicators on productivity, under the restriction that the four instruments affect productivity only indirectly, through policy. Thus, we estimate using two-stage least squares (see chapter 5 for a discussion of this estimation method). In the first stage, the endogenous institutional and policy variables (*GADP* and *YRSOPEN*) are regressed on the four instruments (the same regressions as in columns 3 and 4). In the second stage, productivity is regressed on these institutional and policy variables; the results are displayed in columns 5 and 6. Antidiversion policies (*GADP*) have a strong and significant effect on output per worker, with the expected sign. Trade policies also enter with an expected (positive) sign, but the estimated coefficient is (weakly) statistically significant only in the case of total factor productivity. Note that the fit of the total factor productivity regression is quite low, suggesting that the dependent variable might be measured with considerable error.[10] Finally, the overidentifying restriction for the validity of the four instruments (once more, see chapter 5 for further discussion) is rejected in this sample: according to the data, at least some of the instruments appear to exert a direct influence on productivity over and above their impact on the two policy indicators. That Hall and Jones (1999) could not reject this overidentifying restriction indicates that their results are fragile to the sample of countries.

Some of the variables introduced in earlier sections to explain fiscal policy or rent extraction might also have an effect on productivity, either directly or indirectly through the Hall and Jones (1999) policy indicators. To explore these possibilities, table 3.7 extends the reduced and structural forms of table 3.6, allowing for a less parsimonious specification. As in the previous table, columns 1–4 display results from a reduced-form estimation of productivity and policies. To the four instruments used by Hall and Jones we have added our measure of federalism (*FEDERAL*), our set of colonial-origin dummy variables, and our dummy variables for geographic location.[11]

---

10. Hall and Jones (1999) constrain *GADP* and *YRSOPEN* to enter the productivity equation with the same coefficient, but as shown in table 3.6, this constraint is strongly rejected in our sample. Since there is no a priori reason to impose such a constraint, we let the two policy variables enter with different coefficients.

11. We have not added quality of democracy as an explanatory variable, for it would be endogenous in this setting. But we return to this issue in chapter 7, where we also include the age of democracy in each country among the regressors. We have also experimented with some other regressors used in earlier sections, such as the indicators of religious beliefs and population size, but they do not seem to have robust and general effects on the dependent variables of table 3.6 (except for a hard-to-interpret negative and significant estimated coefficient of the share of protestants [*PROT80*] in the reduced form for total factor productivity).

Table 3.7
Productivity- and growth-promoting policies: Other determinants

	(1)	(2)	(3)	(4)	(5)	(6)
Dependent variable	LOGYL	LOGA	GADP	YRSOPEN	LOGYL	LOGA
GADP					4.26	1.72
					(0.71)***	(0.61)***
YRSOPEN					0.93	1.11
					(0.47)*	(0.43)**
LAT01	1.00	0.31	0.37	−0.01		
	(0.59)*	(0.45)	(0.15)**	(0.52)		
ENGFRAC	0.35	0.05	0.08	0.37		
	(0.25)	(0.21)	(0.05)*	(0.26)		
EURFRAC	0.45	0.52	0.10	0.05		
	(0.24)*	(0.21)**	(0.05)**	(0.17)		
FRANKROM	0.20	0.18	0.04	0.21		
	(0.09)**	(0.07)**	(0.02)	(0.07)***		
FEDERAL	0.46	0.27	0.09	0.07		
	(0.16)***	(0.13)**	(0.03)***	(0.12)		
AFRICA	−1.25	−0.62	−0.11	−0.01		
	(0.33)***	(0.28)**	(0.07)	(0.33)		
ASIAE	−0.48	0.05	−0.06	0.60		
	(0.30)	(0.24)	(0.08)	(0.55)		
LAAM	−0.59	−0.27	−0.21	−0.25	0.92	0.58
	(0.24)**	(0.21)	(0.05)***	(0.21)	(0.18)***	(0.18)***
COL_ESPA	−0.15	−0.70	−0.11	−0.46		
	(0.52)	(0.41)*	(0.15)	(0.44)		
COL_UKA	−0.24	−0.32	−0.03	−0.63		
	(0.21)	(0.18)*	(0.06)	(0.39)		
COL_OTHA	0.34	0.10	0.00	−0.63	0.52	0.33
	(0.29)	(0.24)	(0.07)	(0.36)*	(0.25)**	(0.24)
Chi-square: over-id					6.43	4.28
Method of estimation	OLS	OLS	OLS	OLS	2SLS	2SLS
Number of observations	74	73	75	75	73	73
Adjusted R^2	0.69	0.48	0.65	0.19	0.69	0.37

Note: Robust standard errors in parentheses. "Chi-square: over-id" refers to the statistic for testing the overidentifying restriction that the instruments included in first-stage regressions in columns 3 and 4 do not enter the second-stage regressions in columns 5 and 6.
*significant at 10%; **significant at 5%; ***significant at 1%.

Several interesting results emerge. On the one hand, geography remains relevant: the distance from the equator (measured by *LAT01*) retains its explanatory power, though the coefficient is less precisely estimated than before. But other measures of geography now become highly significant, with Latin America and Africa being associated with lower productivity and worse policies. The relevance of geography is also confirmed by the predicted share of trade from the gravity model (*FRANKROM*), which is now statistically significant with a positive estimated coefficient. History and culture, on the other hand, seem less important than geography: the estimated coefficients on language variables and colonial origin are generally not statistically different from zero, except for *EURFRAC*, which has a positive effect on productivity and institutions. This lack of significance might be due, however, to some of these variables' measuring similar historical heritages. Finally, political centralization also plays an important role, with federal countries having higher productivity and better institutions and policies. The fit of all regressions naturally improves, as we add further regressors, even though they still explain a very small part of the variation in the trade policy variable (*YRSOPEN*).

Columns 5 and 6 of table 3.7 report the two-stage least-squares estimates. The first stage coincides with columns 3 and 4. In the second stage, productivity is regressed on the two policy indicators (*GADP* and *YRSOPEN*), and also on colonial origin other than Britain and Spain/Portugal (*COL_OTHA*) and the dummy variable for Latin America (*LAAM*). The choice of these additional control variables has been made with the criterion of not violating the overidentifying restrictions on the remaining instruments. Thus, with this second-stage specification, the instruments for the two institutional and policy indicators are the four Hall and Jones (1999) instrumental variables (*LAT01*, *ENGFRAC*, *EURFRAC*, and *FRANKROM*), plus federalism, the dummy variables for Africa and Asia, and British and Spanish/Portuguese colonial origin. As shown in columns 5 and 6, with this second-stage specification, we can no longer reject the overidentifying restrictions at the 10% confidence level. The results of the previous specification are confirmed: both institutional and policy variables are highly statistically significant and better policies and institutions are associated with much higher levels of productivity. Antidiversion policies (*GADP*) have an exceptionally strong effect on output per worker. The estimated coefficient of 4.26 implies that the different values of antidiversion policies between, say, Switzerland and Spain can account for twice the difference in output per worker between these two countries. If Spain could improve its institutional environment, cutting the distance to Swiss institutions and policies by half, it would thus have the same output per worker as Switzerland.

Some of the basic insights of Hall and Jones (1999) and the subsequent related literature are thus confirmed in our data set: two indicators of antidiversion and trade policies appear to be strongly associated with economic performance. Countries with better protection of property rights and less corruption (higher values of GADP) and more open access to international trade (higher values of YRSOPEN) also have a higher productivity of labor.

But the identifying assumptions of Hall and Jones (1999) are rejected. This is important, because it implies that other country characteristics, proxied by colonial origin and geographic location, also shape productivity over and above their impact on the two central policy variables. Moreover, the specific constitutional and political determinants of these good economic and institutional environments remain rather mysterious. What is the GADP variable really measuring, and why does it lead to higher levels of productivity and more efficient methods of production? One of the goals of the empirical analysis in chapter 7 is to shed some further light on what specific features of the political constitution (if any) might lead to adoption of better economic and regulatory policies and hence to stronger economic performance.

4

Electoral Rules and Forms of Government

4.1 Introduction

The theory surveyed in chapter 2 attempts to explain how economic policy outcomes are influenced by electoral rules and forms of government. The empirical policy measures introduced in chapter 3 are chosen to correspond as closely as possible to those appearing in the theoretical models. In this chapter, we outline the second piece necessary for solving the empirical puzzle: we describe how to measure and classify observed constitutions in a way consistent with the theoretical constructs.

As already mentioned, it is hard to find enough interesting variation in electoral rules and government regimes at the subnational level, so we focus on constitutions at the nation-state level. We limit ourselves to democracies, because the theories we take as our starting point predict how alternative democratic institutions modify the incentives of voters and politicians. Thus we must first address a primitive question: what do we mean by a democracy? More practically: how do we exclude countries that cannot be regarded as democracies from the two data sets introduced in chapter 3? That question is tackled in section 4.2.

In section 4.3, we discuss how to measure the various characteristics of electoral rules in practice. This leads up to a simple classification of the countries in our samples into those operating under majoritarian, mixed, and proportional electoral rules, as well as two continuous variables measuring the finer details of electoral systems. In addition, we give a short account of the history of electoral systems and recent reforms of them. In section 4.4, we turn to the legislative rules implied by different forms of government and provide a classification of countries into those with parliamentary and those with presidential regimes, also briefly discussing the historical origin of these regimes.

A major feature of our data is that the constitutional measures are not randomly distributed across countries. In section 4.5, we describe the observed correlations between constitutional rules and other variables, including a number of the socioeconomic character- istics included in the previous chapter. We also take a first look at the relation between constitutions and the various policy and perfor- mance measures introduced in chapter 3. At this point, we note some intriguing correlations, but caution the reader not to jump to pre- mature conclusions as to how constitutions might influence policy. As with the material presented in chapter 3, additional details on our data and our sources beyond those provided in the text can be found in the data appendix.

4.2   Which Countries and Years?

Our empirical investigations rely on cross-country data, in either pure cross section or panel format. In view of this, we have an obvi- ous interest in maximizing the number of prospective observations contained in our data set. Given the scarcity of reliable outcome measures, particularly for the period from 1960 onward, our mini- mal requirement for classifying a particular country as a democracy is quite generous. In the coming chapters, however, we check care- fully whether our results are sensitive to the chosen definition of democracy.

We obtain data on democratic governance primarily from two sources. One is the well-known surveys made and published by Freedom House since 1972; the other is the Polity IV data set, first described by Eckstein and Gurr (1975). Freedom House covers a large group of countries but does not go far back in time. The Polity IV data go back to 1800 and are more carefully drafted, and previous codings are updated to take account of subsequent changes in defi- nitions. The Polity IV data set does not, however, cover the very small countries in our sample. For this reason, we rely on the Free- dom House data set to select the 1990s cross section, our sample of contemporary democracies. But we rely mainly on the Polity IV data set to select the 1960–1998 panel and use it exclusively to extract historical information. Where they overlap, the two data sets lead to a similar classification of countries into democracies and non-democracies (see below).

4.2.1 Defining Democracies

To define a democracy in the 1990s cross section of countries, we rely on the annual surveys published by Freedom House. The so-called Gastil indexes of political rights and civil liberties assign values on a discrete scale from 1 to 7, with low values associated with better democratic institutions. Countries scoring 1 or 2 on an index are "free," countries scoring from 3 to 5 are "semi-free," and those scoring 6 or 7 are "nonfree." To arrive at these ratings, Freedom House uses the answers to a number of questions on a specific checklist. For political rights, this checklist involves items such as rulers being elected in free and competitive elections, a substantial role for the opposition, and freedom of organization; for civil liberties, it includes freedom of expression and assembly, rule of law, and so on.[1] We call the average of the two scores *GASTIL*. A drawback of the Freedom House measures is that changes in variable definitions in any given year do not change the codings of previous years, which makes the surveys less useful for comparisons over time than they might otherwise be. In a few cases detailed below, we also need to compute a measure comparable to *GASTIL* for the period 1960–1970, for which Freedom House data are not available. We then rely on the comparable measure compiled by Bollen (1990), available every five years and also going back to that period (we rescale Bollen's measure onto a scale from 1 to 7, equivalent to that of the Freedom House data). Thus, the sources for the variable *GASTIL* in our data set are Freedom House (when available) and Bollen rescaled (for the period 1960–1970).

To include a country in the 1990s cross section, we require a *GASTIL* score lower than an average of 5 for the 1990–1998 period. This rule permits 85 countries to be classified as democracies; we call these our *broad* sample. This sample includes some shady countries, however, such as Belarus and Zimbabwe (which also experienced significant cuts in democratic rights at the end of and after the sample period). For this reason, we always check whether the results of the empirical analysis are robust to imposing a stricter definition

---

1. A more precise description of the methodology Freedom House uses to arrive at its ratings can be found at ⟨http://www.freedomhouse.org/research/freeworld/2000/⟩.

of democracy. Specifically, we define a *narrow* sample that includes only those countries with an average *GASTIL* score lower than 3.5. This cuts 20 countries from the data set, leaving us with 65 prospective observations (subject to the availability of other variables).

For the 1960–1998 panel, we rely instead mainly on the Polity IV data set, as noted above. This represents the fourth wave of the well-known and encompassing historical study of democratic development initiated and first described by Eckstein and Gurr (1975). For each country, the data go back to as early as 1800 or the year of creation of an independent nation. This data set covers (1) all independent nations with (2) a population exceeding half a million people (both [1] and [2] refer to 1998). Specifically, we use the most encompassing POLITY index, which assigns an integer score ranging from −10 to +10 to each country and year, with higher values associated with better democracies. This index in itself constitutes the difference between two separate indexes (DEMOC and AUTOC in the original source). The former is an institutional measure of democracy with values from 0 to 10, based on a country's competitiveness and openness in selecting the executive, political participation, and constraints on the chief executive, whereas the latter scores autocratic limitations from 0 to 10 on the same dimensions of democratic rights. We adopt the original name, *POLITY*, for this index in our two data sets. Whenever Polity IV reconstructs its indexes, any changes in definitions are imposed on the entire historical data set, so as to allow comparability over time.[2]

We rely on the *POLITY* index, with the following slight modification, to define years and countries of democratic rule in our 1960–1998 panel. For five small countries, Bahamas, Barbados, Belize, Malta, and St. Vincent, the *POLITY* index is missing. We therefore use the *GASTIL* scores for these countries whenever available to amend the series, creating the modified index *POLITY_GT*. (Specifically, having rescaled the variable *POLITY* to make it comparable with *GASTIL*, we regress it on *GASTIL* and use the predicted values from this regression to replace the missing observations; since we need to go back in time, the *GASTIL* variable here includes the observations obtained from Bollen 1990). We then restrict our panel to include only those countries and years with values of *POLITY_GT*

---

2. More information about the Polity IV data can be downloaded from the Polity Web site: ⟨http://www.bsos.umd.edu/cidcm/polity/#data⟩.

below or equal to 3.666 (corresponding to positive values of *POL-ITY*). This restriction permits a total of 60 countries in the panel, but some of these enter in some years only. As an example, the rule temporarily excludes countries like Turkey (intermittently in the 1970s and 1980s), Argentina (until 1972 and between 1976 and 1982), and Chile (between 1974 and 1988). Throughout, we treat the censored observations as randomly missing, and we do not attempt to model this aspect of sample selection. We also perform some sensitivity analysis and occasionally restrict the sample with a stricter definition of democracy corresponding to *POLITY* scores above 5 (the boundary suggested by Polity IV for a stable democracy).

Table 4.1 lists the sample of 85 countries included in the 1990s cross section and the average quality of democracy in the 1990s as measured by *GASTIL* and *POLITY*. Whether each of the 85 countries also belongs to the 1960–1998 panel is indicated in the last column of the table.

Our two alternative measures of democracy imply similar, albeit not identical, classifications of democracies and nondemocracies for the 1990s cross section (where both indicators are available). An alternative criterion for inclusion in our 1990s cross section, consistent with our criterion for the 1960–1998 panel, is to insist on positive average values of *POLITY*. The resulting classification is somewhat stricter than the broad Gastil rule described above; it defines a set of 77 countries, in which all observations have a *GASTIL* value below 4.3. The countries (with more than half a million inhabitants) excluded by this Polity IV rule but included in our broad sample of democracies are Belarus, Gambia, Ghana, Malaysia, Peru, Singapore, Uganda, and Zimbabwe. Some sensitivity analysis suggests that the results reported in chapters 6 through 8 are robust to this small modification of our default sample.

4.2.2 Dating Democracies

The countries in our sample also differ on another important dimension, namely, *how long* they have been democracies. This could be of empirical importance: mature democracies might adopt systematically different policies than young ones. For example, although welfare state programs may be predominantly associated with democracies, it may take considerable time for a country to decide on and build up programs such as public pension systems. A link between age of democracy and social transfers is also suggested

Table 4.1
Age and quality of democracies

Country	GASTIL	POLITY	DEM_AGE	1960–1998 PANEL?
Argentina	2.3	7.0	1983	Yes
Australia	1.0	10.0	1901	Yes
Austria	1.0	10.0	1946	Yes
Bahamas	1.7		1973	Yes
Bangladesh	3.2	4.8	1991	No
Barbados	1.0		1966	Yes
Belarus	4.9	0.9	1991	No
Belgium	1.2	10.0	1853	Yes
Belize	1.1		1981	Yes
Bolivia	2.4	9.0	1982	Yes
Botswana	1.9	9.0	1966	Yes
Brazil	3.0	8.0	1985	Yes
Bulgaria	2.4	8.0	1990	No
Canada	1.0	10.0	1867	Yes
Chile	2.1	8.0	1989	Yes
Colombia	3.5	8.0	1957	Yes
Costa Rica	1.3	10.0	1841	Yes
Cyprus	1.0	10.0	1960	Yes
Czech Republic	1.7	10.0	1918	No
Denmark	1.0	10.0	1915	Yes
Dominican Republic	2.9	6.4	1978	Yes
Ecuador	2.6	8.9	1979	Yes
El Salvador	3.0	6.9	1984	Yes
Estonia	2.1	6.0	1991	No
Fiji	3.8	5.0	1990	Yes
Finland	1.0	10.0	1917	Yes
France	1.5	9.0	1946	Yes
Gambia	4.4	0.2	1965	Yes
Germany	1.5	10.0	1949	Yes
Ghana	4.3	−0.6	1996	No
Greece	1.8	10.0	1975	Yes
Guatemala	4.0	4.7	1986	Yes
Honduras	2.7	6.0	1982	Yes
Hungary	1.7	10.0	1990	No
Iceland	1.0	10.0	1944	Yes
India	3.3	8.4	1950	Yes
Ireland	1.1	10.0	1921	Yes
Israel	2.0	9.0	1948	Yes
Italy	1.4	10.0	1948	Yes

Table 4.1
(continued)

Country	GASTIL	POLITY	DEM_AGE	1960–1998 PANEL?
Jamaica	2.3	9.3	1959	No
Japan	1.6	10.0	1868	Yes
Latvia	2.3	8.0	1991	No
Luxembourg	1.0	10.0	1879	Yes
Malawi	4.2	0.0	1994	No
Malaysia	4.6	10.0	1957	Yes
Malta	1.0		1964	Yes
Mauritius	1.6	10.0	1968	Yes
Mexico	3.8	2.7	1994	Yes
Namibia	2.4	8.0	1990	No
Nepal	3.3	5.0	1990	Yes
Netherlands	1.0	10.0	1917	Yes
New Zealand	1.0	10.0	1857	Yes
Nicaragua	3.4	6.9	1990	Yes
Norway	1.0	10.0	1898	Yes
Pakistan	4.3	7.8	1988	No
Papua New Guinea	2.8	10.0	1975	Yes
Paraguay	3.3	5.8	1989	Yes
Peru	4.4	2.1	1980	Yes
Philippines	2.9	7.9	1987	Yes
Poland	1.8	8.1	1989	No
Portugal	1.1	10.0	1976	Yes
Romania	3.6	6.0	1990	No
Russia	3.5	3.3	1992	No
St. Vincent & the Grenadines	1.4		1978	Yes
Senegal	4.0	−1.0	1975	No
Singapore	4.7	−2.0	1965	No
Slovak Republic	2.5	7.2	1993	No
South Africa	2.9	7.9	1910	No
South Korea	2.2	6.2	1988	No
Spain	1.3	10.0	1978	Yes
Sri Lanka	4.2	5.0	1948	Yes
Sweden	1.0	10.0	1917	Yes
Switzerland	1.0	10.0	1848	Yes
Taiwan	3.0	5.8	1992	No
Thailand	3.4	7.2	1992	Yes
Trinidad & Tobago	1.3	9.0	1962	Yes
Turkey	4.1	8.1	1983	Yes
Uganda	4.9	−4.3	1994	No

Table 4.1
(continued)

Country	GASTIL	POLITY	DEM_AGE	1960–1998 PANEL?
Ukraine	3.4	6.4	1991	No
United Kingdom	1.5	10.0	1837	Yes
United States	1.0	10.0	1800	Yes
Uruguay	1.7	10.0	1985	Yes
Venezuela	2.6	8.2	1958	Yes
Zambia	3.8	2.7	1991	No
Zimbabwe	4.9	−6.0	1989	No

Note: Values of *POLITY* missing for countries with less than half a million inhabitants (in 1998).

by the panel estimates in chapter 3, which show that the quality of democracy (positively) affects overall and welfare state spending only when democratic transitions are included in the sample. Alternatively, older democracies might have a better system of checks and balances than younger ones for fighting corruption and abuse of power.

We date the birth of democracy in a particular country by defining the variable *DEM_AGE* as the first year of a string with uninterrupted positive yearly *POLITY* values until 1990, given that the country is also an independent nation. In defining this variable, we do not regard foreign occupation during World War II as an interruption of democracy, as it was imposed externally rather than being the result of a coup. (Because Polity IV goes back to the year 1800, the minimum value of *DEM_AGE* is 1800.) For the five smaller countries not included in the Polity IV data set, we rely on the modified *POLITY_GT* variable to identify the date when a country first became a democracy (all five of these countries are young nations that gained their independence after 1960, and they can typically be classified as democracies from the year of their independence).

The resulting birth-of-democracy dates are listed in the column labeled *DEM_AGE* in table 4.1. They reflect historical waves of democratization that have swept over the world.[3] Some countries

---

3. A classic work on different waves of democratization is Samuel Huntington's book from more than a decade ago (Huntington 1991).

are very old democracies, with democratic rule dating back well into the 19th century. Apart from these, a number of European states, such as the Nordic and Benelux countries, obtained stable-democracy status, by extending the franchise, dismantling weighted votes, and undertaking other reforms, in the 20 years from the turn of the 19th century until the aftermath of World War I. Another set, including Germany, Italy, and other countries relapsing into dictatorship in the interwar period, consolidated their democracies after World War II. Some former European colonies became stable democracies in the 1960s and 1970s. Finally, many former Latin American and communist dictatorships became democracies through reforms in the last two decades of the 20th century.

The historical information discussed in this section will be exploited in the empirical analysis, when we require instrumental variables for constitutions (i.e., variables correlated with constitutional features but not with unobserved determinants of policy outcomes; see chapter 5). We also include the age of democracy as an explanatory variable in the empirical analysis of chapters 6 and 7 (based on DEM_AGE, we define $AGE = (2000 - DEM\_AGE)/200$, so that AGE varies between 0 and 1). As suggested above, we expect age of democracy to be correlated with measures of performance, such as corruption and government spending.[4] Age of democracy might influence performance in nonlinear ways, and the definition of the variable AGE may not capture the full impact of the age of democracy. For this reason, in some specifications we check the robustness of our results by including both a linear and a squared term in the AGE variable.

4.3 Electoral Rules

Our theoretical discussion in chapter 2 involved three aspects of electoral rules: (1) how many legislators get elected in each district (district magnitude), (2) how vote shares are converted into seat shares (electoral formula), and (3) how voters cast their ballot on the spectrum from single individuals to party lists (ballot structure). Although these aspects are analytically distinct from one another, they are correlated across countries in the real world, as noted in

---

4. For instance, Treisman (2000) reports that democracies older than 45 years have significantly less corruption compared to younger democracies.

chapter 2. In particular, electoral formulas and ballot structures are closely correlated: plurality rule is typically associated with voting over alternative individual candidates, whereas PR is typically implemented through a system of party lists. But district magnitudes and electoral formulas also covary systematically. The single most common form of legislative elections in the world is the traditional U.K. first-past-the-post system, which combines single-member constituencies with plurality rule in the elections to the lower house of the Parliament. On the other side of the spectrum, the 120 members of Israel's Knesset and the 150 members of the Dutch lower house are elected in single national districts in which legislative seats are awarded through PR. Moreover, in full PR systems with smaller primary voting districts, regular seats are often combined with "adjustment seats" awarded in secondary (most often national) districts, so as to obtain a closer relation between overall national vote shares and seat shares in the legislature.

But the correlations among the three aspects are certainly not perfect. In particular, we find a number of "mixed" electoral systems. A well-known example is Germany, where voters have two ballots, electing half the 656 members of the Bundestag through plurality in single-seat electoral districts and the other half through PR at a national level, so as to achieve proportionality between the national vote and seat shares.[5] Furthermore, a few PR systems, such as the Irish one (see below), do not rely on party lists.[6]

According to the theory presented in chapter 2, correlated aspects of electoral rules may either pull in the same or in different directions, depending on the performance measure employed. For the composition of fiscal policy, larger voting districts and the associated greater reliance on PR both pull the outcome in the direction of broad, rather than targeted, policies. But in the case of rent extraction, larger districts pull toward lower levels of rents, whereas the associated greater reliance on party list–oriented ballots pulls toward higher levels of rents. This motivates us to compile alternative measures of electoral rules.

---

5. The minimal number of seats in the German lower house is 656. The actual number is often higher because of the so-called Überhangsmandate, used to achieve an outcome closer to full proportionality.

6. See, for instance, Blais and Massicotte 1996 and Cox 1997 for recent and extensive overviews of the electoral systems employed in the world's various countries.

4.3.1 Basic Measures of Electoral Rules

We classify a country's rules for electing its *lower house*. In the event that reforms to a country's electoral system have been enacted, we date them by the year in which the first election took place under the new electoral rule, irrespective of when the reform was actually passed (more on this below).

Our most basic measure is a simple classification of the *electoral formula* into "majoritarian," "mixed," or "proportional" electoral rules, resulting in two binary indicator (dummy) variables, *MAJ* and *MIXED*. More precisely, years when a country elected its lower house exclusively through plurality rule in the most recent election are coded as $MAJ = 1$, whereas other (mixed or proportional) rules are coded $MAJ = 0$. The alternative indicator variable *MIXED* is also defined on the basis of a country's electoral formula, taking on a value of 1 only in the electoral systems relying on a mixture of plurality rule and PR and a value of 0 in pure plurality or PR systems. Data for these two binary variables are relatively easy to collect, and we have an entry for all countries and years in the 1960–1998 panel, as well as in the 1990s cross section. Another reason (beyond ease of collection) for relying on binary variables is that a binary measure is required by some of the statistical methods used to allow for a systematic (nonrandom) selection into different constitutions (to be discussed in chapter 5). Table 4.2 displays the values of the *MAJ* and *MIXED* indicators for the 85 countries in our 1990s cross section.

For a few countries in the table, *MAJ* and *MIXED* take on values between 0 and 1. Because the entries in the table are computed as an average from 1990 to 1998, these are the countries that undertook sufficiently substantial electoral reforms in the last decade to change their classification according to our indicators. Four of these countries—Japan (in 1994), New Zealand, the Philippines, and Ukraine (all three in 1996)—moved from a system in which every lower-house legislator was individually elected by plurality rule to a German-style mixed system in which some, but not all, legislators are instead elected via party lists and PR.[7] Only Fiji (in 1994) went

---

7. The prereform Japanese system was based on the single nontransferable vote. Unlike other multiseat plurality elections, in which each voter in a district has as many votes as the number of seats, Japanese voters had only one vote in districts with three to five seats, which were awarded to the candidates with the highest number of votes. Although the classification of this system is subject to some dispute, most political scientists include the prereform Japan system among the plurality rule systems.

Table 4.2
Electoral rules and forms of government

Country	MAJ	MIXED	MAGN	PIND
Argentina	0.00	0.00	0.09	0.00
Australia	1.00	0.00	1.00	1.00
Austria	0.00	0.00	0.05	0.00
Bahamas	1.00	0.00	1.00	1.00
Bangladesh	1.00	0.00	0.91	1.00
Barbados	1.00	0.00	1.00	1.00
Belarus	1.00	0.00	1.00	1.00
Belgium	0.00	0.00	0.14	0.00
Belize	1.00	0.00	1.00	1.00
Bolivia	0.00	0.22	0.07	0.12
Botswana	1.00	0.00	1.00	1.00
Brazil	0.00	0.00	0.05	0.00
Bulgaria	0.00	0.00	0.13	0.00
Canada	1.00	0.00	1.00	1.00
Chile	1.00	0.00	0.50	1.00
Colombia	0.00	0.00	0.21	0.00
Costa Rica	0.00	0.00	0.12	0.00
Cyprus	0.00	0.00	0.11	0.00
Czech Republic	0.00	0.00	0.04	0.00
Denmark	0.00	0.00	0.11	0.00
Dominican Republic	0.00	0.00	0.25	0.00
Ecuador	0.00	0.33	0.26	0.00
El Salvador	0.00	0.00	0.18	0.00
Estonia	0.00	0.00	0.11	0.00
Fiji	0.56	0.44	0.64	0.79
Finland	0.00	0.00	0.09	0.01
France	1.00	0.00	1.00	1.00
Gambia	1.00	0.00	0.98	1.00
Germany	0.00	1.00	0.52	0.50
Ghana	1.00	0.00	1.00	1.00
Greece	0.00	0.00	0.19	0.00
Guatemala	0.00	0.00	0.24	0.00
Honduras	0.00	0.00	0.14	0.00
Hungary	0.00	1.00	0.51	0.46
Iceland	0.00	0.00	0.13	0.00
India	1.00	0.00	1.00	1.00
Ireland	0.00	0.00	0.25	0.00
Israel	0.00	0.00	0.01	0.00
Italy	0.00	0.56	0.46	0.42
Jamaica	1.00	0.00	1.00	1.00
Japan	0.33	0.67	0.38	0.87
Latvia	0.00	0.00	0.05	0.00
Luxembourg	0.00	0.00	0.07	0.00
Malawi	1.00	0.00	1.00	1.00

Table 4.2
(continued)

Country	PINDO	YEARELE	PRES	YEARREG
Argentina	0.00	1983	1	1983
Australia	1.00	1901	0	1901
Austria	0.00	1945	0	1945
Bahamas	1.00	1973	0	1973
Bangladesh	1.00	1991	0	1991
Barbados	1.00	1966	0	1966
Belarus	1.00	1991	1	1991
Belgium	0.00	1899	0	1853
Belize	1.00	1981	0	1981
Bolivia	0.12	1982 (1996)	1	1982
Botswana	1.00	1966	0	1966
Brazil	1.00	1988	1	1988
Bulgaria	0.00	1991	0	1991
Canada	1.00	1867	0	1867
Chile	1.00	1989	1	1989
Colombia	0.00	1957	1	1957
Costa Rica	0.00	1953	1	1949
Cyprus	1.00	1981	1	1960
Czech Republic	0.00	1993	0	1993
Denmark	0.00	1920	0	1915
Dominican Republic	0.00	1966	1	1978
Ecuador	0.00	1979 (1996)	1	1979
El Salvador	0.00	1984	1	1984
Estonia	1.00	1992	0	1992
Fiji	0.79	1990 (1994)	0	1990
Finland	1.00	1917	0	1917
France	1.00	1986	0	1958
Gambia	1.00	1965	1	1965
Germany	0.50	1949	0	1949
Ghana	1.00	1992	1	1992
Greece	1.00	1975	0	1975
Guatemala	0.00	1985	1	1985
Honduras	0.00	1982	1	1982
Hungary	0.46	1990	0	1990
Iceland	0.00	1944	0	1944
India	1.00	1950	0	1950
Ireland	1.00	1937	0	1937
Israel	0.00	1948	0	1948
Italy	0.86	1945 (1994)	0	1945
Jamaica	1.00	1962	0	1962
Japan	0.87	1952 (1994)	0	1952
Latvia	0.00	1991	0	1991
Luxembourg	1.00	1918	0	1879
Malawi	1.00	1994	1	1994

Table 4.2
(continued)

Country	MAJ	MIXED	MAGN	PIND
Malaysia	1.00	0.00	1.00	1.00
Malta	0.00	0.00	0.20	0.00
Mauritius	1.00	0.00	0.33	1.00
Mexico	0.00	1.00	0.60	0.60
Namibia	0.00	0.00	0.17	0.00
Nepal	1.00	0.00	1.00	1.00
Netherlands	0.00	0.00	0.12	0.00
New Zealand	0.67	0.33	0.85	0.85
Nicaragua	0.00	0.00	0.13	0.00
Norway	0.00	0.00	0.12	0.00
Pakistan	1.00	0.00	1.00	1.00
Papua New Guinea	1.00	0.00	1.00	1.00
Paraguay	0.00	0.00	0.23	0.00
Peru	0.00	0.00	0.01	0.00
Philippines	0.89	0.11	0.98	0.98
Poland	0.00	0.00	0.11	0.00
Portugal	0.00	0.00	0.09	0.00
Romania	0.00	0.00	0.12	0.00
Russia	0.00	1.00	0.50	0.50
St. Vincent & the Grenadines	1.00	0.00	1.00	1.00
Senegal	0.00	1.00	0.25	0.43
Singapore	1.00	0.00	0.30	1.00
Slovak Republic	0.00	0.00	0.03	0.00
South Africa	0.00	1.00	0.02	0.00
South Korea	0.00	1.00	0.78	0.78
Spain	0.00	0.00	0.15	0.01
Sri Lanka	0.00	0.00	0.10	0.00
Sweden	0.00	0.00	0.08	0.00
Switzerland	0.00	0.00	0.13	0.03
Taiwan	0.00	1.00		0.78
Thailand	1.00	0.00	0.42	1.00
Trinidad & Tobago	1.00	0.00	1.00	1.00
Turkey	0.00	0.00	0.19	0.00
Uganda	1.00	0.00	1.00	1.00
Ukraine	0.80	0.20	0.90	0.90
United Kingdom	1.00	0.00	1.00	1.00
United States	1.00	0.00	1.00	1.00
Uruguay	0.00	0.00	0.11	0.00
Venezuela	0.00	0.67	0.45	0.33
Zambia	1.00	0.00	1.00	1.00
Zimbabwe	1.00	0.00	1.00	1.00

Note: Years within parentheses in *YEARELE* column are years of electoral reforms in the 1990s, where the reforms are significant enough to charge the country's classification according to *MAJ* or *MIXED*.

Table 4.2
(continued)

Country	PINDO	YEARELE	PRES	YEARREG
Malaysia	1.00	1957	0	1957
Malta	1.00	1964	0	1964
Mauritius	1.00	1968	0	1968
Mexico	0.60	1994	1	1994
Namibia	0.00	1990	1	1990
Nepal	1.00	1990	0	1990
Netherlands	0.00	1917	0	1917
New Zealand	0.85	1906 (1996)	0	1906
Nicaragua	0.00	1990	1	1990
Norway	0.00	1919	0	1898
Pakistan	1.00	1988	1	1988
Papua New Guinea	1.00	1975	0	1975
Paraguay	0.00	1992	1	1992
Peru	0.00	1979	1	1979
Philippines	0.98	1987 (1996)	1	1987
Poland	1.00	1989	0	1989
Portugal	0.00	1976	0	1976
Romania	0.00	1989	0	1989
Russia	0.50	1992	1	1992
St. Vincent & the Grenadines	1.00	1978	0	1978
Senegal	0.43	1975	0	1975
Singapore	1.00	1965	0	1965
Slovak Republic	1.00	1993	0	1993
South Africa	0.00	1994	0	1994
South Korea	0.78	1988	1	1988
Spain	0.01	1978	0	1978
Sri Lanka	1.00	1978	1	1948
Sweden	0.00	1917	0	1917
Switzerland	1.00	1918	1	1874
Taiwan	0.78	1992	0	1992
Thailand	1.00	1978	0	1992
Trinidad & Tobago	1.00	1962	0	1962
Turkey	0.00	1982	0	1982
Uganda	1.00	1994	1	1994
Ukraine	0.90	1991 (1996)	0	1991
United Kingdom	1.00	1837	0	1837
United States	1.00	1800	1	1800
Uruguay	0.00	1985	1	1985
Venezuela	0.33	1958 (1993)	1	1958
Zambia	1.00	1991	1	1991
Zimbabwe	1.00	1989	1	1989

in the opposite direction, replacing a mixed-member system with an exclusive reliance on plurality rule (and only single-member districts, beginning with the 1998 election). If we also add the four countries that changed their status according to the *MIXED* measure, the movement toward "middle-of-the-road" mixed-member systems becomes even more apparent. Bolivia (1996), Ecuador (1996), Italy (1994), and Venezuela (1993) all replaced full PR with mixed-member systems. In addition, following the fall of communism, some new democracies, like Russia and Hungary, introduced a mixed-member system in their first free elections.[8]

The 1990s were, however, an exceptional decade in terms of the frequency of electoral reform, at least when it comes to the basic features of electoral systems. For instance, in our panel data set, the 1980s show only two electoral reforms: Cyprus going from plurality rule ($MAJ = 1$) to PR ($MAJ = 0$) in 1981 and a brief experiment in which France temporarily replaced plurality rule with PR during 1985–1986. Moreover, in the 1960s and 1970s, we register no electoral reform sufficiently important to change any country's coding according to *MAJ*. All this stability reflects an inertia of electoral systems that is sometimes referred to as an "iron law" by political scientists. We will return to this stability in several places throughout the book, as it has important consequences for how to design a convincing empirical strategy for identifying the causal effect of electoral rules on policy outcomes.

In the 85-country cross section, our observations do not refer to a particular year but are averages over the period 1990–1998. As mentioned above, some of our statistical tools (to be discussed in chapter 5) require that we measure a country's constitution as a binary (0 or 1) variable. The question then arises of whether to treat the constitutions of countries that underwent a reform in the 1990s as 0s or 1s. Our rule in such cases is to measure the constitution according to *the earlier* part of the sample, on the argument that it takes some time before constitutional reform changes such slowly moving variables as the size of government or the average perception of corruption. Thus Italy and Japan, both of which had elections under their new rules in 1994, are coded as proportional and

---

8. See Shugart 2001 and the collection of studies in Shugart and Wattenberg 2001 for a discussion of the forces behind the reforms and the political consequences of reform in these countries.

majoritarian, respectively, since that was the prevailing rule until their 1994 elections. Using an alternative timing convention produces similar empirical results.

In the remainder of this chapter and in the empirical analyses to follow, we always use and refer to the values of *MAJ* and *MIXED* (and the regime indicator *PRES*, to be defined in the next section) as strictly equal to 0 or 1, unless otherwise noted, constructed with the dating convention stated above (namely, we code a country's constitution before any reform that may have been enacted).

According to our classification of electoral systems, 52 countries have proportional elections, and 33 have majoritarian elections. Only 9 countries in the cross-sectional sample have mixed electoral systems; all the others are either strictly majoritarian or strictly proportional. The small number of observations in the mixed group makes it difficult to estimate empirically differences between mixed systems and either strictly majoritarian or strictly proportional ones. For this reason, much of the empirical analysis in later chapters focuses on the effects of the *MAJ* indicator, namely, on differences between strictly majoritarian countries, on the one hand, and mixed plus proportional countries, on the other. In general, as noted below, the data do not reject the hypothesis that mixed and proportional countries can be lumped together as far as their policy outcomes are concerned. But with only 9 countries in the data set having mixed systems, the alternative hypothesis of important differences between proportional and mixed systems may be hard to refute.

4.3.2 Dating of Electoral Rules

It is not surprising that history has played an important role in shaping the electoral rules observed today. Some of the historical and cultural circumstances that have shaped the electoral systems in our data set are peculiar to each individual country,[9] whereas other determinants may be common for all countries in the data set. The various forces shaping constitutional rules—such as experience by other democracies, prevalent political and judicial doctrines, and

---

9. Lijphart (1984b) and, more recently, Colomer (2001), provide useful discussions of the history behind past and present electoral rules in a number of countries. Boix (1999) and earlier Rokkan (1970) suggest strategic-choice theories based on the balance of power between existing and prospective political forces at the time of democratization.

academic thinking—may shift systematically over time. These time-varying historical determinants may be very hard to gauge in terms of observable variables (although we make some attempts in this direction in chapters 5 and 6). Because of the stability of electoral rules, however, these determinants are likely to show up in systematically different distributions of electoral rules, if we compare constitutions dating back to different historical epochs.

To look for such systematic historical patterns in the data, we date the origin of a country's electoral rules as classified by the variable *MAJ*. Specifically, we proceed as follows. First, we obtain the earliest possible date of the electoral rule for a particular country by checking two separate conditions: (1) when the country became an independent nation and (2) the value of *DEM_AGE* (i.e., the year from which democracy has been uninterrupted through 1998, as defined by the *POLITY* rule described above). We then take the later date of (1) and (2). If the *MAJ* classification for the country in that year is the same as today, without intervening changes, that year gives the age of the electoral rule. If the electoral rule has been reformed in the interim, the most recent reform date, provided that it changed the value of *MAJ*, gives the age of the electoral rule. When repeating this procedure for each country in our data set, we obtain a new variable, called *YEARELE*. Its value for each country in our 1990s cross section is presented in table 4.2.

For the few countries pursuing electoral reforms in the 1990s, we display two values in table 4.2: the original date of the current electoral rule (in parentheses), as well the original date of the prereform rule. For example, Japan's previous plurality rule system (based on the single nontransferable vote) originated in 1952 but was reformed in 1994 in favor of a mixed-member system, so both years are presented in the table.

Does the distribution of current electoral rules vary with the age of these rules? To answer this question, we consider four broad time periods suggested by the discussion in section 4.2: before 1920, 1921–1950, 1951–1980, and after 1981. The frequency of majoritarian rules $(MAJ = 1)$ does indeed appear to be systematically related to the age of the electoral rule.[10] Although the overall frequency of majoritarian electoral rules in our 1990s cross section is slightly

---

10. As noted above, for the countries that underwent a reform in the 1990s, we code *MAJ* according to the rule existing before the reform.

above one-third (33 countries out of 85), it is much lower (one-seventh) in the 1921–1950 period, but much higher (one half) in the 1951–1980 period. We exploit this pattern in the empirical work to follow by constructing three dummy variables, corresponding to the periods 1921–1950, 1951–1980, and after 1981, which take a value of 1 if the current electoral rule originated in the respective period, and 0 otherwise. Other factors than timing have certainly played an important role in the selection of electoral rules, but a pure timing effect as captured by these dummy variables generally retains predictive value, even as we hold constant other geographical and cultural variables.

4.3.3 Continuous Measures of Electoral Rules

The binary variable *MAJ* is based on electoral formula (aspect (2) in our discussion at the beginning of this section) but correlated with district magnitude (aspect (1) in that discussion). This variable may be sufficient for investigating the predicted constitutional effect on fiscal policy, as the theory tells us that these aspects of the electoral system pull policy in the same direction. But the *MAJ* variable may be too blunt when the theoretical predictions are more subtle and concern detailed features of the electoral system, as in the case of rent extraction. Therefore, we have also constructed three continuous measures; one measuring district magnitude, the other two measuring ballot structure.

Like several related measures in the political science literature, *MAGN* gauges the average size of voting districts in terms of the number of legislative seats in the district. Specifically, let *DISTRICTS* be the number of districts, primary as well as secondary (and tertiary if applicable), in a country, and *SEATS* the number of seats in the country's lower house. Then, we define *MAGN* for that country as

$$MAGN = \frac{DISTRICTS}{SEATS}.$$

Thus, our measure is the *inverse* of district magnitude as commonly defined by political scientists; it ranges between 0 and 1, taking a value of 1 in a U.K.-style system with single-member districts and a value slightly above 0 in an Israel-style system with a single national district, where all legislators are elected. By construction, the endpoints of the range of *MAGN* coincide with the two possible values of *MAJ*, which simplifies the interpretation of the empirical results.

To check whether our results are robust, we also rely on an alternative measure of district magnitude collected and discussed by Seddon et al. (2001). The variable *SDM* is defined like traditional measures of district magnitude (i.e., as $\frac{SEATS}{DISTRICTS}$), except that district magnitude is, in the case of *SDM*, a weighted average, where the weight on each district magnitude in a country is the share of legislators running in districts of that size. Seddon et al. (2001) argue that this measure better reflects differences across electoral systems in the incentives for the typical legislator of appealing to a narrow constituency.

To gauge the ballot structure, we define two measures called *PIND* and *PINDO*. Like *MAGN* (and *SDM*), these variables will mostly be used to investigate rent extraction (corruption) by politicians. In line with the theoretical career concern model discussed in chapter 2, we focus on the incidence of voting for individuals rather than party lists to capture the notion of individual rather than collective accountability.

Specifically, our first measure is designed to capture the free-rider effect on the incentives of individual candidates associated with belonging to a party list. It is defined by

$$PIND = 1 - \frac{LIST}{SEATS},$$

where *LIST* denotes the number of lower-house legislators elected through party lists (open or closed). We thus measure the proportion of legislators elected by plurality rule via a vote on individuals (as opposed to party lists). Like our continuous measure of district magnitude, this measure of ballot structure ranges between 0 and 1, taking a value of 1 in the United Kingdom (where all of the legislators are elected by individual votes under plurality rule), a value of approximately 0.5 in Germany (where only about half of the legislators are elected in that way), and a value of 0 in Poland (where all of the legislators are elected in party lists even though voters' preferences determine the ranking in the elected list).[11]

---

11. The precise party list allocation formulas for distributing seats within each district (D'Hondt, modified St. Laguë, LR-Hare, etc.) do not immediately affect the individual candidate's career concern, and we therefore do not distinguish among them.

This continuous measure is based both on the ballot structure and on the electoral formula. With a proportional electoral formula, the number of candidates elected from a list depends on the votes received by the whole list, and this gives rise to a free rider problem. Thus, proportional electoral systems that rely on the single transferable vote (such as the Dáil Eireann in Ireland, or the similar electoral system in Malta) are classified as $LIST = 1$ (and $PIND = 0$) even if voters are obliged to rank-order individual candidates. Conversely, the single non-transferable vote system used for the lower houses in Taiwan (part of the house) and Japan (before mid-1990s reform) are based on plurality rule and thus are classified as $LIST = 0$ (and $PIND = 1$). Finally, we have to deal with a borderline case. The hybrid system in Chile formally has party lists in two-member districts. But the seats are won based on individual votes (open list), and the system has plurality in the sense that a first-ranked list collecting more than twice as many votes as a second-ranked list obtains both seats in a district. We treat this as plurality rule on individual ballots, setting $LIST = 0$ (and $PIND = 1$) for Chile.

Our second measure of the ballot structure, $PINDO$, is designed to reflect the effect of closed lists only. It is defined as the proportion of legislators in the lower house elected individually or on open lists. The legislators elected in closed lists are instead coded as 0. Thus:

$$PINDO = 1 - \frac{LIST}{SEATS} CLIST$$

where $CLIST$ is a dummy variable taking a value of 1 if the list is closed, and 0 if it is open. This different definition of individual accountability discriminates between ballots in which voters choose among individuals and those where they don't, irrespective of whether or not there is a free rider problem. Thus, here the United Kingdom is still coded as 1 and Germany as 0.5, but now Poland (that votes on open lists) is coded as 1.

The variables $PIND$ and $PINDO$ take on different values in thirteen countries: those using a semi-proportional STV-system, plus those where voters have to vote for individual politicians in open-list or panachage systems. In these thirteen countries, $PIND = 0$ but $PINDO > 0$.[12]

Once more, we use an alternative variable compiled by Seddon et al. (2001) to check for robustness. This variable is called *SPROPN* and measures the share of legislators elected in national (secondary or tertiary) districts rather than subnational (primary) districts. As the forces of collective rather than individual accountability (the theoretical concepts stressed in chapter 2) may be at their largest for a politician running on a national party list, we sometimes use *SPROPN* as an alternative to *PIND* (naturally expecting the opposite sign in the estimated coefficient).

Information on current electoral arrangements for most countries is readily available from public sources, such as the Inter-Parliamentary Union or the International Institute for Democracy and Electoral Assistance. But the detailed information required for coding *MAGN*, *PIND*, and *PINDO* is less easily available as we move back in time. In many cases, we must consult national sources to obtain reliable data. Moreover, these variables will be of most use when we are investigating the constitutional determinants of rent extraction by politicians, and as discussed in chapter 3, reliable data on corruption are mostly available only for the 1990s. For these reasons, we have limited data collection to this later period, so that the three continuously measured variables only enter the 85-country cross section. Table 4.2 presents the values of these three variables.

4.4   Forms of Government

The theoretical studies surveyed in chapter 2 highlight two features of the legislative rules entailed in different forms of government. One

---

12. Party list voting can be of three types: closed lists, open lists (or preference vote), and panachage. Closed lists do not allow the voters to express a preference for individual candidates, so we set *PINDO* = 0. A preference on open lists may be prescribed (as in Finland), or allowed (as in Sweden) with the party list still being the default option for the voter. We code as *PINDO* = 1 only those systems, where the ranking on the party lists is exclusively decided by the preferential votes (Brazil, Cyprus, Estonia, Finland, Greece, (pre-reform) Italy, Poland, Slovakia, and Sri Lanka). The panachage (used in Luxembourg and Switzerland) also gives voters the option of expressing preferences across parties. Here we set *PINDO* = 1. Finally, the PR systems in Ireland and Malta based on the single transferable vote are classified as *PINDO* = 1. We do not discriminate on the basis of the precise party-list allocation formulas for distributing seats within each district (D'Hondt, modified St. Laguë, LR-Hare, etc.), since they do not immediately affect the individual candidate's career concerns. See also the discussion in Carey and Shugart (1995), who take a somewhat different perspective.

is the separation of powers in the legislative process among different political offices and different groups of legislators, which produces a more effective accountability of politicians toward voters. The other is the presence of a confidence requirement that makes the executive accountable to the legislature, thereby producing greater incentives for legislative cohesion (i.e., to form stable majority coalitions of legislators that support the government and vote together on economic policy decisions to avoid triggering a costly government crisis).

Our prototype of a presidential regime has a directly elected president fully in charge of the executive, with the executive not being accountable to the legislature for its survival, and with a clear separation of powers, not only between the president and congress, but also among congressional committees holding proposal (agenda-setting) powers in different spheres of policy. On the other hand, in our prototype of a parliamentary regime, the executive is not directly elected but formed out of the majority of the legislature. Thus it needs the continued confidence of a majority in the parliament to maintain its powers throughout an entire election period and has considerable powers to initiate legislation.

Several real-world constitutions mandate political systems that correspond closely to these prototypes. The United States is one example of a presidential regime, but not the only one. Most countries with an elected president have no confidence requirement, and the executive can hold on to its powers without the support of a majority in the congress. Likewise, in many real-world parliamentary regimes, government formation must be approved by the parliament, which can also dismiss the government through a vote of no-confidence, and legislative proposals made by the government get preferential treatment in the agenda of the parliament.

Nevertheless, even more than in our classification of electoral rules, some observed constitutions cannot easily be assigned to one of our models or the other. First, when it comes to the confidence requirement, the political science literature emphasizes that semipresidential regimes, such as France, combine an elected president with considerable executive powers and an important role for the government held accountable by the legislature (Duverger 1980). Within the group of semipresidential countries, a further distinction between premier-presidential and president-parliamentary regimes is sometimes made on the basis of who holds the government

accountable (Shugart and Carey 1992) and who controls its formation. Moreover, among parliamentary states, the precise constitutional mechanisms for holding the executive accountable to the
legislature, and thus the incentives for maintaining stable coalitions,
also vary considerably. For example, the German requirement for a
constructive vote of confidence (any coalition voting the government
out of office must come up with a new coalition) makes it more difficult to break up the government (Diermeier, Eraslan, and Merlo
2000) and thus weakens incentives for legislative cohesion.

Second, when it comes to separation of powers, Shugart and Carey
(1992) identify important differences in the relative powers of the
president and the legislature, even among clear-cut presidential
regimes. In Argentina and the United States, for example, the president has relatively weak legislative powers deriving mainly from
his authority to veto legislative bills as a whole (package veto). Other
presidents, like Brazil's, have more extensive legislative powers,
including line item veto rights, restrictions on congressional rights to
amend bills, and the possibility of legislating by decree. As stressed
by Strom (1990), parliamentary countries also vary considerably
in the extent to which agenda-setting powers are concentrated in
the government versus vested in parliamentary committees. For
instance, U.K. and French cabinets clearly dominate the parliaments
in those countries, but Belgian and Danish governments must live
with relatively powerful parliamentary committees that also grant
the opposition an influence (see Strom 1990, the contributions in
Döring 1995, Powell 1989, and Powell 2000).

4.4.1 A Basic Measure of Forms of Government

As the above discussion indicates, it would be interesting to develop
detailed measures of the two constitutional features, separation of
powers and presence of a confidence requirement, discussed above.
One would be based on different constitutional rules introducing
separation of legislative powers, which promotes electoral accountability. The other would be based on constitutional provisions such
as different confidence requirements and rules for government formation, which promote legislative cohesion in the form of stable
majorities. Fragmentary measures along these lines for subsets of the
countries in our data sets do exist in the political science literature
(see the work mentioned above and the sources cited therein). But
building detailed measures with a comprehensive coverage of the

countries in our data sets is a daunting task well beyond the scope of this study.

We therefore limit ourselves to the less ambitious task of making a crude classification of constitutions into presidential and parliamentary regimes. Thus, we introduce a binary variable called *PRES* that takes on values of either 1 (in presidential regimes) or 0 (otherwise). Because data on the separation of powers are not readily available—and perhaps disputable—we take our starting point in the other feature suggested by the theory, namely, the existence of a government subject to a confidence requirement. If this feature is absent, we call the country presidential (*PRES* = 1), if present, we call it parliamentary (*PRES* = 0).

In most cases, the classification is straightforward, even though it sometimes leads to results somewhat different from the popular conception. Thus using the confidence requirement as a decisive criterion leads us to classify one or two countries without a popularly elected president as presidential. This is the case with Switzerland, where a coalition government is appointed by each newly elected assembly but cannot be revoked before the next election. Similarly, in some circumstances, the Bolivian congress, rather than the voters, elects the president, who, in turn, forms the executive and is not subject to a censure vote from the legislature.

The situation is less clear-cut for some of the semipresidential countries, however, where both the president and the legislative assembly have some control over the appointment and/or dismissal of the executive. In these cases, we classify a regime as parliamentary or presidential depending on whether such control primarily rests with the president or the legislative assembly.[13] Specifically, suppose that the legislative assembly has the right to censure the government but shares this right with the president and plays no role in government formation. (This situation applies to Colombia, Ecuador, and Peru.) Then the right of censure is less likely to be exercised by the assembly, and the incentives to maintain stable legislative coalitions seem correspondingly weaker. We therefore code such regimes as presidential. Suppose instead that the legislative assembly has an exclusive right of censure and that the president does not have an exclusive and predominant role in government

---

13. In principle, and according to some literature, the classification of these countries might also change over time, depending on whether the president and the assembly belong to the same party. But we abstain from such complications in what follows.

formation. Then the right of censure can be used in the assembly as a credible threat to hold a legislative coalition together, and the incentives for legislative cohesion seem much stronger. According to this criterion, France and Portugal are coded as parliamentary, since the legislature in these countries has an exclusive and unrestricted right of censure and the president nominates the government (or has an influence over it), but parliament must approve it. Finally, Finland and Iceland fall somewhere in between, since the assembly has an exclusive and unrestricted right of censure, as in France, but the president has a full right of appointment without requiring parliamentary approval, as in Peru. Since the right of censure is likely to be strategically more important than the right of appointment, we classify these regimes as parliamentary. The information underlying the classification of these borderline cases is extracted from Shugart and Carey 1992 (chap. 8).[14]

We have collected data for the *PRES* indicator annually both for the countries in the 1990s cross section and for those in the longer panel. The values for the 85 countries in our 1990s cross section are listed in table 4.2. Under our rules for classification, we have a total of 33 presidential and 52 parliamentary regimes.

4.4.2   Dating of Forms of Government

Consistent with constitutional inertia in the broad features of political institutions, we observe almost no change in our classifications of constitutional regimes over time. Bangladesh shifts from a parliamentary to a presidential regime in 1991 (although it enters the data set before 1991 only according to the broad Gastil rule, not according to the Polity rule). No other change in regime classification is observed in the panel for the earlier decades, except a brief experiment with parliamentary rule in Brazil in 1961–1963.

As in the case of electoral rules, we want to know how the distribution across presidential and parliamentary regimes depends on the age of their constitutional provision. To that end, we determine the original date of the present regime classification (according to *PRES*) for each country. The procedure is completely analogous to

---

14. More precisely, we use the classification of nonlegislative powers in table 8.2 of Shugart and Carey 1992. The borderline semipresidential cases are those assigned a score of 0 in the column "Censure." Regimes scoring a combined sum of 8 in the columns "Cabinet Formation" and "Dismissal" are coded as presidential, and those scoring a sum of 4 or less, as parliamentary (no country has a score between 4 and 8).

that used in dating the present electoral rule classification (according to *MAJ*). Thus, we create another variable, *YEARREG*, the values of which are displayed in table 4.2.

Here, we do find a monotonic development over time, in the frequency of alternative arrangements, if we divide history into the same broad time periods as in the previous section. A total of 13 present regimes have their constitutional origin in the period up to 1920. Only two of these, Switzerland and the United States, are presidential. Similarly, 2 out of 9 stable regimes that date from the 1921–1950 period are presidential, namely, Costa Rica and Sri Lanka. But the 1951–1980 period produced 7 stable presidential regimes out of a total of 23. The two most recent decades have brought a further increase in relative frequency: more than half, 22 out of 41, of the democratic regimes born since 1981 are presidential.

Naturally, forces other than the vogue of each historical time period may explain the higher frequency of presidentialism at later birth dates of regimes. For example, whereas the early birth dates of stable political regimes are associated with countries located in the Old World, later birth dates are increasingly associated with countries in the New World, where the influence of European cultural and political traditions is presumably smaller. Furthermore, observers such as Linz (1990) claim that presidential regimes are more prone to military coups and other breakdowns of democracy than parliamentary regimes, which would bias the outcome toward a higher frequency of older (surviving) parliamentary regimes. The accuracy of this claim is far from settled, however (it is disputed by Shugart and Carey [1992], for example). Be that as it may, we shall see that a pure time effect remains even as we hold constant country characteristics such as continental location and colonial history, as well as age of democracy (as measured by *AGE*, defined above).

Comparing the values of *YEARELE* and *YEARREG* in table 4.2, we see that only six countries have an electoral rule and a form of government dating back to different periods (according to the period classifications used above). For all other countries, both constitutional features date back to the same period (most often the broad period that gave birth to the democratic state), another confirmation that fundamental constitutional features, such as those captured by our classifications, are stable and rarely change. To reduce the number of variables measuring the historical aspects of constitutions, we summarize the origin of *both* constitutional features, that is, the electoral rule and form of government, by means of a single categorization. Specifically, we create three indicator variables (*CON2150*, *CON5180*, and *CON81*) corresponding to the three periods mentioned above (1921–1950, 1951–1980, and post-1981); these indicator variables take a value of 1 if *either* the current form of government *or* the current electoral rule (as measured by *PRES* and *MAJ*) originate in the relevant subperiod and a value of 0 otherwise. Chapter 5 explains the statistical reasons for reducing the number of these historical-constitutional variables.

4.5 Our Political Atlas

It is convenient to summarize with a map the simple classifications we have made of political institutions. Figure 4.1 thus illustrates the values of our indicators *MAJ* and *PRES* as coded in 1998, the last year of data in the computation of the cross-sectional average for the 1990s. The colored portions of the map represent the 85 countries in the 1990s data set. Solid areas indicate presidential regimes (*PRES* = 1) and striped areas parliamentary regimes (*PRES* = 0), notwithstanding the shade. A darker shade indicates majoritarian elections (*MAJ* = 1) and a lighter shade proportional elections (*MAJ* = 0), notwithstanding the pattern. As revealed by the map, the least common system is the U.S.-style (gray-striped) combination of a presidential regime with majoritarian elections, with only 11 countries having such a system. But each of the other three combinations is well represented in the sample: 22 countries are proportional and presidential, 23 majoritarian and parliamentary, and 30 proportional and parliamentary.

Even a cursory look at the map presented in figure 4.1 indicates that different types of constitutions do not appear to have been randomly selected, geographically and historically speaking. Electoral rule does not exhibit a particular pattern in terms of development, but most Anglo-Saxon countries and former U.K. colonies are majoritarian, whereas most of Europe and South America are proportional. Presidential regimes are largely confined to non-OECD countries (the only presidential regimes in the OECD are the United States and Switzerland). Moreover, presidential regimes are overrepresented in the Americas, though the 1990s cross section also includes several parliamentary Caribbean countries. Other presiden-

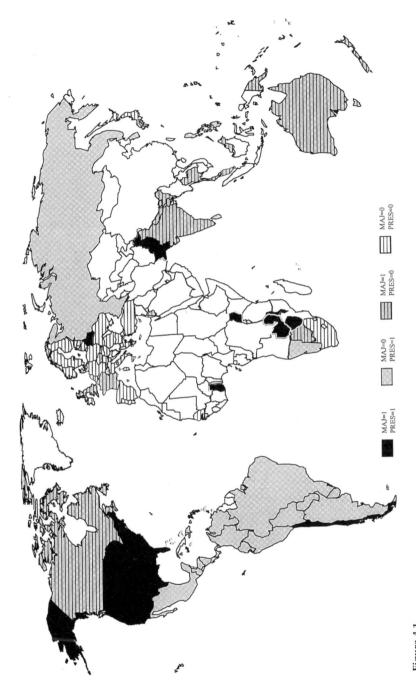

Figure 4.1
Electoral rules and forms of government, 1998.

Table 4.3
Constitutional rules across the world

	COL_UK	COL_ESP	LAAM	ASIAE	AFRICA	OECD
MAJ	0.73	0.13	0.30	0.69	0.73	0.30
PRES	0.33	1.00	0.74	0.31	0.64	0.09

Note: Fractions of majoritarian (*MAJ*) and presidential (*PRES*) constitutions in each group.

tial regimes are found in Africa and Asia and in former Spanish and Portuguese colonies.

Table 4.3 confirms this visual impression by reporting the fractions of majoritarian and presidential political systems by colonial origin, continental location, and level of development. All former Spanish colonies are nowadays presidential regimes, whereas more than 70% of the former U.K. colonies have majoritarian electoral rules. Perhaps more surprisingly, more than 70% of the Asian and African countries in our sample have majoritarian elections. Many (but not all) countries in Latin America are presidential regimes. And OECD countries are prevalently parliamentary-proportional democracies.

Exploiting these and other historical and geographic variables, we can indeed explain a considerable fraction of the cross-country variance in constitutional rules. Table 4.4 reports the results of probit regressions on our two main constitutional indicators (*MAJ* and *PRES*) under two specifications. One is more parsimonious and includes British colonial origin, an indicator for Latin America, and the three dummy variables defined above corresponding to the birth of the current constitutional features in the various countries of the sample, plus the age of democracy.[15] The second is more comprehensive, adding another measure of geography (*LAT01*) and two indicators of cultural heritage, namely, the fraction of the population whose mother tongue is English (*ENGFRAC*) or a European language (*EURFRAC*); these variables are available only for a smaller number of countries than the first set of variables. Table 4.5 shows that historical and cultural variables predominantly explain the electoral rule, whereas geographic variables tend to explain the regime type. As expected, British colonial origin and English mother

---

15. The other colonial-origin indicators and continental dummy variables were not included; if they had been, we could perfectly have predicted the constitutional state of several countries.

Table 4.4
Determinants of constitutional rules: Probit estimates

	(1)	(2)	(3)	(4)
Dependent variable	PRES	PRES	MAJ	MAJ
CON2150	0.52	0.15	−1.72	−1.38
	(0.63)	(0.72)	(0.69)**	(0.82)*
CON5180	0.59	−0.04	0.10	0.13
	(0.58)	(0.63)	(0.62)	(0.68)
CON81	1.83	1.52	0.03	0.23
	(0.62)***	(0.73)**	(0.72)	(0.72)
AGE	1.61	3.83	0.74	0.14
	(1.15)	(1.51)**	(1.27)	(1.48)
COL_UKA	−0.08	−0.05	2.15	1.02
	(0.45)	(0.67)	(0.45)***	(0.62)
LAAM	1.51	1.61	−0.38	−1.96
	(0.40)***	(0.63)***	(0.36)	(0.80)**
LAT01		−5.15		−4.19
		(1.79)***		(1.57)***
ENGFRAC		−3.26		2.62
		(1.02)***		(0.90)***
EURFRAC		0.71		0.74
		(0.61)		(0.72)
Sample	1990s, broad	1990s, broad	1990s, broad	1990s, broad
Number of observations	85	78	85	78
Pseudo-R^2	0.26	0.51	0.31	0.50

Note: Robust standard errors in parentheses.
*significant at 10%; **significant at 5%; ***significant at 1%.

tongue always significantly contribute to predicting majoritarian electoral rules (and in the case of ENGFRAC, also parliamentary governments), whereas presidential regimes are more likely to be found in Latin America and close to the equator. This last result, that countries closer to the equator are more likely to be presidential, might seem surprising. A possible interpretation is that closeness to the equator is associated with a later wave of colonialization by the West and hence a weaker influence of the predominant form of government in Europe.

Note that the three dummy variables dating the origin of the current constitution remain statistically significant (jointly and in some cases even individually) in all specifications, even after the other geographic and historical or cultural variables are controlled for. We

Table 4.5
Policy outcomes and constitutions: Variation across countries

	(1)	(2)	(3)	(4)	(5)	(6)	(7)	(8)	(9)
Dependent variable	MAJ	MIXED	PROP	p(MAJ, MIXED)	p(PROP, MIXED)	p(MAJ, PROP)	PRES	PARL	p(PRES, PARL)
CGEXP	25.6 (8.2)	27.1 (11.6)	31.4 (11.3)	0.676	0.323	0.016	22.2 (7.2)	33.3 (10.0)	0.000
SSW	4.7 (5.4)	7.1 (6.8)	10.7 (6.5)	0.330	0.195	0.000	4.8 (4.6)	9.9 (7.0)	0.002
SPL	−1.1 (4.3)	−3.0 (2.7)	−2.8 (2.8)	0.229	0.821	0.053	−2.0 (2.7)	−2.3 (3.9)	0.708
GRAFT	4.3 (1.9)	4.3 (1.4)	4.0 (2.0)	0.959	0.687	0.594	5.3 (1.5)	3.4 (1.8)	0.000
GADP	0.7 (0.2)	0.7 (0.1)	0.7 (0.2)	0.559	0.780	0.649	0.6 (0.2)	0.8 (0.2)	0.000
LOGYL	8.9 (1.1)	9.3 (0.7)	9.5 (0.7)	0.295	0.543	0.007	8.8 (0.9)	9.5 (0.8)	0.000
LOGA	8.0 (0.8)	8.2 (0.4)	8.3 (0.5)	0.359	0.622	0.024	7.9 (0.6)	8.3 (0.5)	0.003

Note: $p(X, Y)$ is the probability of falsely rejecting equal means in groups X and Y, under the maintained hypothesis of equal variances. Standard deviations in parentheses. MAJ refers to countries coded $MAJ = 1$, $MIXED$ to those coded $MIXED = 1$, $PROP$ to those coded $MAJ = 0$, PRES to those coded $PRES = 1$, and PARL to those coded $PRES = 0$.

exploit this result in later chapters, when we try to isolate exogenous variation in (finding instruments for) constitutional rules.

The nonrandom pattern of constitutional rules we have uncovered in our data sets raises a fundamental question. Can we really treat constitutions as exogenous in the empirical analysis of policy performance? This question and related concerns are a major theme in the empirical analysis of subsequent chapters. But before we address this issue, let us see how constitutions correlate with policy outcomes and other variables that are, a priori, likely to influence these outcomes.

4.6 Constitutions, Performance, and Covariates: A First Look

4.6.1 Constitutions and Outcomes
In this section, we take a provisional look at how the policy and performance measures introduced in chapter 3 vary across constitutions. Table 4.5 shows the mean and standard deviation of fiscal policy, rent extraction, and productivity outcomes in our 1990s cross section, grouped according to the binary indicators of regime ($PRES$) and electoral rule (MAJ and $MIXED$) introduced in this chapter.

The first six columns of the table split this cross-sectional sample according to electoral rule. Columns 1–3 report the mean values of each policy outcome by electoral rule. Columns 4–6 report the p-values for equal-means tests across electoral systems, comparing majoritarian versus mixed, mixed versus proportional, and majoritarian versus proportional electoral systems, respectively. Notice that these tests should be interpreted just as a convenient way of describing the data and should definitely *not* be given any causal interpretation (see below).

Majoritarian elections ($MAJ = 1$) are associated with a smaller overall size of government ($CGEXP$), smaller welfare spending (SSW), and larger budget surpluses (smaller deficits) (SPL) than proportional and mixed systems. The differences between majoritarian and proportional countries are large (and statistically significant): 5% of GDP for the two spending variables, and almost 2% of GDP for the budget deficit. Mixed electoral systems ($MIXED = 1$) fall in between the two extremes as far as the two spending variables are concerned and have an even larger deficit than proportional countries. Given the small number of countries with mixed electoral rules, the standard errors are large, however, so we cannot reject the hypothesis that they have the same mean for all fiscal policy variables as either proportional or majoritarian countries. Rent extraction (*GRAFT*) and our indicator of antidiversion policies (*GADP*) do not seem to vary systematically with electoral rule, however. Nevertheless, labor and total factor productivity (*LOGYL* and *LOGA*, respectively) are correlated with electoral rules: both measures of productivity are lower in majoritarian countries, though the difference by electoral rule is not very large. In this case, mixed systems are very similar to proportional countries.

The last three columns of table 4.5 split the 1990s cross section according to form of government. Parliamentary regimes (*PRES* = 0) have much larger governments than presidential regimes (*PRES* = 1); the difference is as large as 11% of GDP. The same is true for welfare spending, with the difference as large as 5% of GDP. Moreover, parliamentary regimes are less corrupt (*GRAFT* is lower, which corresponds to the perception of a less widespread abuse of power), and they have policies more conducive to growth (*GADP* is higher, which corresponds to better policies). The differences between the two types of regimes on these variables are also large. Finally, parliamentary regimes are associated with higher values of labor and total factor productivity. Only budget deficits do not seem correlated with forms of government.

As discussed in chapter 3, we are also interested in the *time variation* of the fiscal policy measures. Table 4.6 gives the results for the full 60-country panel and breaks those results down according to forms of government and electoral rules. It then displays the average values of fiscal policy outcomes in each group of countries for five-year subperiods between 1960 and 1998.

Table 4.6a considers size of government, displaying both the average value of central government spending (*CGEXP*) in each five-year period and its cumulative change (*DCGEXP*) over the period, expressed as percentages of GDP. Since the number of countries varies over time according to data availability, the time variation in size of government is best captured by the cumulative change. In the early 1960s, parliamentary countries already have larger governments than presidential countries, whereas governments in proportional and majoritarian countries are about equal in size. As discussed in chapter 3, government spending increases in all countries in the 1970s and the first half of the 1980s. The growth of government is especially rapid in parliamentary countries, but such growth also occurs in proportional countries. (A further breakdown into four constitutional groups shows that the most rapid growth indeed takes place in the proportional-parliamentary subgroup.) Moreover, the acceleration starts earlier (in the mid-1960s) in the parliamentary and proportional groups, and later (in the mid-1970s) in the presidential and majoritarian groups. The late 1980s and the 1990s are periods of government retrenchment everywhere. All in all, parliamentary governments grow about twice as much as presidential governments in the entire sample period.

Similar patterns are observed in social security and welfare spending, as shown in table 4.6b, which starts in 1970 because of data unavailability prior to that year. Both the proportional and parliamentary groups have much larger welfare states initially than the other groups, and these differences grow over time. It is somewhat harder to identify a common time pattern, though welfare spending keeps growing until the mid-1990s in almost all groups.

Finally, table 4.6c considers budget surpluses (also as a percentage of GDP). All groups look very similar in terms of budget surpluses until the mid-1970s. In the 1970s, deficits grow everywhere, but the increase is more pronounced among proportional and parliamentary countries. These groups continue to have larger deficits in the 1980s and 1990s.

Altogether, table 4.6 shows the relation between the constitution and government fiscal policy to be one that changes over time. Some important differences in fiscal policy among constitutional groups are already apparent in the 1960s. But something special occurs in the 1970s and 1980s that has a different effect on constitutional groups, and this has lasting consequences well into the 1990s. This pattern suggests that, to fully understand constitutional effects on fiscal policy, we also need to pay attention to time variation in the data.

Both tables 4.5 and 4.6 reveal important similarities between majoritarian electoral rules and presidential forms of government and some stark differences relative to proportional and parliamentary countries. Majoritarian and presidential countries have smaller governments, smaller welfare states, smaller deficits, and lower productivities than parliamentary and proportional countries. Parliamentary regimes are also less corrupt than presidential regimes, and their policies are more conducive to growth.

It is tempting to relate these performance patterns to the theoretical predictions put forward in chapter 2, a temptation that should,

Table 4.6
Fiscal policy outcomes and constitutions: Variation over time

a. Size of government

	Full sample		Presidential		Parliamentary		Majoritarian		Proportional	
	CGEXP	DCGEXP	CGEXP	DCGEXP	CGEXP	DCGEXP	CGEXP	DCGEXP	CGEXP	DCGEXP
1960–1964	18.3	0.7	14.6	−0.4	20.5	1.4	19.2	1.5	18.7	0.5
1965–1969	20.0	1.8	15.7	1.0	22.7	2.4	21.0	0.6	20.4	2.4
1970–1974	22.2	3.0	16.7	1.1	25.8	4.3	22.1	1.5	22.9	3.6
1975–1979	26.0	3.6	18.3	2.1	30.6	4.5	26.3	3.0	26.3	4.0
1980–1984	29.8	4.1	21.7	4.1	34.4	4.0	28.6	3.5	30.6	4.5
1985–1989	29.3	−2.4	20.7	−3.0	33.9	−2.0	27.3	−1.5	30.2	−2.9
1990–1994	29.1	1.2	20.0	1.5	34.4	1.0	27.5	−0.3	29.9	1.9
1995–1998	28.5	−0.8	20.3	−0.1	33.4	−1.2	25.9	0.2	29.9	−1.4
All years	25.8	11.9	18.7	7.4	30.1	14.7	25.4	8.6	26.5	13.3
Number of countries	60	60	22	22	38	38	21	21	39	39

b. Social security and welfare spending

	Full sample		Presidential		Parliamentary		Majoritarian		Proportional	
	SSW	DSSW	SSW	DSSW	SSW	DSSW	SSW	DSSW	SSW	DSSW
1970–1974	5.9	0.9	3.7	−1.1	7.2	2.2	3.8	−0.9	6.8	1.6
1975–1979	6.4	1.0	3.6	0.1	8.2	1.6	4.7	0.8	7.6	1.1
1980–1984	8.0	0.7	4.9	0.3	9.4	0.9	5.6	1.0	9.6	0.5
1985–1989	7.7	−0.1	3.8	−0.6	9.4	0.1	5.1	−0.5	9.0	0.1
1990–1994	8.1	1.5	4.9	1.7	9.8	1.3	5.4	0.6	9.5	1.9
1995–1998	8.1	−0.5	6.0	0.0	9.2	−0.7	4.6	−0.2	9.9	−0.6
All years	7.4	5.2	4.4	1.8	9.0	7.0	5.0	2.7	8.8	6.5
Number of countries	50	49	18	17	32	32	18	17	32	32

Constitutions, Performance, and Covariates

c. Budget surplus

	Full Sample	Presidential	Parliamentary	Majoritarian	Proportional
	SPL	SPL	SPL	SPL	SPL
1960–1964	-1.5	-1.2	-1.7	-1.9	-1.4
1965–1969	-2.0	-1.7	-2.3	-1.9	-2.2
1970–1974	-2.4	-2.1	-2.7	-3.0	-2.3
1975–1979	-3.7	-2.6	-4.4	-3.5	-3.9
1980–1984	-5.0	-4.3	-5.4	-4.2	-5.5
1985–1989	-3.2	-3.7	-2.9	-1.7	-3.9
1990–1994	-2.8	-1.7	-3.4	-1.5	-3.4
1995–1998	-2.0	-1.3	-2.4	-0.8	-2.6
All years	-3.0	-2.4	-3.3	-2.5	-3.3
Number of countries	60	22	38	21	39

Note: "Number of countries" denotes the number of countries in 1990–1994 (this number changes over time). DCGEXP and DSSW denote the average cumulative changes of CGEXP and SSW, respectively, in the rows for different subperiods, as a percentage of GDP, and the average cumulative change over the whole time period in the "All years" row.

however, be strongly resisted. If the grouping of countries according to different constitutional rules were entirely random, we could use the unconditional comparisons in tables 4.5 and 4.6 for inference, for if that were the case, we might trust that other country character- istics would not systematically influence our policy and performance measures. But given the correlations between constitutions and other cultural, historical, or geographic variables, discussed in section 4.5, random selection of constitutional rules is not an assumption we can seriously entertain. Inference about the causal effect of constitu- tions on policy outcomes requires additional assumptions and more sophisticated statistical techniques than simple tabulation. These issues will be discussed in the next three chapters. But before turning our attention to statistical issues and methods, we will complete our provisional discussion of the data by considering some additional differences among our constitutional groups.

4.6.2   Constitutions and Other Covariates

In chapter 3, we showed policy outcomes to be systematically corre- lated with several economic and social characteristics, such as per capita income, demographics, and openness to international trade. How different are the countries in our constitutional groups when it comes to those characteristics? Table 4.7 displays means and stan- dard deviations of some prominent policy determinants by political regimes and electoral rules.

Starting with the split of the sample according to electoral rules (the first six columns of the table), we find some stark differences. Majoritarian electoral rules are clearly found in poorer countries (*LYP*), in worse democracies (*GASTIL*), and in societies with more Catholics (*CATHO80*) and younger populations (*PROP65*); only the differences between majoritarian and pure proportional countries tend to be statistically significant. As indicated by the results in chapter 3, younger populations might explain the smaller govern- ments and welfare states of majoritarian countries found in tables 4.5 and 4.6. But openness to international trade (*TRADE*) is not corre- lated with the electoral rule, contrary to the widespread expectation that more open economies prefer PR because they need stability to survive in world markets, as argued by Rogowski (1987) and others. Although there is a positive correlation between PR and openness among the 24 developed OECD democracies Rogowski studied, no apparent correlation is present in our more extensive data set, and if

Table 4.7
Country characteristics and constitutions

	(1)	(2)	(3)	(4)	(5)	(6)	(7)	(8)	(9)
	MAJ	MIXED	PROP	p(MAJ,MIXED)	p(PROP,MIXED)	p(MAJ,PROP)	PRES	PARL	p(PRES,PARL)
LYP	8.1	8.5	8.6	0.395	0.792	0.058	7.9	8.7	0.000
	(1.1)	(0.9)	(0.8)				(0.9)	(0.9)	
TRADE	85.2	67.3	78.8	0.386	0.415	0.580	62.5	89.1	0.011
	(59.6)	(24.3)	(40.2)				(27.5)	(54.2)	
PROP65	6.6	7.7	9.9	0.563	0.234	0.003	5.6	10.3	0.000
	(4.4)	(5.1)	(4.8)				(3.5)	(4.8)	
CATHO80	23.0	23.9	55.7	0.924	0.039	0.000	57.8	29.8	0.001
	(24.5)	(32.0)	(42.4)				(39.2)	(34.5)	
PROT80	16.7	18.1	18.3	0.847	0.980	0.791	9.9	22.3	0.028
	(18.5)	(19.0)	(31.7)				(15.9)	(29.2)	
AGE	0.2	0.1	0.2	0.280	0.194	0.926	0.2	0.3	0.056
	(0.2)	(0.1)	(0.2)				(0.2)	(0.2)	
GASTIL	2.8	2.9	2.1	0.752	0.043	0.027	3.1	2.0	0.000
	(1.4)	(1.0)	(1.1)				(1.2)	(1.1)	

Note: $p(X, Y)$ is the probability of falsely rejecting equal means across groups X and Y, under the maintained hypothesis of equal variances. Standard errors in parentheses. Group headings at top of columns defined as in table 4.5.

anything, the correlation seems to be negative. Note also that we do not find differences in age of democracy (*AGE*) across electoral rules.

Continuing with the split of the sample according to form of government (the last two columns of table 4.7), we see that countries with parliamentary regimes are richer and more open to international trade and have a larger percentage of old people than countries with presidential regimes (all differences are statistically significant). As chapter 3 showed, these factors all tend to correlate with larger governments. The higher spending in parliamentary regimes revealed in table 4.6 might simply reflect these socioeconomic differences. On average, parliamentary regimes also have smaller proportions of Catholics and larger proportions of Protestants; moreover, they are older and better democracies. These features are all expected to correlate with lower levels of corruption (again recall chapter 3), which might account for the lower unconditional level of corruption in parliamentary regimes.

These cautionary remarks—and earlier remarks on nonrandom constitution selection—remind us of the common danger in social science research of attributing causal interpretations to simple correlations. As a minimum requirement, we should be very careful in holding constant other determinants of the outcomes we study when we test the constitutional effects our theory might suggest. The next chapter presents a more systematic discussion of the assumptions necessary to draw causal inference from cross-country data in the presence of nonrandom selection.

Cross-Sectional Inference: Pitfalls and Methods

5.1 Introduction

As we have seen in chapter 4, the broad features of electoral rules and forms of government are very stable over time. Because of this stability, we have an insufficient number of "constitutional experiments" to isolate the causal effects of constitutional reforms from variation in performance over time. Instead, we must infer the causal effects of constitutions from cross-country comparisons, a task undertaken in the next two chapters. But the road to secure inference from cross-country data is riddled with statistical difficulties. We therefore devote the present chapter to a discussion of the most important statistical pitfalls we may encounter and to a presentation of methods that may provide ways around them. Readers mainly interested in the substantive results and willing to trust our choice of methodology can probably skip parts of this chapter without compromising their ability to follow the subsequent arguments. Similarly, econometrically skilled readers may choose to skim the material in the chapter that is already familiar to them. To get a sense of where we are going, however, both the econometrically uninterested and the econometrically proficient should read this introduction. They should also read the final parts of sections 5.4.1, 5.4.2, and 5.5, which speak most directly to the practical implementation of the methods that will be used in chapters 6 and 7. More extensive discussions of the econometric methodology introduced in this chapter can be found in Angrist and Krueger 1999 and 2001, Heckman, Lalonde, and Smith 1999, Ichino 2002, and Wooldridge 2002 (chap. 18).

Which questions on constitutions and policy outcomes do we pose to the data? We are not interested in correlations per se, but in what they reveal about underlying causation. For the policy and performance measures introduced in chapter 3, we would thus like to answer counterfactual questions like the following: "Suppose we pick a country at random in our sample and, going back in history, change its constitution. How would this alter its current performance?" In section 5.2, we show how to pose such questions in a precise way and discuss a fundamental difficulty that crops up as we attempt to provide an answer.

At the end of chapter 4, we pointed out that constitutional features are correlated with country characteristics that also determine policy outcomes and stressed the importance of holding these common determinants constant in cross-country comparisons. But confounding constitutions with other unobserved socioeconomic determinants of performance is certainly not the only pitfall that we may encounter in separating correlation from causation. It is just one instance of a general statistical phenomenon known as "simultaneity," namely, the notion that our inference becomes biased if the variation in constitutional rules used to explain performance is related to the random (unexplained) component of performance. Simultaneity problems can take the form of *reverse causation*, different forms of *selection bias*, and *measurement error*.

Direct reverse causation (i.e., a causal link from policy outcomes to constitutions) is probably not a major concern in our context. If it were, we would probably not observe so much stability of political institutions over very long time periods, despite pretty substantial changes in policy. The constitutional stability highlighted in chapter 4 indicates that it may be correct to treat electoral rules and political regimes as given by history and not plagued by reverse causation from outcomes to constitutions. In that way, stability may be a blessing.

Historically predetermined constitutional rules certainly do not rule out problems of selection bias, however. As chapter 4 made eminently clear, constitutional choices do not appear to have been random. It is quite possible that countries self-selected into constitutions on the basis of cultural traits and historical experience, which also shape long-run collective preferences and thus influence policy and performance even today. For instance, Botswana's history as a U.K. colony may have fostered its selection of a first-past-the post electoral system, as well as its tradition (by African standards) of resistance to corruption, and this preselection might bias our inference toward finding a negative link between majoritarian elections and corruption. This is why it is crucial to hold constant prospective determinants of constitutional choices that may also influence policy performance. The Botswana example—and more generally the evidence from the equal-means tests and probit estimates in section 4.5—suggests that is important to control for measures like colonial history and continental location. We try to achieve such control when estimating constitutional effect via simple linear regression analysis with many right-hand-side variables. Although this way of approaching the data is the most common empirical strategy in economics and (probably) in political science, it does rely on very strong underlying assumptions. In section 5.3, we clarify and discuss these *identifying* assumptions.

Specifically, holding observable constitutional determinants constant may not be enough. Suppose, for example, that Sweden's history of equal opportunity, broad education, and widespread ownership of land (relative to other countries) fostered a common culture of equality that has promoted the selection of a proportional electoral system as well as a preference for a welfare state. Because such underlying determinants might be very hard to identify or measure, we may encounter a problem of selection on *unobservables*. Although this is a notoriously difficult problem, social scientists have developed some methods for dealing with selection bias: isolating sources of truly exogenous variation in constitution through instrumental variables or correcting the estimation of constitutional effect through an adjustment for systematic self-selection. Instrumental-variable estimation is also a classical method for dealing with one of the other sources of simultaneity bias, namely, measurement error in the causal variable of interest. Section 5.4 introduces and discusses these statistical methods in the context of our problem and explains how they are used in chapters 6 and 7.

A final concern is that our attempts to estimate a causal effect of constitutions involve "comparing the incomparable," a critique frequently leveled by some political scientists against statistical work in comparative politics. Suppose the effect of a political reform (say, going from a parliamentary to a presidential regime) depends on culture, geography, and history. For example, the same constitutional reform might have different effects on policy outcomes in, say, Latin America versus Europe, or in good versus bad democracies. Then we may indeed run into inference problems, even if the most relevant constitutional determinants are fully observed and held constant. In the wake of such interaction effects, or nonlinearities, the fact that presidential regimes are (much) more common in Latin America and in worse democracies makes it dangerous to extrapolate from their experience to that of good parliamentary democracies in Europe. To handle this problem of selection on *observables*, we need a method that is robust to functional form and handles systematic selection by focusing on appropriate "local" comparisons. Nonparametric matching methods with these properties are introduced in section 5.5, where we also explain how these methods will be applied to our problem in subsequent chapters.

In most of the chapter, we simplify the formal statistical discussion by considering the estimation of a single constitutional effect at a time. Section 5.6 briefly deals with the extensions to multiple constitutional features.

5.2   The Question

5.2.1   Primitives

For the sake of argument, assume that there is only one constitutional rule, S, and it can take on only two values, $S = 0, 1$. At any point in time, country i belongs to one of these two constitutional states, denoted by the indicator S_i. Thus, country i could be Botswana and S could be the electoral rule, as measured by the binary variable MAJ, in which case we would have $S_i = 1$.

Suppose that the constitution selection by country i can be described by the index model

$$S_i = \begin{cases} 1 & \text{as } G(\mathbf{W}_i) + \eta_i \geq 0 \\ 0 & \text{as } G(\mathbf{W}_i) + \eta_i < 0 \end{cases}, \tag{5.1}$$

where $\mathbf{W}$ is a set of *observed* variables influencing the observed choice of constitution. Members of $\mathbf{W}$ would involve variables, such as those discussed in chapter 4, describing continental location, colonial history, culture, and the pure timing of constitutional choice. Other *unobserved* country-specific factors are summarized by the random variable η_i. Throughout, we assume that η and $\mathbf{W}$ are uncorrelated.

Let Y_i^S denote the *potential* policy outcome or performance of country i in constitutional state S. Thus, Y could be corruption, with Y_i^1 and Y_i^0 and denoting corruption in Botswana under majoritarian and proportional elections, respectively. Potential performance is not observed, as each country can have only one constitution at any given moment in time. We observe *actual* performance only in one of the two constitutional states, Y_i:

$$Y_i = S_i Y_i^1 + (1 - S_i) Y_i^0. \tag{5.2}$$

Thus we observe corruption in Botswana under its actual majoritarian electoral rule, but not under its *counterfactual* proportional rule. This distinction between actual and potential performance is crucial to the statistical problems to be discussed in this chapter, so we return to it below.

The stochastic process determining potential performance in constitutional state S and country i is

$$Y_i^S = F^S(\mathbf{X}_i) + \varepsilon_i^S, \qquad S = 0, 1, \tag{5.3}$$

where $\mathbf{X}$ is a vector of observed variables (say, the educational attainment and predominant religion in the population), $F^S(\cdot)$ is a function that is allowed to depend on constitutional state, and ε^S is a random variable capturing the effect of all the unobserved determinants of performance. The observed determinants in $\mathbf{X}$ could interact with constitutional state in influencing policy or performance in many ways. But, by assumption, the observable variables in $\mathbf{X}$ are not causally affected by constitutional state.[1]

Importantly, the unobserved determinant of performance, ε^S, is allowed to depend on constitutional state. For instance, corruption could depend on unobservable social norms, but the effect of social norms on corruption is also influenced by the constitution, so that $\varepsilon_i^1 \neq \varepsilon_i^0$. In this case, the effect of constitutions on performance can differ across countries even if they have identical observables. In the special case in which $\varepsilon_i^1 = \varepsilon_i^0$ for all i, the influence of the constitution on performance is instead homogenous for countries with similar observables $\mathbf{X}$, since the influence does not interact with ε_i. Even if we allow ε^1 and ε^0 to differ, we always assume that both have a mean of zero in the *full population* of countries. We also assume that ε^S is uncorrelated with $\mathbf{X}$ (for $S = 0, 1$).

1. The assumption that there is no effect of S on $\mathbf{X}$ is admittedly very strong. It is more plausible for some variables entering our actual $\mathbf{X}$ vector than for others. If the assumption fails, the estimated effect of S on performance that we discuss below has the interpretation of a direct effect on performance (a partial derivative), holding constant the values of $\mathbf{X}$, rather than a reduced-form effect (a total derivative). But in that case, other estimation problems arise on top of those discussed in this chapter: see Heckman, Lalonde, and Smith 1999.

With this notation, each country in our sample is fully described by a realization of the vector $(\mathbf{W}, \mathbf{X}, \eta, \varepsilon^1, \varepsilon^0)$. The random variables contained in this vector (some of them unobserved) are the primitive objects that define our population of countries. Through equations (5.1) and (5.3), these primitives then determine a realization of (S, Y^1, Y^0), and together with (5.2) they define a vector of observables $(S, Y, \mathbf{X}, \mathbf{W})$. In the rest of the chapter, we discuss what restrictions need to be placed on the joint distributions of these random variables to enable us to draw unbiased inferences from observable data. But before we can do that, we must define more precisely the parameter we want to estimate.

5.2.2 The Parameter of Interest

Suppose that we pick a country at random with characteristics $\mathbf{X}$ and switch its constitutional state from $S = 0$ to $S = 1$. The expected effect of constitutional reform in this particular country is now given by the (conditional) expectation

$$\alpha(\mathbf{X}) = \mathsf{E}(Y^1 - Y^0 \mid \mathbf{X}), \tag{5.4}$$

where the expectations operator E refers to potential performance, Y^S, $S = 0, 1$.[2]

Naturally, it would be very interesting to estimate the effect of constitutional reform on performance for many different values of $\mathbf{X}$. But given the rich set of relevant determinants in $\mathbf{X}$ and the relative scarcity of observed democracies, we simply do not have enough data for such conditional estimation. What can be more realistically estimated is the *average* effect of constitutional reform on performance for all countries in our sample. Thus, we define our parameter of interest, α, as the *average* value of $\alpha(\mathbf{X})$ in our population, namely:

$$\alpha = E\{\mathsf{E}(Y^1 - Y^0 \mid \mathbf{X})\} = \mathsf{E}(Y^1 - Y^0). \tag{5.5}$$

In (5.5), the outer expectations operator E is taken over the actual unconditional distribution of $\mathbf{X}$ in our sample, and the second equality follows from the law of iterated expectations. Throughout the chapter, we refer to α as the *constitutional effect*. It tells us the expected effect of constitutional reform on performance for a country

---

2. In terms of our primitives, a constitutional reform can be thought of as a hypothetical experiment in which we change the realization of the unobserved determinant of the constitution, η, so that the constitutional state switches from $S = 0$ to $S = 1$.

drawn at random from the population of countries. In the corruption example above, this is the average (or expected) effect on corruption of a particular electoral reform, switching from proportional to majoritarian elections.[3]

Given our assumption that ε^S has zero mean in the population, $S = 0, 1$, by (5.3) and (5.5) we can rewrite the constitutional effect as

$$\alpha = E[F^1(\mathbf{X}) - F^0(\mathbf{X})],$$

where again the expectations operator is taken over the distribution of $\mathbf{X}$ in the whole sample of countries. This formulation makes clear that our question ultimately concerns how the function $F^S(\cdot)$, which determines performance, varies with constitution. But since we don't know $F^S(\cdot)$, we have to estimate it from observable data. This is the problem we turn to next.

5.2.3 Estimation

As already noted, we observe only *actual* performance, not *potential* performance. Yet we are interested in the determinants of potential performance: the function $F^S(\cdot)$. We would like to know how changing the electoral rule would affect corruption in, say, Botswana. But we observe Botswana only under majoritarian electoral rule, not under a hypothetical proportional rule.

The consequences of this "missing-data problem" can best be seen by rewriting equation (5.5) as

$$\alpha = P \cdot [E(Y^1 \mid S = 1) - E(Y^0 \mid S = 1)]$$

$$+ (1 - P) \cdot [E(Y^1 \mid S = 0) - E(Y^0 \mid S = 0)], \tag{5.6}$$

where P is the probability of observing a country with $S = 1$ in the sample. The first bracketed term in (5.6) is the effect of constitutional reform in countries currently in state $S = 1$, and the second bracketed term is the effect for countries currently in state $S = 0$. In the above example, $S = 1$ denotes majoritarian electoral rule, and $S = 0$ denotes proportional electoral rule. Equation (5.6) says that the effect of electoral reform on the whole sample is the weighted average of

---

3. Readers familiar with the program evaluation literature will recognize this expression as the *average treatment effect*. See Heckman, Lalonde, and Smith 1999 for a discussion of this and other statistical definitions of a causal effect in program evaluation. Wooldridge (2002, chap. 18) provides an advanced textbook treatment of different approaches to estimating average treatment effects.

the effect of electoral reform on the two groups of countries, those currently under majoritarian rule (the first term) and those under proportional rule (the second term), each weighted by the relative frequency of that type of rule among the countries in the sample.[4] Clearly, we can easily estimate the factual outcomes $E(Y^1 | S = 1)$ and $E(Y^0 | S = 0)$ from, say, the sample mean of observed corruption under each electoral rule. But how should we proceed with the unobserved counterfactuals $E(Y^1 | S = 0)$ and $E(Y^0 | S = 1)$? This difficult question is sometimes referred to as the "fundamental problem of causal inference."

In a world where the constitution was randomly assigned to countries, the problem would have a simple solution. Random selection would imply that constitutional rules S were independent of outcomes Y; moreover, it would balance the distribution of X across the two constitutional groups. As a result, we could safely set $E(Y^1 | S = 0) = E(Y^1 | S = 1) = E(Y^1)$, thereby replacing unobservable counterfactual performance with observable actual performance, as the two would be (close to) equal. Similarly, we could set $E(Y^0 | S = 1) = E(Y^0 | S = 0) = E(Y^0)$. For example, we could comfortably assume that the average *potential* corruption in the whole population under, say, majoritarian rule could be measured by the average *actual* corruption in *currently majoritarian* countries. Making these substitutions in (5.6), we would thus simply compute the constitutional effect as $\alpha = E(Y^1 | S = 1) - E(Y^0 | S = 0)$. The constitutional effect on corruption would be evaluated as the observed difference in average corruption between majoritarian and proportional countries.

But as highlighted in chapter 4, the world of random constitution assignment is not the real world. Constitution selection is certainly not random, so we need to make additional assumptions in order to evaluate unobservable counterfactuals. At a general level, these assumptions can be described with reference to the model in equations (5.1)–(5.3), which define constitution selection and performance. One set of assumptions concerns the *unobserved determinants*

---

4. The first effect is also known in the program evaluation literature as the "average effect of treatment *on the treated*," whereas the second term is called the "average effect of treatment *on the controls (untreated).*" Note that these two effects are *not* necessarily symmetric if selection of the constitution is not random and not independent of the policy outcome. The average treatment effect is thus a weighted average of the average effect of treatment on the treated and the average effect of treatment on the controls.

of outcomes and constitutional choices, as captured by the joint distribution of the random components η and ε^S, $S = 0, 1$.[5] Another set of assumptions concerns the *functional forms* of $G(\cdot)$ and $F^S(\cdot)$, $S = 0, 1$, and their exact specification (i.e., which variables are excluded from one equation but included in the other). As we explain below, when constitutional selection is nonrandom, making accurate assumptions regarding these distributions and functional forms is crucial to obtaining unbiased estimates of constitutional effect, α. The different estimation methods described in the following three sections implicitly trade off less restrictive assumptions in one of these dimensions against more restrictive assumptions in the other.

5.3 Simple Linear Regressions

Linear regression analysis is routinely applied in empirical work by most economists and many political scientists. Does it give reliable results if applied to our problem? This section discusses a set of identifying assumptions that guarantee an unbiased estimate of the causal effect of constitutional reform on performance.

5.3.1 Conditional Independence

A standard and convenient assumption in applied econometrics is *conditional independence*. Loosely speaking, this assumption says that the selection of constitutions is random, once we have controlled for the vector of observable variables in $\mathbf{X}$. Specifically, suppose that the variables entering $\mathbf{W}$ in the index model of selection (5.1) are a subset of the variables in $\mathbf{X}$ influencing performance in (5.3). Then conditional independence is satisfied if the random terms in (5.1) and (5.3), η and ε^S, are uncorrelated. We can also state the assumption in a different way, namely, as *recursivity* of the model consisting of (5.1) and (5.3).

In chapter 4, we saw that a number of observable variables likely to influence performance are indeed correlated with electoral rules

---

5. In fact, as noted by Wooldridge (2002), the assumptions about the unobserved determinants of constitution selection and performance needed to identify and estimate the constitutional effect (i.e., the average treatment effect) can be stated in terms of the means of Y^S, conditional on S and $\mathbf{X}$, without imposing any kind of model on the joint distributions of our primitive variables $(\mathbf{X}, \mathbf{W}, \eta, \varepsilon^1, \varepsilon^0)$. Of course, these assumptions imply specific conditions on the underlying joint distribution of the primitive variables, and in some cases we will explicitly spell out such conditions.

and forms of government. This is the case for colonial history and continental location, and also for levels of income, openness, and quality of democracy. The critical assumption is thus that when these observables have been taken into account, the unexplained influence on constitution selection is not systematically related to the unexplained influence on potential performance. As a result, conditional independence is known as *ignorability* or as *selection on observables*.

More precisely, we assume the following:

$$E(Y^1 \mid \mathbf{X}, S = 0) = E(Y^1 \mid \mathbf{X}, S = 1) = E(Y^1 \mid \mathbf{X}),$$

$$E(Y^0 \mid \mathbf{X}, S = 1) = E(Y^0 \mid \mathbf{X}, S = 0) = E(Y^0 \mid \mathbf{X}). \tag{5.7}$$

This assumption is sometimes called "conditional *mean* independence" to emphasize that it is slightly weaker than conditional independence. It says that once we have conditioned on $\mathbf{X}$, expected *potential* performance in state S, Y^S, is the same for all countries irrespective of their *actual* constitutional state. Conditional mean independence is implied by orthogonality of ε^S and η: if ε^S and η are uncorrelated, then $E(\varepsilon^1 \mid S = 0) = E(\varepsilon^1 \mid S = 1) = 0$, and taking expectations of (5.3), we satisfy (5.7).[6]

This assumption allows us to replace the unobservable counterfactuals in each constitutional state entering into (5.6) with an estimate obtained from the actual performance in each state. That estimate should take into account the observable variables in $\mathbf{X}$ and thus, all variables $\mathbf{W}$ systematically correlated with constitutional rules.

5.3.2 Linearity

But how exactly should we separate constitutional effects from the effects of other determinants of performance; that is, how should we control for $\mathbf{X}$? A particular concern is that constitutional effect could interact with other determinants of performance in subtle ways. For instance, electoral rule could be a more important determinant of corruption in more developed democracies and economies. As some developing countries have democratic institutions that are more dubious than others, the influence of electoral rules in those coun-

---

6. We could also get by with the weaker assumption $E(\varepsilon^1 \mid S = 0) = E(\varepsilon^1 \mid S = 1)$, possibly different from 0, according to which ε^1 (and ε^0) would be correlated with η in the same way across states.

tries might be less important than that of implicit or unwritten norms, when we are comparing such countries with more developed countries. Alternatively, the effect of income inequality on the size of government might depend on the electoral rule. Since the Meltzer and Richard (1981) model relies on the median-voter theorem, it may be more applicable in countries with first-past-the post elections, as plurality rule in single-member districts promotes two-party systems, in which the logic of two-candidate electoral competition for the median voter is more likely to apply.

Formally, such interactions between constitutions and other determinants of performance would show up as nonlinearities in $F^S(\mathbf{X})$. If we knew the precise functional form of $F^S(\mathbf{X})$, through which $\mathbf{X}$ affects the performance in each state, this would not be a problem. But we do not, so again we need additional assumptions. The most parsimonious assumption is that the constitution has only a *direct* effect on performance, which is always the same, irrespective of the values taken by the variables in $\mathbf{X}$. In other words, we assume away any interaction effect between constitution and conditioning variables. This is indeed our assumption when we estimate constitutional effects in a linear regression.

More precisely, suppose that the data-generating process $F^S(\mathbf{X})$ determining performance in state S is linear with constant coefficients, except for a constitution-dependent intercept. Thus, equation (5.3) takes the forms

$$Y_i^1 = F^1(\mathbf{X}_i) + \varepsilon_i^1 = \alpha^1 + \boldsymbol{\beta}\mathbf{X}_i + \varepsilon_i^1,$$
$$Y_i^0 = F^0(\mathbf{X}_i) + \varepsilon_i^0 = \alpha^0 + \boldsymbol{\beta}\mathbf{X}_i + \varepsilon_i^0. \tag{5.8}$$

Under this assumption, the constitutional effect is just

$$\alpha = E\{\mathsf{E}(Y^1 - Y^0 \mid \mathbf{X})\} = \alpha^1 - \alpha^0. \tag{5.9}$$

A less restrictive formulation would allow some of the slope coefficients $\boldsymbol{\beta}$ in (5.8) to differ across the constitutional states. Denoting these coefficients by $\boldsymbol{\beta}^S$, we would then define the constitutional effect as

$$\alpha = E\{\mathsf{E}(Y^1 - Y^0 \mid \mathbf{X})\} = \alpha^1 - \alpha^0 + (\boldsymbol{\beta}^1 - \boldsymbol{\beta}^0)E(\mathbf{X}). \tag{5.10}$$

In the regression analyses conducted in chapters 6 and 7, we will mainly impose the linearity assumption behind (5.9) but will experiment somewhat with nonlinear specifications.

5.3.3 Ordinary Least Squares

The simplest linearity assumption, together with conditional independence, allows us to estimate the constitutional effect α as the coefficient on S in a linear regression of Y on $\mathbf{X}$ and S. We now explain why. Recall that we observe $Y_i = S_i Y_i^1 + (1 - S_i) Y_i^0$. Exploiting linearity, we can replace Y_i^1 and Y_i^0 with the corresponding expressions in (5.8) to get:

$$Y_i = S_i(\alpha^1 + \boldsymbol{\beta}\mathbf{X}_i + \varepsilon_i) + (1 - S_i)(\alpha^0 + \boldsymbol{\beta}\mathbf{X}_i + \varepsilon_i)$$

$$= \alpha^0 + \boldsymbol{\beta}\mathbf{X}_i + S_i(\alpha^1 - \alpha^0) + e_i, \tag{5.11}$$

where the error term e_i is defined by $e_i = \varepsilon_i^0 + S_i(\varepsilon_i^1 - \varepsilon_i^0)$.

Equation (5.11) looks very familiar. It is tempting to jump to the conclusion that we can easily uncover the constitutional effect α as the estimated coefficient $\hat{\alpha}$ on the binary variable S in an ordinary least squares (OLS) regression. But the error term of this equation is highly nonstandard, since it has a component that switches on and off with S. To see what could go wrong with the estimate, consider the special case with $\alpha^0 = 0$ and no conditioning variables $\mathbf{X}$, such that $Y_i = S_i\alpha + e_i$. The probability limit of the OLS estimate is then[7]

$$\text{plim}(\hat{\alpha}) = \frac{\text{Cov}(Y, S)}{\text{Var}(S)} = \alpha + \frac{\text{Cov}(e, S)}{\text{Var}(S)}$$

$$= \alpha + \mathsf{E}(\varepsilon^1 \mid S = 1) - \mathsf{E}(\varepsilon^0 \mid S = 0). \tag{5.12}$$

This is where the assumption of conditional independence is essential. By (5.7), $\mathsf{E}(\varepsilon^1 \mid S = 1) = \mathsf{E}(\varepsilon^1 \mid S = 0) = 0$, and likewise for ε^0. Both of the last two terms in the right-most expression of (5.12) are thus equal to zero, which guarantees an unbiased OLS estimate of α.

---

7. To derive the last equality in (5.12), note that

$$\text{Cov}(e, S) = \mathsf{E}(eS) - \mathsf{E}(e)\mathsf{E}(S)$$
$$= P\mathsf{E}(\varepsilon^1 \mid S = 1) - P^2\mathsf{E}(\varepsilon^1 - \varepsilon^0 \mid S = 1)$$

and that

$$\text{Var}(S) = \mathsf{E}(S^2) - [\mathsf{E}(S)]^2 = P(1 - P).$$

Moreover, $\mathsf{E}(\varepsilon^0) = 0$ implies

$$P\mathsf{E}(\varepsilon^0 \mid S = 1) = -(1 - P)\mathsf{E}(\varepsilon^0 \mid S = 0).$$

Using these expressions and simplifying, we obtain (5.12). The same expression for the OLS bias could be derived if other conditioning variables $\mathbf{X}$ entered the regression.

To appreciate which possible sources of bias in OLS estimates we are ruling out by means of the conditional-independence assumption, rewrite the last two terms on the right-most side of (5.12) as

$$[\mathsf{E}(\varepsilon^0 \,|\, S = 1) - \mathsf{E}(\varepsilon^0 \,|\, S = 0)] + \mathsf{E}(\varepsilon^1 - \varepsilon^0 \,|\, S = 1). \tag{5.13}$$

First, consider the two terms inside the square brackets. These would be nonzero if there were a nonzero correlation between ε^0 and S, a version of the common problem of omitted variables. To pick up the earlier Botswana example, this problem would arise if, in a corruption regression, we were to leave out some determinants, such as colonial history, that were also likely to have influenced the selection of electoral rule. Notice that the direction of this selection bias has the same sign as the correlation between the unobserved determinants of performance and constitution selection, ε^0 and η. In the example, former British colonies (such as Botswana) are more likely to have majoritarian elections than other countries. If they also have less corruption, and colonial history is not included in the corruption regression, the correlation between ε^0 and η is negative. As former British colonies tend to have less corruption (lower ε^0) and are more likely to be majoritarian (high η), we are more likely to observe majoritarian rule ($MAJ = 1$) where corruption is low; conversely, we are more likely to observe proportional rule ($MAJ = 0$) where corruption is high. Because we do not observe the random determinants of corruption (colonial history), we mistakenly attribute the lower levels of corruption under majoritarian rule to a causal effect, when in fact it is due to the selection of constitution on unobservables. Hence, the difference inside the square brackets in (5.13) is a negative number, and our estimate of α is biased downward.

Next, consider the last term in (5.13). This second prospective source of bias is more subtle. It arises if constitutional choices are systematically related to the *heterogeneous* component of the effect of constitutional reform, $\varepsilon_i^1 - \varepsilon_i^0$. This could occur if there were reverse causation, that is, if constitution selection is driven by the desire to improve performance in the particular dimension measured by Y. As discussed in chapter 2, the political science literature suggests that the choice of majoritarian ($S = 1$) rather than proportional ($S = 0$) elections may foster better accountability at the expense of less widespread representation. Suppose, therefore, that countries in which accountability has a particularly strong effect on corruption (i.e., $\varepsilon_i^1 - \varepsilon_i^0$ is negative) choose majoritarian rule, whereas those where such effect is weak (i.e., $\varepsilon_i^1 - \varepsilon_i^0$ is positive) choose proportional rule. Such choices would imply a negative value of $\mathsf{E}(\varepsilon^1 - \varepsilon^0 \mid S = 1)$, which would once more bias our OLS estimate of α toward finding a negative effect of majoritarian elections on corruption.

Both biases are ruled out under conditional-independence assumptions. The only remaining nonstandard econometric feature is that we are estimating a "random coefficient" model: even though the error term e is uncorrelated with S, country-specific heterogeneity in constitutional effect remains, unless we assume that $\varepsilon_i^1 = \varepsilon_i^0$ for all i. In other words, we have a heteroscedastic error term and should take that into account when computing standard errors.

In chapters 6 and 7, we frequently regress performance on a constitutional dummy variable and other controls $\mathbf{X}$ to estimate our parameter of interest. The resulting estimates rely on the assumptions of linearity and conditional independence. Clearly, the latter assumption becomes more credible if the performance regression includes a large number of variables in $\mathbf{X}$ that are likely to be correlated with constitutional origin. The former, parsimonious assumption on functional form makes such a strategy feasible.

5.4   Relaxing Conditional Independence

Although both common and convenient, the conditional-independence assumption is nonetheless very strong. In chapter 4, we saw that countries in different constitutional groups differ systematically in terms of the observable variables known (from chapter 3) to influence policy outcomes. But how do we know that we have controlled for all such common determinants? It could very well be that some unobserved determinants of policy also differ systematically across constitutional groups.

If the conditional-independence assumption is violated, we have seen that OLS estimates of the constitutional effect become biased. Clearly, this is an instance of a well-known problem in econometrics known as *selection bias*. In the context of our application, we present two ways of dealing with this problem. One relies on finding instrumental variables that isolate some truly exogenous variation in constitutional rules. The other relies on adjusting our estimates of the constitutional effect for "self-selection," that is, for any correlation between selection and performance that remains after controlling for observables.

5.4.1   Instrumental Variables

How can instrumental variables solve the selection bias problem?[8] That is, how can some truly exogenous variation in constitutional rules be isolated and used in the estimation of constitutional effects? Suppose we find a variable—an instrument—Z that is correlated with the constitutional state S, but not with the error term e, in (5.11). Formally, we thus require $\text{Cov}(Z, S) \neq 0$, but $\text{Cov}(Z, e) = 0$. Under these conditions, we can find a consistent estimate of the coefficient on the constitutional dummy variable in (5.11) and hence, of the true constitutional effect, α. To see the main idea, consider again the simple special case presented in section 5.3.3 with $\alpha^0 = 0$ and no conditioning variables $\mathbf{X}$, such that $Y_i = S_i \alpha + e_i$. Then we have $\text{Cov}(Z, Y) = \alpha \, \text{Cov}(Z, S) + \text{Cov}(Z, e)$. Now if $\text{Cov}(Z, S) \neq 0$ and $\text{Cov}(Z, e) = 0$, we can uncover the true value of the constitutional effect as $\alpha = \text{Cov}(Z, Y)/\text{Cov}(Z, S)$ (given that we can consistently estimate the two covariances in this ratio in our sample).

A set of valid instruments $\mathbf{Z}$ must thus satisfy two requirements. First—and corresponding to $\text{Cov}(Z, S) \neq 0$ above—they must be *relevant*. That is, they should help predict constitutional state once we control for $\mathbf{W}$, the subset of controls $\mathbf{X}$ influencing both performance and constitution. In other words, the set of instruments should enter the selection process of the constitutional rule:

$$S_i = \begin{cases} 1 & \text{as } G(\mathbf{W}_i, \mathbf{Z}_i) + \eta_i \geq 0 \\ 0 & \text{as } G(\mathbf{W}_i, \mathbf{Z}_i) + \eta_i < 0 \end{cases}. \tag{5.14}$$

We may readily check this requirement, for example, by estimating a linear probability model for (5.14), as we do below, and testing whether the partial correlation between S and $\mathbf{Z}$ is equal to 0.

Second—and corresponding to $\text{Cov}(Z, e) = 0$ above—the set of valid instruments $\mathbf{Z}$ must be *exogenous*, that is, the instruments should be uncorrelated with the error term e in (5.11). This requirement is more tricky in our context, as e is not a primitive object but instead is given by $e = \varepsilon^0 + S(\varepsilon^1 - \varepsilon^0)$. Therefore, an exogenous instrument must satisfy two distinct conditions that correspond to

---

8. Most modern mainstream econometrics texts, such as Green 2000, Ruud 2000, and Wooldridge 2002, provide a general treatment of instrumental variables, and Stock 1999 and Angrist and Krueger 2001 give easily accessible introductions. For the specific problems involved in using instrumental variables to estimate average treatment effects under conditions of self-selection, see Wooldridge 2002 (chap. 18), Heckman, Lalonde, and Smith 1999, and Angrist and Krueger 1999.

the two possible sources of bias in the OLS estimates, which are captured by the two terms discussed in connection with (5.13).[9] The first is standard: $\text{Cov}(\varepsilon^0, \mathbf{Z}) = 0$; namely, the instruments must not help predict the unobserved component of performance in constitutional state 0. The second condition is

$$\text{Cov}(S(\varepsilon^1 - \varepsilon^0), \mathbf{Z})) = \text{Prob}(S = 1 \mid \mathbf{Z}) \cdot \text{E}[(\varepsilon^1 - \varepsilon^0) \mid \mathbf{Z}, S = 1] = 0.$$

As discussed in section 5.3.3, the term $(\varepsilon^1 - \varepsilon^0)$ is the country-specific, unobserved change in performance associated with constitutional reform from $S = 0$ to $S = 1$. Conditional on being in state $S = 1$, this change must be uncorrelated with the instruments. Phrased differently, when controlling for $\mathbf{Z}$, the remaining random component of constitution selection must become uncorrelated with $\varepsilon^1 - \varepsilon^0$. This second requirement could be violated even if the first one is met.

If we have more instruments in $\mathbf{Z}$ than the number of constitutional features S, the model is overidentified, and we can test for the exogeneity of the *additional* instruments (i.e., those beyond the number of features in S). Note, however, that the test is valid only under the null hypothesis that *at least one* of the instruments in $\mathbf{Z}$ is uncorrelated with the error term e in the performance equation. Hence, a rejection of the overidentifying restrictions implies that some of the instruments in $\mathbf{Z}$ are not valid. But we cannot, on the other hand, interpret a failure to reject the overidentifying restrictions as a proof of the validity of all instruments. It might be the case that we fail to reject, and yet no instrument is valid. The assumption that there is at least one exogenous instrument in $\mathbf{Z}$ is nontestable.

Even if a specific set of instruments is determined to be exogenous, a possible problem in our application is that of *weak instruments*. This problem refers to the common situation where the instruments $\mathbf{Z}$, although exogenous, are relatively weakly correlated with the constitution S, given the variables in $\mathbf{W}$. As the correlation between $\mathbf{Z}$ and S becomes weaker, the partitioning of S into exogenous and endogenous components becomes more arbitrary, and when the correlation goes to 0, the bias in the instrumental-variables estimates approaches the OLS selection bias.[10] Clearly, this problem might

---

9. We rule out the remote possibility that the two terms in (5.13) sum to zero even though each of them is nonzero.

10. Staiger and Stock (1997) also show that the ratio of the finite sample bias of the instrumental-variables estimator to that of the OLS estimator can be estimated as $1/F$, where F is the F-statistic on the excluded instruments in the first stage.

become worse if the vector $\mathbf{W}$ contains many variables and these are correlated with the instruments $\mathbf{Z}$. A possible remedy is to choose a parsimonious formulation of the selection equation, excluding most variables from $\mathbf{W}$, so as to preserve a strong correlation between $\mathbf{Z}$ and S. This would not be a good idea if the problem motivating the instrumental-variables estimation were one of reverse causation. In that case, we must set $\mathbf{W} = \mathbf{X}$ (i.e., the first stage should include all exogenous variables in the outcome relation). Our main simultaneity problem is not reverse causation, however, but omitted variables. In this case, the model is recursive, and using a parsimonious first-stage relation with few variables beyond the instruments $\mathbf{Z}$ is fine. For more on this point, see Wiggins 2000.

Concretely, our estimates of constitutional effects on outcomes in chapters 6 and 7 rely on the method of two-stage least squares. In the first of the two stages, we estimate a model such as (5.14) to decompose the variation in S into an "exogenous" and an "endogenous" component. In the second stage, the exogenous variation in S (namely, the projection of S on the instruments) is exploited to estimate a constitutional effect. Because the dependent variable in the first stage takes values between 0 and 1, like our electoral dummy MAJ, this procedure amounts to imposing the so-called linear probability model. That is, the first stage effectively estimates the probability that a particular country i will have a majoritarian electoral rule as a linear function of its characteristics $(\mathbf{W}_i, \mathbf{Z}_i)$. The assumption of a linear first-stage model is more robust to functional form specification than the assumption of a probit or logit first-stage model (Angrist and Krueger 2001).

In chapters 6 and 7, we use this instrumental-variables technique to isolate exogenous variation in electoral rules and forms of government when we estimate constitutional effect on fiscal policy, rent extraction, and productivity. Unless noted otherwise, we use six instruments for our two binary constitutional variables ($PRES$ and MAJ). The first three are the indicator variables for the historical periods when the current electoral rules and political regimes were adopted (1921–1950, 1951–1980, post-1981). We also include three other measures of geography or cultural heritage already discussed (in chapter 4), namely, the distance from the equator ($LAT01$) and the percentage of the population whose mother tongue is English ($ENGFRAC$) or a European language ($EURFRAC$). To diminish the problem of weak instruments, we typically restrict the first-stage regression to these six instruments plus age of democracy (AGE), thus omitting all other controls in $\mathbf{X}$.[11]

Are these six instruments exogenous? For the three timing variables for constitutional origin, we think the likely answer is yes. There is little reason to expect the pure timing of constitutional adoption to have a systematic effect on fiscal performance, corruption, or productivity. To allow age of democracy to exercise an effect on constitutional choices (constitutional reforms are often adopted at the verge of democratization), we include this variable (measured by AGE) among the first-stage regressors on top of our instruments. Because we do this, the three timing variables should really pick up the pure effect of history on constitutional selection (rather than the birth date of the democracy). Naturally, more distantly adopted electoral rules or political regimes might be correlated with older, and perhaps stronger, democracies, which might have systematically different policies than other democracies. For these reasons, however, variables such as age and quality of democracy also enter in the vector $\mathbf{X}$ and are thus held constant in the second-stage outcome regressions. It is plausible that the remaining unexplained portion of performance is uncorrelated with our timing dummies.

The verdict on exogeneity may be different for the other three instruments ($LAT01$, $ENGFRAC$, and $EURFRAC$). Like Hall and Jones (1999) and, more recently, Acemoglu, Johnson, and Robinson (2001), we would like to argue that these instruments reflect the depth of European cultural influence on institutions. Acemoglu et al. show latitude to be strongly correlated with the incidence of tropical disease among early European conquerors, and therefore with their propensity for exploitation as opposed to settlement. Geography might thus have influenced subsequent constitutional choices, with less influence on territories closer to the equator. The current fractions of English and European speakers in a country are likely to reflect the historical penetration of British and (continental) Euro-

---

11. As anticipated in chapter 4, the problem of weak instruments is addressed by defining the dummy variables dating the origin of the constitution so that each dummy variable takes a value of 1 if *either PRES or MAJ* originated in a certain historical period. This change of definition is relevant for only six countries: all other countries have the same date of origin for both *PRES* and *MAJ* anyway. The definition allows us to reduce the number of instruments relative to the number of endogenous variables, which, in turn, reduces the likely bias of instrumental-variables estimators in the presence of weak instruments (see Angrist and Krueger 2001).

pean culture on the country's society, more generally, and its constitutional choices, more specifically. Admittedly, these variables could be correlated with other unobserved historical determinants of fiscal policy or corruption. To diminish the correlation with the second-stage error term, we try to include variables such as continental location or colonial origin in the second-stage performance relation. Moreover, as we are confident about the exogeneity of the time dummies for constitutional adoption, we can test the validity of the additional instruments by exploiting the overidentifying restrictions. When this is done systematically in chapters 6 and 7, we typically do not reject the hypothesis that the additional instruments are exogenous.

Are these six instruments relevant, in the sense of being correlated with constitutional state? Above, we have tried to argue that there are strong a priori arguments to expect that they will be. In practice, we have seen in chapter 4 that the relative frequencies of alternative electoral rules and political regimes do indeed differ across time periods of constitutional adoption and that the other three instruments are strongly correlated with constitutional selection. Columns 1 and 2 of table 5.1 report our estimates of a linear regression of *MAJ* and *PRES* on our six instruments, plus age of democracy (*AGE*), for the sample of countries in our 1990s cross section for which these seven variables are available. The results are very similar for other subsamples defined by the availability of our different performance measures. Overall, the regression explains 40–50% of the variation in *PRES* and *MAJ*.

As the table shows, the three cultural influence variables (*LAT01*, *ENGFRAC* and *EURFRAC*) we use have a great deal of explanatory power with regard to both constitutional features under consideration, and the signs of their coefficients conform to prior expectations. Indeed, their explanatory power is a strong reason for using them as instruments along with the three indicator variables dating origin of constitution. If we use only the timing variables, these explain relatively little of the variation in *PRES* and *MAJ*. In the regression for presidential regimes displayed in the table, none of the three constitutional timing variables is significant in isolation, but an *F*-test comfortably rejects the hypothesis that they do not jointly belong to the regression. Their partial correlation with majoritarian elections is considerably weaker, however, and the *F*-test cannot

Table 5.1
Constitution selection: OLS and Probit estimates

	(1)	(2)	(3)	(4)
Dependent variable	PRES	MAJ	PRES	MAJ
CON2150	−0.04	−0.16	0.15	−1.38
	(0.14)	(0.16)	(0.72)	(0.82)*
CON5180	−0.12	0.07	−0.04	0.13
	(0.18)	(0.24)	(0.63)	(0.68)
CON81	0.27	0.06	1.52	0.23
	(0.20)	(0.25)	(0.73)**	(0.72)
LAT01	−1.37	−0.88	−5.15	−4.19
	(0.33)***	(0.39)**	(1.79)***	(1.57)***
ENGFRAC	−0.69	0.92	−3.26	2.62
	(0.12)***	(0.12)***	(1.02)***	(0.90)***
EURFRAC	0.42	−0.35	0.71	0.74
	(0.11)***	(0.13)**	(0.61)	(0.72)
AGE	0.54	0.20	3.83	0.14
	(0.31)*	(0.29)	(1.51)**	(1.48)
COL_UKA			−0.05	1.02
			(0.67)	(0.62)
LAAM			1.61	−1.96
			(0.63)**	(0.80)**
Sample	1990s, broad	1990s, broad	1990s, broad	1990s, broad
Method of estimation	OLS	OLS	Probit	Probit
F: all $CON = 0$	3.66**	0.52		
Number of observations	78	78	78	78
R^2	0.48	0.40	0.51	0.50

Note: Robust standard errors in parentheses. "F: all $CON = 0$" refers to the F-statistic for the test that the coefficients on $CON2150$, $CON5130$, and $CON81$ are all zero in columns 1 and 2. R^2 (unadjusted) for OLS, pseudo-R^2 for probit.
*significant at 10%; **significant at 5%; ***significant at 1%.

reject the hypothesis that the coefficients on the timing variables are zero.[12]

When interpreting the results presented in the next chapter, we should thus bear in mind that the instrumental-variables estimates of the constitutional effects of majoritarian elections may be less reliable. The major sources of variation in the first-stage regression are our cultural influence variables (*LAT01*, *ENGFRAC*, and *EURFRAC*), and we are not certain that this variation is truly exogenous to outcomes. The problem is smaller in our estimates of the constitutional effect of presidential regimes, in which the timing variables for constitutional origin play a more important role in the first stage.

5.4.2 Adjusting for Selection

A second way, in addition to the use of instrumental variables, around the presence of selection bias is first to estimate the bias in (5.13) and then correct our estimates of the constitutional effect.[13] To simplify the exposition of this method, we assume that $\varepsilon_i^1 = \varepsilon_i^0 = \varepsilon_i$: the unexplained part of performance is common across constitutional states and denoted by ε; that is, we abstract from the country-specific, heterogenous part of constitutional effect. (With a heterogenous constitutional effect, a similar estimator to the one below can be developed under additional assumptions, as discussed in Wooldridge 2002, section 18.4.)

Maintaining the linearity assumption in the outcome relation, the equation to be estimated (5.11) can be rewritten as a so-called switching regression model:

$$Y_i = \alpha^1 + \boldsymbol{\beta}\mathbf{X}_i + \varepsilon_i, \quad \text{if } S_i = 1,$$
$$Y_i = \alpha^0 + \boldsymbol{\beta}\mathbf{X}_i + \varepsilon_i, \quad \text{if } S_i = 0. \tag{5.15}$$

Inferring a constitutional effect from the estimated coefficient of S in an OLS regression (5.11) is equivalent to estimating a constitutional effect from $\hat{\alpha} = \mathsf{E}(Y\,|\,\mathbf{X}, S = 1) - \mathsf{E}(Y\,|\,\mathbf{X}, S = 0)$. This is almost like estimating the two equations in (5.15) separately and then

---

12. Specifically, a regression of *PRES* on the three timing variables and a constant has an R^2 of 0.124 and an F-statistic with a p-value of 0.012, whereas the same regression for *MAJ* has an R^2 of 0.065 and an F-statistic with a p-value as high as 0.135.

13. Maddala 1983 is the classic reference on econometrics with so-called limited-dependent variables. It includes an exhaustive discussion of estimation techniques to address prospective selection-bias problems in a variety of models.

subtracting the second estimated intercept from the first. If conditional independence is violated, however, the terms $E(\varepsilon \mid S = 1)$ and $E(\varepsilon \mid S = 0)$ are not zero. Just as before, this biases the OLS estimate, which converges to

$$\text{plim}(\hat{\alpha}) = \alpha + [E(\varepsilon \mid S = 1) - E(\varepsilon \mid S = 0)]. \tag{5.16}$$

The last term in (5.16) constitutes the selection bias discussed in section 5.3. Heckman (1974, 1976a, 1979) pioneered the development of methods for dealing with the problem of selection bias.[14] These methods rely on an assumption about functional form. Specifically, suppose that the unobserved determinants of performance, ε, and constitution selection, η, are jointly normally distributed, with correlation coefficient ρ and standard errors σ_ε and σ_η, respectively. Following the argument in Maddala 1983, these assumptions imply that

$$E(\varepsilon \mid \mathbf{W}, \mathbf{Z}, S = 1) = E(\varepsilon \mid \eta > -G(\mathbf{W}, \mathbf{Z})) = \rho\sigma_\varepsilon M^1(G(\mathbf{W}, \mathbf{Z})). \tag{5.17}$$

The first equality follows from (5.14). The second follows from the formula for the conditional mean of a truncated bivariate normal, where $M^1(G(\mathbf{W}, \mathbf{Z})) = \phi(G(\mathbf{W}, \mathbf{Z}))/\Phi(G(\mathbf{W}, \mathbf{Z}))$ is the ratio of the density, ϕ, to the cumulative, Φ, of a standard normal distribution evaluated at the point $G(\mathbf{W}, \mathbf{Z})$, an expression also called the (inverse) Mills ratio. Similarly,

$$E(\varepsilon \mid \mathbf{W}, \mathbf{Z}, S = 0) = E(\varepsilon \mid \eta < -G(\mathbf{W}, \mathbf{Z})) = \rho\sigma_\varepsilon M^0(G(\mathbf{W}, \mathbf{Z})), \tag{5.18}$$

where $M^0(G(\mathbf{W}, \mathbf{Z})) = -\phi(G(\mathbf{W}, \mathbf{Z}))/[1 - \Phi(G(\mathbf{W}, \mathbf{Z}))]$.

If we knew the value taken by the right-hand side of (5.17) and (5.18), we could correct for the selection bias in (5.16) and obtain an unbiased estimate of the true constitutional effect. Expressions $M^S(\cdot)$ are known functions of $G(\mathbf{W}, \mathbf{Z})$, whereas parameters ρ and σ_ε and those of the function $G(\cdot)$ are unknown. These parameters are identified, however, and can be jointly or sequentially estimated from the constitution selection equation (5.14) and the performance equations

---

14. In fact, a problem quite similar to ours of identifying a true constitutional effect appears in another early paper by Heckman (Heckman 1976b). Landes (1968) had analyzed how the existence of fair employment laws affected the status of blacks across U.S. states. Relying on methods like those presented in this section, Heckman argued that Landes's estimates would be biased if the possibility of selection bias is not taken into account (states in which blacks are better treated could be more likely to have fair employment laws, or the demand for such laws could be higher in states in which they are treated badly).

(5.15). Heckman-style adjustment procedures amount to precisely this kind of correction.

In chapters 6 and 7, we pursue the following approach. We estimate a probit model for the constitutional selection equation (5.14) with a linear specification of $G(\cdot)$. From these estimates, we can retrieve consistently estimated values of the two Mills ratios for each country in the sample M_i^S, $S = 0, 1$. We estimate the parameters ρ, σ_ε, α^S, $\boldsymbol{\beta}$ using (5.15), augmenting each equation by the estimated Mills ratios according to (5.17) and (5.18).[15] The constitutional effect α is then just the difference between the estimates of α^1 and α^0. Note that this procedure also enables us to test the null hypothesis of conditional independence, namely, that the correlation coefficient ρ is zero. The estimation can be made either using maximum likelihood, or else using a two-step procedure in which the probit selection equation is estimated in the first step and the (augmented) outcome relation in the second.

The procedure presented in the previous paragraph has drawbacks, however. For one thing, the estimates and test statistics it employs are sensitive to the distributional assumptions made regarding ε and η and to the assumed linearity of the performance equation.[16] The reason for this sensitivity is that the outcome relation now includes a specific and highly nonlinear function of the variables $\mathbf{W}$ that, in turn, is a subset of the controls $\mathbf{X}$ influencing constitutional selection. This critique applies most forcefully when we have no valid instrument (the set of variables $\mathbf{Z}$ is empty). Identification of α is then achieved *only* through a functional-form assumption. Specifically, the nonlinearity of the subset $\mathbf{W}$ of variables in the second step reflects only the Mills ratio and not the performance equation, which is instead assumed to be linear. A set of valid instruments $\mathbf{Z}$ makes the identification more robust, as the instruments are excluded from the outcome regression. Nevertheless, if the

---

15. These parameters can be separately estimated from the two regimes in (5.15) by rewriting each regime S as

$$Y_i = \alpha^S + \boldsymbol{\beta}\mathbf{X}_i + \rho\sigma_\varepsilon \hat{M}_i^S + v_i,$$

where $\hat{M}_i^S = M^S(\hat{G}(\mathbf{W}_i, \mathbf{Z}_i))$ is the Mills ratio estimated in the first step. Since the Mills ratios have been consistently estimated, the error term v_i now has a zero mean and is uncorrelated with the included variables.

16. In fact, the critical assumptions are that the error term η of the constitution selection equation is normal and that the mean of ε conditional on η is a linear function of η; both assumptions are satisfied if η and ε are bivariate normal.

normality assumption for η and the linearity assumption for the outcome regression fail, our correction for selection bias could be off—possibly way off—and we could falsely reject the null hypothesis of zero correlation between ε and η (see Maddala 1983 for an extensive discussion).

Another drawback of the above procedure is that it fails to address the possibility of a heterogenous treatment effect (i.e., the second source of bias due to $\varepsilon_i^1 \neq \varepsilon_i^0$). Although the adjustment for selection could be extended to this more general case, we believe that our data set is too small for such an extension to be meaningful.[17]

A final issue when applying the adjustment for selection in chapters 6 and 7 is how to specify the probit for constitution selection. Our specification reflects some concern for the above-mentioned fragility with respect to functional form. To address this fragility in the identification, we always include the six instrumental variables (corresponding to $\mathbf{Z}$) discussed in section 5.3.1. Otherwise, we choose a parsimonious specification (few variables in $\mathbf{W}$), adding only the age of democracy (AGE) and two other variables correlated with both constitutional features, namely, British colonial origin and a dummy variable for Latin America. Columns 3 and 4 of table 5.1 show the coefficient estimates of these probit regressions. (Indeed, these columns coincide with one of the specifications displayed in table 4.4 and are reproduced here only for convenience.) The general sign and significance picture is the same as for the linear probability model in columns 1 and 2. But the inclusion of British colonial origin and Latin American location strengthens the relation between the timing variables and constitutional outcomes.

5.5 Relaxing Linearity

Imposing linearity in applied econometrics is so common that the assumption of linearity almost seems innocuous. But is it? As argued above, there are many a priori reasons to expect that the constitutional effect on performance is not only direct, but the result of an

---

17. More precisely, we would allow for separate distributions for ε_i^1 and ε_i^0. Imposing the assumption of trivariate normality, we would allow for separate correlation coefficients ρ^0 and ρ^1 between these errors and η. These would enter separately in the expressions for (5.17) and (5.18) and be estimated along with the other parameters in an augmented outcome relation, much as in the procedure explained above. (See Wooldridge 2002, section 18.4.)

interaction with many other variables, such as demographics or economic development. We can still disregard these nonlinearities and approximate the performance equation with a linear regression. But a linear approximation of a nonlinear model is reliable only locally, within a certain neighborhood of the point where the approximation is taken. Once we move away from that point, the approximation can become very bad, and the assumption of linearity very restrictive.

In our context, we rely on the linearity assumption as an approximation of two possibly nonlinear relations: the function $Y^1 = F^1(\mathbf{X}) + \varepsilon^1$, determining performance as a function of controls $\mathbf{X}$ in constitutional state $S = 1$; and the same performance equation, $Y^0 = F^0(\mathbf{X}) + \varepsilon^0$, in constitutional state $S = 0$. As explained above, an assumption commonly maintained in regression analysis is that F^1 and F^0 in equation (5.8) differ only by an intercept. This assumption may be innocuous if we approximate F^1 and F^0 in the neighborhood *of the same point*. Unfortunately, the appeal to a local approximation may not be valid in our application. In chapter 4, we saw that the variables in $\mathbf{X}$ have very different distributions for different constitutional states. Recall the tests in table 4.7, where we rejected equality of means between presidential and parliamentary regimes for seven covariates out of seven and between majoritarian and proportional countries for four covariates out of seven. In other words, presidential and parliamentary countries (or majoritarian and proportional countries) differ in several relevant dimensions.

The importance of the linearity assumption can also be stated in terms perhaps more familiar to political scientists (see also the discussion in King and Zeng 2001). At any given moment in time, we observe the policy performance of a given country only in one constitutional state. But we still seek the answer to a counterfactual question: how would performance change in a country of our sample, drawn at random, in the event of constitutional reform? For the purpose of answering this question, we compare the performance of countries currently in different constitutional states. We try to draw from this comparison inferences about counterfactuals: would the most corrupt countries in western Europe and Latin America, namely, Belgium and Paraguay, be less corrupt if they had majoritarian rather than proportional elections? But such inferences can be made only by observing performance in countries ruled by other types of constitutions. Thus, if the counterfactual of interest is very far from what we observe—if Belgium and Paraguay differ from currently majoritarian countries in many respects—then our inference is fragile with respect to the functional-form assumption. As the data reveal, the counterfactual of interest can indeed be quite far from what we observe: on average, majoritarian and proportional countries do differ from one another in some respects, whereas presidential and parliamentary regimes differ from one another even more.

With such systematic differences, linearity cannot be regarded just as a convenient local approximation; it is really a binding and important functional-form assumption. How can it be relaxed?

5.5.1   Matching Estimators

The central idea in matching is to approach the evaluation of causal effects as one would in a controlled experiment. If we are willing to make a conditional-independence assumption, we can largely re-create the conditions of a randomized experiment, even though we have access only to observational data. We start by splitting our observations into two groups, often called "treated" and "controls," as in an experiment. (In this context, however, that terminology is less useful, as the assignment of "treatment" and "control" labels would be quite arbitrary.) The countries in our sample are divided into two groups according to their constitution ($S = 1$ or $S = 0$), say majoritarian versus proportional electoral rule. The crucial point is that as a result of conditional independence, constitution selection is random and uncorrelated with performance once we control for $\mathbf{X}$. Consider countries with the same set of characteristics $\mathbf{X}$. Some of these have constitution $S = 1$, others $S = 0$. The constitutional effect on performance for this group of countries is

$$\alpha(\mathbf{X}) = \mathsf{E}(Y^1 - Y^0 \mid \mathbf{X}) = \mathsf{E}(Y^1 \mid S = 1, \mathbf{X}) - \mathsf{E}(Y^0 \mid S = 0, \mathbf{X}), \qquad (5.19)$$

where the second equality follows from conditional independence (5.7). The average constitutional effect for the whole sample is then just $\alpha = E\{\alpha(\mathbf{X})\}$, where the expectation is now taken over the $\mathbf{X}$s.

In other words, if we are willing to assume conditional independence and consider countries with similar conditioning variables $\mathbf{X}$, the counterfactual distribution of performance is the same as the observed distribution of performance. This enables us to derive the right-most side of (5.19) so that it contains no counterfactual. The unobservable counterfactual outcome for a specific country is then estimated from the actual outcomes among countries with similar observable attributes.

Once more, the basic idea is that we should compare the performance of similar countries, because their selection into different constitutions is largely random, as in an experiment. Thus for each country with a particular constitutional rule, we try to find its "twin" or a "set of close relatives" to it with the alternative constitutional rule. In the above example, we try to find countries with majoritarian elections that are as similar as possible to Belgium and Paraguay in respect to their other characteristics. Practically, $\alpha = E\{\alpha(\mathbf{X})\}$ could be computed by dividing the sample into different groups, each defined by countries with similar values of $\mathbf{X}$. A separate estimate of the constitutional effect is then computed within each group, and the overall constitutional effect is a weighted average of the constitutional effects for all groups.

Note that this argument does not impose any functional-form assumption on the performance equation. In fact, we can estimate the constitutional effect nonparametrically by comparing (weighted) mean outcomes. This is the central difference between the method of matching and a linear regression. Matching allows us to draw inferences from *local* comparisons only: as we compare countries with similar values of $\mathbf{X}$, we rely on counterfactuals that are not very different from the factuals observed. Relaxing the functional-form assumption comes at the price of reduced efficiency in our estimates. Compared to linear regressions, we should thus expect matching estimates of constitutional effects to be associated with larger standard errors.

5.5.2 Propensity Scores

There is a difficulty in this matching methodology, however, and it is easily seen in our application. We have already stressed that countries differ in many attributes that may correlate with observed policy outcomes as well as observed constitutional states (i.e., the relevant dimension of $\mathbf{X}$ is high). Finding similar countries to compare under different constitutional rules would therefore tax the available data beyond its capacity. An important result due to Rosenbaum and Rubin (1983) provides a way around this problem, however. It implies that comparing countries with the same *probability of selecting* a specific constitutional rule, given the relevant controls $\mathbf{X}$, is equivalent to comparing countries with similar values of $\mathbf{X}$.

Specifically, let

$$p_i = p(\mathbf{X}_i) = \text{Prob}[S_i = 1 \,|\, \mathbf{X}_i]$$

be the conditional probability that country i is in constitutional state $S_i = 1$, given the vector of controls $\mathbf{X}_i$. This conditional probability is also called the country's *propensity score*. Assume the propensity score to be bounded away from 0 and 1 for all countries, the so-called *common-support* condition:

$$0 < p(\mathbf{X}_i) < 1, \quad \text{for all } \mathbf{X}_i.$$

Rosenbaum and Rubin (1983) show that conditioning on vector $\mathbf{X}$ is equivalent to conditioning on the scalar p, in the sense that conditional independence (5.7) implies

$$\mathsf{E}(Y^0 \,|\, S = 0, p(\mathbf{X})) = \mathsf{E}(Y^0 \,|\, S = 1, p(\mathbf{X})), \tag{5.20}$$

and similarly for Y^1. That is, for countries with similar propensity scores, constitution selection is random and uncorrelated with the potential outcomes (Y^1, Y^0). Hence, we can replace the unobserved counterfactual $\mathsf{E}(Y^0 \,|\, S = 1, p(\mathbf{X}))$ with its observed counterpart $\mathsf{E}(Y^0 \,|\, S = 0, p(\mathbf{X}))$.

This result has an important practical implication: when applying the method of matching, we can match countries with similar propensity scores, rather than those with similar values of the full vector $\mathbf{X}$. The curse of dimensionality is reduced as the one-dimensional propensity score p becomes a sufficient statistic for the full-dimensional vector $\mathbf{X}$.

Repeating the argument in section 5.5.1, the constitutional effect for countries with propensity score $p(\mathbf{X})$ is

$$\alpha(p(\mathbf{X})) = \mathsf{E}(Y^1 - Y^0 \,|\, p(\mathbf{X})), \tag{5.21}$$

and the effect for the whole population is

$$\alpha = \mathsf{E}(Y^1 - Y^0) = E\{\alpha(p(\mathbf{X}))\}, \tag{5.22}$$

where the expectations operator E is taken over the distribution of $p(\mathbf{X})$. (We return to the evaluation of this expression in section 5.5.3). As in direct matching, the method forces us to draw inferences from *local* comparisons of similar countries. But now we have a simple metric, the propensity score, for measuring similarity. For our purposes, two countries are similar and comparable if they have similar conditional probabilities of being in the same constitutional state S.

But what does "similar propensity scores" mean in practice? If two countries are too distant from one another in terms of propensity score, we can no longer perform local comparisons appealing to (5.21). In such cases, Rosenbaum and Rubin (1983) prove a second result that is very useful: under the common-support assumption, and *conditional on the propensity score*, the observable covariates X are uncorrelated with the constitutional state S. Countries with the same propensity score $p(X)$ should thus have the same distribution of X, irrespective of their constitutional state. This result, known as the *balancing property*, suggests a practical test. We can rank countries in terms of their estimated propensity scores and partition this ranking into different "strata." Within each stratum, according to the balancing property, the distribution of covariates X should be the same for all countries, irrespective of their constitution. If this version of the balancing property is rejected, either the partition into strata is too coarse and should be refined or something is wrong with the estimated propensity scores.

The latter possibility brings us to our next point. The entire preceding discussion presupposes that we know the propensity score of each country in our sample. But we do not. Estimation of countries' propensity score thus becomes a crucial step in our methodology. This estimation could be conducted by a simple probit or logit, as in chapter 4. But which variables should we include in X? There are two concerns with respect to this question.

The first of these concerns is crucial: we must respect the conditional-independence assumption. The appropriate specification will thus vary with the particular measure of performance we are investigating. It will also differ from the specification of the selection equation in the Heckman procedure, discussed in section 5.4. In the specification of the selection equation in the Heckman procedure, we worry about correlation between the variables W included in the probit regression (5.1) and the error term η of that same regression. Thus we should not omit any variables that really drive selection. To get robust identification in the second stage of the specification, we should also include some variables (instruments) uncorrelated with performance. In the procedure, discussed above, we worry about conditional independence. Thus we should not omit any variables that really drive performance and should try to include in X all variables correlated with performance, conditional on constitutional state. This speaks in favor of an inclusive logit or probit specification.[18]

The second concern in estimating the propensity score is the common-support condition. If we explain constitutional choice "too well," we shrink the region of overlapping propensity scores between countries belonging to different constitutional groups: for some $S_i = 1$ countries, the estimated propensity score can be very close to 1, for some $S_i = 0$ countries, it can be very close to 0. Matching then becomes difficult for these extreme observations, because there are no comparable cases (i.e., no otherwise similar countries in the opposite constitutional state). Preserving enough randomness in the propensity scores thus speaks for a parsimonious logit or probit specification.

5.5.3   Implementation

In chapters 6 and 7, we experiment with different specifications when estimating the propensity scores. For example, when estimating the constitutional effect of electoral rule on size of government, we estimate the probability of majoritarian election as a function of four socioeconomic covariates—level of income (LYP), proportion of old people ($PROP65$), quality of democracy ($GASTIL$), and the indicator for federal states ($FEDERAL$)—plus the indicators for previous British colonies (COL_UKA) and Latin American location ($LAAM$), all factors likely to correlate with the size of government. Table 5.2a lists the 82 countries for which all of these variables are available in the 1990s cross-section, as well as their actual value for the electoral-rule indicator (MAJ). The countries are ranked by their estimated propensity scores, which are also listed in the table. Notice that the countries with *low* estimated probabilities of majoritarian elections are mostly located in continental Europe and Latin America, regions where elections are indeed most often conducted according to proportional rule. In contrast, countries with higher scores are more

---

18. The contrast between the specification of the propensity score equation and that of the first stage of the instrumental-variables estimation is even starker. In the instrumental-variables estimation, we want to avoid correlation between the instruments included in the first stage and the error term of the second stage. In the propensity score equation, we instead want to avoid correlation between the error terms of the two equations.

often previous British colonies and, as we move down the ranking, more often poor countries with young populations not located in Latin America. We use table 5.2a in the discussion below, but for completeness, table 5.2b shows a similar listing of countries in the order of their propensity scores for the form-of-government indicator ($PRES$), estimated by means of a probit over the same six variables.

Now that we have an estimate of propensity score, p, how do we impose the common-support condition in practice? To be on the safe side, we define the *estimated* common support as the interval between the minimum estimated p_i among the $S = 1$ countries and the maximum estimated p_i among the $S = 0$ countries. All observations outside this estimated common support are discarded as noncomparable in terms of observable attributes. In table 5.2a, for example, we discard the six proportional countries ($MAJ = 0$) at the very top of the table, which all have a propensity score lower than that of the United Kingdom, the majoritarian country with the lowest actual estimated probability (about 0.08) of being majoritarian. In the same way, we discard the seven majoritarian countries ($MAJ = 1$) at the very bottom of the table, all of which have a higher propensity score than that of Fiji, the proportional country with the highest actual estimated probability (about 0.85) of being majoritarian. This procedure reduces an already small sample, but it has the advantage of excluding outliers, as we drop countries that may be anomalous in their social and economic conditions. It reinforces the idea that matching estimation relies on inference from local comparisons among similar countries.[19]

Another important question, besides the common-support condition, in the practical implementation is how well propensity score matching eliminates observable differences among countries. In other words, does the balancing property hold up empirically? To answer this question, we follow the approach suggested in section 5.5.2 for a given estimate of the propensity score. Consider the propensity score for majoritarian elections, estimated by the probit formulation underlying table 5.2a and the three strata defined in that table, namely, countries with low ($p < 0.33$), medium ($0.33 < p < 0.67$) and high ($p > 0.67$) estimated propensity scores, given that

---

19. When imposing the common-support condition for forms of government in the specification used for fiscal policy, we are forced to discard a large number of presidential regimes in Latin America; see table 5.2b.

Table 5.2
Estimated propensity scores

a. Majoritarian elections

Country	PSCORE	MAJ
Uruguay	**0.052**	**0**
Sweden	**0.070**	**0**
Greece	**0.073**	**0**
Bulgaria	**0.075**	**0**
Italy	**0.077**	**0**
United Kingdom	0.078	1
Romania	0.083	0
Peru	0.084	0
Belgium	0.090	0
Norway	0.090	0
France	0.093	1
Spain	0.095	0
Latvia	0.101	0
Portugal	0.104	0
Denmark	0.105	0
Hungary	0.106	0
Japan	0.108	1
Colombia	0.112	0
Estonia	0.114	0
Guatemala	0.115	0
Czech Republic	0.126	0
Luxembourg	0.127	0
Chile	0.128	1
Argentina	0.132	0
Finland	0.132	0
Paraguay	0.133	0
Slovak Republic	0.141	0
Nicaragua	0.148	0
Dominican Republic	0.152	0
Netherlands	0.153	0
Ecuador	0.157	0
Germany	0.160	0
Russia	0.161	0
Poland	0.177	0
Bolivia	0.181	0
Honduras	0.185	0
Mexico	0.194	0
Austria	0.199	0
Iceland	0.212	0
Switzerland	0.214	0
Turkey	0.220	0
Brazil	0.230	0

Table 5.2
(continued)

Country	PSCORE	MAJ
Costa Rica	0.240	0
El Salvador	0.258	0
Thailand	0.264	1
Venezuela	0.292	0
United States	0.297	1
Senegal	0.320	0
Nepal	0.337	1
South Korea	0.355	0
Bangladesh	0.371	1
Philippines	0.377	1
Namibia	0.419	0
Barbados	0.496	1
New Zealand	0.568	1
Jamaica	0.582	1
Ireland	0.617	0
Canada	0.641	1
Singapore	0.659	1
Israel	0.673	0
Sri Lanka	0.674	0
Trinidad & Tobago	0.694	1
Australia	0.735	1
South Africa	0.757	0
Cyprus	0.759	0
Malta	0.760	0
Bahamas	0.763	1
Pakistan	0.781	1
Uganda	0.790	1
Gambia	0.794	1
Ghana	0.797	1
Zimbabwe	0.808	1
Belize	0.812	1
Fiji	0.828	0
Malawi	**0.831**	**1**
St. Vincent & the Grenadines	**0.856**	**1**
Zambia	**0.856**	**1**
Malaysia	**0.857**	**1**
Mauritius	**0.873**	**1**
India	**0.886**	**1**
Papua New Guinea	**0.904**	**1**
Botswana	**0.924**	**1**

Note: PSCORE is the predicted value of a logit regression of MAJ on LYP, PROP65, FEDERAL, GASTIL, LAAM, and COL_UKA. Observations for countries in boldface type are discarded to impose common support.

Table 5.2
(continued)

b. Presidential regimes

Country	PSCORE	PRES
Cyprus	0.017	1
New Zealand	0.017	0
Malta	0.018	0
Ireland	0.018	0
Sweden	0.024	0
Norway	0.024	0
Luxembourg	0.027	0
Denmark	0.029	0
Israel	0.029	0
Belgium	0.031	0
Finland	0.036	0
Italy	0.036	0
United Kingdom	0.037	0
Netherlands	0.038	0
France	0.039	0
Japan	0.042	0
Mauritius	0.045	0
Spain	0.046	0
Iceland	0.047	0
Portugal	0.047	0
Greece	0.072	0
Australia	0.096	0
Hungary	0.100	0
Singapore	0.104	0
Canada	0.107	0
Bulgaria	0.132	0
Czech Republic	0.137	0
Botswana	0.150	0
Barbados	0.153	0
Poland	0.153	0
Germany	0.163	0
Switzerland	0.169	1
United States	0.182	1
Austria	0.182	0
South Korea	0.185	1
Slovak Republic	0.191	0
Latvia	0.197	0
Fiji	0.208	0
Estonia	0.212	0
South Africa	0.225	0
Trinidad & Tobago	0.249	0
Papua New Guinea	0.250	0

Table 5.2
(continued)

Country	PSCORE	PRES
Bahamas	0.252	0
Sri Lanka	0.305	1
Belize	0.337	0
Thailand	0.425	0
Namibia	0.430	1
Romania	0.454	0
Pakistan	0.477	1
St. Vincent & the Grenadines	0.481	0
Turkey	0.519	0
Uruguay	0.532	1
Zimbabwe	0.541	1
Ghana	0.545	1
Jamaica	0.559	0
Zambia	0.567	1
Gambia	0.576	1
Philippines	0.582	1
Bangladesh	0.632	0
Malawi	0.640	1
Malaysia	0.653	0
Nepal	0.699	0
Uganda	0.699	1
Chile	0.708	1
Costa Rica	0.746	1
India	0.769	0
Senegal	0.784	0
Russia	**0.836**	**1**
Ecuador	**0.866**	**1**
El Salvador	**0.868**	**1**
Colombia	**0.895**	**1**
Dominican Republic	**0.901**	**1**
Bolivia	**0.903**	**1**
Paraguay	**0.925**	**1**
Argentina	**0.931**	**1**
Honduras	**0.933**	**1**
Guatemala	**0.946**	**1**
Peru	**0.948**	**1**
Nicaragua	**0.954**	**1**
Venezuela	**0.959**	**1**
Brazil	**0.975**	**1**
Mexico	**0.978**	**1**

Note: PSCORE is the predicted value of a logit regression of *PRES* on *LYP, PROP65, FEDERAL, GASTIL, LAAM,* and *COL_UKA*. Observations for countries in boldface type are discarded to impose common support.

they belong to the estimated common support. We test whether the means of a number of covariates are equal in the groups of majoritarian ($MAJ = 1$) and proportional ($MAJ = 0$) countries in each of these three strata. The upper part of table 5.3 shows the results of such equal-means tests for nine variables. The first six (LYP, $PROP65$, $GASTIL$, $FEDERAL$, COL_UKA, and $LAAM$) all enter into the estimation of the propensity score, but the other three, openness to trade ($TRADE$) and the shares of Protestants and Catholics in the population ($PROT80$ and $CATHO80$, respectively) do not. Column 1 shows that, for the full sample, we reject equal means for four of these nine variables at the 5% level (and for five of nine at the 10% level). What about the three strata defined by the estimated propensity scores? Here we reject equal means only in two cases out of twenty-seven (nine variables in three strata) at the 5% level. (Admittedly, we have fewer observations in each stratum than in the full population, so a statistical rejection of equal means is more difficult in the strata than in the full sample.) But the ranking based on the propensity score appears successful in balancing the distribution of observables, and even at the 10% significance level, we still reject only two cases out of twenty-seven. Interestingly, the balancing property appears to extend also to those variables not actually included in the estimation of the propensity score, giving some hope that other (and genuinely unobservable) characteristics may also be balanced out by the matching procedure.

The lower half of table 5.3 shows the results when we use the same stratification and test procedure given the estimated propensity scores for presidential regimes displayed in table 5.2b. As column 1 shows, the observable differences between presidential and parliamentary countries are very pronounced in the full sample: we clearly reject equal means at the 5% level for seven covariates out of nine. Once we go to the strata, however, the covariates seem more balanced. We now reject equal means at the 5% level in only two cases out of twenty-seven (and in three out of twenty-seven at the 10% level). Once again, the few rejections might partly reflect a lack of degrees of freedom in some strata, but the balancing of the distribution extends to the variables not included in the estimation of the propensity score.

Now that we have a metric (the propensity score) that appears to capture similarities among countries and a sample of reasonably comparable countries (those on the common support), the question

Table 5.3
Balancing property: Equal-means tests for different constitutional groups

	Whole sample	$p < 0.33$	$0.33 < p < 0.67$	$0.67 < p$
$MAJ = 1$ versus $MAJ = 0$				
LYP	0.04	0.04	0.62	0.21
PROP65	0.01	0.32	0.90	0.04
GASTIL	0.08	0.33	0.55	0.37
FEDERAL	0.93	0.79	0.57	0.48
COL_UKA	0.00	0.69	0.42	0.35
LAAM	0.34	0.27	0.39	0.17
TRADE	0.44	0.13	0.93	0.31
PROT80	0.94	0.56	0.75	0.37
CATHO80	0.00	0.11	0.46	0.83
$PRES = 1$ versus $PRES = 0$				
LYP	0.00	0.87	0.01	0.54
PROP65	0.00	0.34	0.39	0.86
GASTIL	0.00	0.59	0.22	0.71
FEDERAL	0.22	0.07	0.30	0.27
COL_UKA	0.44	0.88	0.56	0.83
LAAM	0.00	0.53	0.23	0.22
TRADE	0.01	0.33	0.34	0.40
PROT80	0.03	0.65	0.60	0.22
CATHO80	0.00	0.28	0.24	0.02

Note: Table presents probabilities of falsely rejecting the hypothesis of equal means across constitutional groups under the hypothesis of equal variances. Strata defined on the common support of propensity scores p, estimated by logit regressions, including LYP, PROP65, GASTIL, FEDERAL, COL_UKA, and LAAM.

is exactly how we should compare performance among similar countries. There are many possible ways of doing this, and each method of comparison corresponds to a specific matching estimator.

A simple method for comparing performance is *stratification*. Countries are ranked on the basis of their estimated propensity scores, then grouped into different strata, indexed by q. In our applications for electoral rules, we use same three strata as those defined in table 5.2a, namely, low (from the U.K. score to 0.33), intermediate (0.33–0.67), and high (from 0.67 to the Fiji score) propensity scores. Naturally, the proportion of actual majoritarian countries is lower in the bottom stratum, $q = 1$ (7/42 countries), than in the top stratum, $q = 3$ ($12/18$ countries). Within each stratum q, we then compute the difference in average performance between $S = 1$ and $S = 0$ countries, $\alpha(q)$, as in (5.21). The overall constitutional effect is thus the weighted average of the $\alpha(q)$ across strata, with weights given by the fraction of countries in each stratum:

$$\alpha = \sum_{q=1}^{3} \alpha(q) \frac{N_q}{N},$$

where N is the number of countries on the common support and N_q is the total number of countries in stratum q (counting both $S = 1$ and $S = 0$ countries).

Although easily computed, this estimator has the drawback that, in small samples, it can be sensitive to the precise definition of the strata. Hence, we also rely on two other estimators. To explain their logic, it is useful to exploit the law of iterated expectations and rewrite equations (5.21) and (5.22) as

$$\alpha = P \cdot E\{\mathsf{E}(Y^1 \mid p(\mathbf{X}), S = 1) - \mathsf{E}(Y^0 \mid p(\mathbf{X}), S = 1)\}$$
$$+ (1 - P) \cdot E\{\mathsf{E}(Y^1 \mid p(\mathbf{X}), S = 0) - \mathsf{E}(Y^0 \mid p(\mathbf{X}), S = 0)\}. \qquad (5.23)$$

As in the similar equation (5.6), $P = \mathrm{Prob}(S = 1)$ denotes the (unconditional) probability of observing the constitutional state $S = 1$ in a country drawn at random. The first term in (5.23) is the effect of constitutional reform in countries currently in state 1. We need to replace the unobservable counterfactual $\mathsf{E}(Y^0 \mid p(\mathbf{X}), S = 1)$ with an observable quantity. As above, conditional independence allows us to use the observed expression $\mathsf{E}(Y^0 \mid p(\mathbf{X}), S = 0)$, if it is computed from countries in the opposite state ($S = 0$) that are sufficiently similar in terms of $p(\mathbf{X})$, to replace this unobserved counterfactual. A similar substitution can be made in the case of the second term in (5.23), which captures the effect of constitutional reform in the $S = 0$ countries.

The *nearest-neighbor* method defines "sufficiently similar" in a simple and intuitive way. For each country with $S = 1$, we just find its "closest twin" in the opposite state: the $S = 0$ country with the closest estimated value of p. A given $S = 0$ country can be used as a match a number of times, if it happens to be the closest match for several $S = 1$ countries. This will increase the size of the standard errors but is preferable in terms of reduced bias. Countries currently in $S = 0$ that are not the closest twin to any $S = 1$ country are discarded from the estimation as incomparable. This allows us to compute an estimate of the constitutional effect for countries currently in $S = 1$ simply as the average difference in performance between these matched countries. To compute the constitutional effect among the countries currently in state $S = 0$—the second term in (5.23)—we proceed in reverse. For each country with $S = 0$, we find its closest twin in the opposite state: the $S = 1$ country with the closest estimated value of p. Again, each $S = 1$ country can be used several times, and $S = 1$ countries that are not the closest twin of any $S = 0$ country are discarded from the estimation. The overall constitutional effect, α, is the weighted average of the constitutional effects for countries currently in states $S = 1$ and $S = 0$, as in (5.23), with weights P and $(1 - P)$, respectively. Weights P and $(1 - P)$ are estimated from the *relative frequency* in our sample of countries in states $S = 1$ and $S = 0$, respectively.

In the example we presented at the beginning of section 5.5, S refers to the electoral rule (as classified by *MAJ*). Which among the majoritarian countries are the best match for the two proportional countries discussed above, Belgium and Paraguay, in nearest-neighbor matching? With the estimated propensity scores in table 5.2a, we can see that France is the best match for Belgium, and Chile is the best match for Paraguay (in both cases, majoritarian countries with observable characteristics similar to those of the proportional countries to which they are matched). As the table shows, France is also the best match for other proportional Western European countries such as Spain and Portugal, and Chile is the nearest match for several other proportional Latin American countries such as Nicaragua and Ecuador. (Admittedly, not all matches suggested by the table are equally intuitive.)

The nearest-neighbor estimator is intuitively appealing. In a small sample, however, it could be quite fragile: small changes in the specification of the propensity score could change the ranking of countries, thereby switching which countries are more heavily used as close matches for others. This fragility in small samples may imply large swings in the weights assigned to different countries in our estimation of constitutional effect as we change the estimated propensity scores of the countries in our sample.

To achieve more robustness, we also rely on a third matching method, namely, *kernel-based* matching. The logic of kernel-based matching is quite similar to that of the nearest-neighbor method. The overall constitutional effect can be expressed as the weighted average of the constitutional effect in the $S = 1$ and $S = 0$ countries, once more with weights given by P and $(1 - P)$. But in kernel-based matching, the match for any particular $S = 1$ country is a weighted average of (the Y values for) all $S = 0$ countries within a certain distance of the propensity score of that country, with weights declining in that distance (and conversely when matching the $S = 0$ countries). Specifically, we use a radius of 0.25 (also imposing the condition that countries belong to the estimated common support). In the example of table 5.1, this means that proportional Belgium is matched against seven majoritarian countries. The countries that are the closest matches to Belgium, like France and the United Kingdom, have a high weight in the average, whereas the more distant ones within the radius, such as Thailand and the United States, have a low weight.

5.6   Multiple Constitutional States

In our discussion in the previous sections, we have treated the case involving only one constitutional feature, measured by a binary variable, $S = 0, 1$. But we are interested in two aspects of the constitution, electoral rules and forms of government. Under the assumption that the constitutional effects of these two features are additive, some of the methods illustrated in this chapter extend directly and without additional assumptions to the case of two constitutional features. The case of OLS is straightforward and requires just the inclusion of both constitutional dummy variables, MAJ and $PRES$, in the same regression. Similarly, when estimating with instrumental variables, we treat both electoral rules (as measured by MAJ) and forms of government (as measured by $PRES$) as endogenous variables appearing in the same performance equation and jointly apply an instrumental-variables estimation to them. Finally, when estimating by means of matching via propensity scores, we match separately in one constitutional dimension at a time and with no loss of generality (because of the additivity assumption).

To apply the simple Heckman procedure to two binary variables, however, we need additional assumptions besides additivity. In chapters 6 and 7, we adjust for selecting one constitutional dimension at a time; the other constitutional dimension is treated as a control generally included in the performance equation, but not in the selection equation. For instance, when estimating the effect of the electoral rule (as measured by *MAJ*), we include the indicator variable for the form of government (*PRES*) in the performance equation and treat it as one of the control variables, without adjusting for its endogenous selection. Thus, besides additivity, we also impose, when estimating the effect of electoral rule, the assumption that the second constitutional feature (*PRES* in the example above) is randomly assigned to countries, and when estimating the effect of form of government, we impose the assumption that the electoral rule is randomly assigned.

Absent additivity, we really have four groups of countries, not just two. Can the methods discussed above be generalized if that is the case? In the case of linear regressions and instrumental-variables estimation, discussed in sections 5.3 and 5.4, the extension is relatively straightforward. We just define three indictor variables—say, *PROPRES*, *MAJPAR*, and *MAJPRES*, in obvious notation—rather than two and proceed basically as indicated above, with the proviso that we should be careful in drawing inferences from small groups (we have only 11 countries that are presidential and majoritarian; the other three groups contain about the same number of countries). The Heckman adjustment presented in section 5.4 can, in principle, be extended to deal with self-selection into more than one state. We will not pursue this extension here, however, mainly because of lack of sufficient data to do so. For the same reason, we will not extend the analysis of matching presented in section 5.5 to multiple constitutional states, although this can also be done (see Persson and Tabellini 2002 for details).

6   Fiscal Policy: Variation across Countries

6.1   Introduction

Armed with the methods introduced in the last chapter, we now proceed to estimating constitutional effects on policy outcomes from cross-country comparisons. Our estimations mostly use the data from the 85 democracies in the 1990s cross-section. But when the data so permit, we also check the robustness of the results we obtain in cross sections based on our longer panel going back to 1960. In this chapter, we study fiscal policy, namely, the size and composition of government spending and budget surplus. The next chapter studies constitutional effects on political rents and productivity.

Our goal is to estimate the effects of constitutional reforms, that is, changing form of government or electoral rule. The theories reviewed in chapter 2 suggest specific hypotheses about the effect of such reforms on fiscal policy. Switching from a parliamentary to a presidential form of government is expected to reduce the size of government and, in particular, the size of spending programs with many beneficiaries (such as general public goods and broad welfare programs). Under a presidential regime, the majority of voters are not residual claimants on additional tax revenues. Spending is directed toward powerful minorities (rather than toward programs benefiting many), and voters/taxpayers can exploit the checks and balances of a presidential regime to keep overall government spending down. No specific prediction has been formulated with regard to the budget deficit.

Switching from proportional to majoritarian electoral rule is also expected to have significant effects on fiscal policy. The predicted effects are similar to those expected from a switch to presidentialism, though the reasons for the effects are different. Many theories predict that plurality rule and small electoral districts (i.e., majoritarian elections) induce spending targeted toward small, but pivotal, geographic constituencies. Proportional elections instead induce political parties to seek consensus in broad groups of the population and hence naturally lead to programs with many beneficiaries. Some theories also predict that majoritarian elections make it easier to limit both the size of government and the size of budget deficits. One reason imposing such limits is easier under majoritarian elections (though not the only one) is related to the party structure: majoritarian elections reduce the number of parties in countries that hold them and the frequency of coalition governments, which, in turn, helps in resolving the common-pool problems that might be at the root of large governments and deficits.

Throughout this chapter, we do not attempt to discriminate among different theories, nor do we consider the detailed mechanisms through which constitutions shape policy outcomes. Instead, we estimate a variety of reduced forms where constitutions are allowed to have a direct effect on the policy outcome of interest. Thus, we seek to quantify these constitutional effects, motivated by a set of theoretical priors, but without testing one specific model against another. Since this exercise is repeated for a variety of policy outcomes (in this chapter, as well as in the two following) our empirical results, in the end, paint a comprehensive picture that can be fruitfully contrasted with the theoretical priors. We defer a general discussion of this picture, however, to the last chapter of the book, after having revealed and discussed all the relevant results.

As discussed in chapter 5, the effect of changing form of government and electoral rule is estimated using the coefficients of the two binary indicator variables defined in chapter 4: PRES and MAJ, respectively. The estimated coefficient of PRES measures the constitutional effect of switching from a parliamentary to a presidential system, holding constant the electoral rule and under the assumption that the electoral rule itself is of no importance for this comparison (i.e., under the additivity assumption that the effect of changing the form of government is the same whatever the rule for electing the legislative assembly). Similarly, the estimated coefficient on the variable MAJ measures the constitutional effect of switching from proportional or mixed to majoritarian electoral rule for the legislative assembly, holding constant the form of government and under the assumption that the effect is the same irrespective of the form of government.[1] In some estimations in this chapter, we relax the additivity assumption and allow interactions between the two constitutional reforms we consider. The constitutional effects estimated under these more general assumptions correspond to the estimated coefficients of the dummy variables *MAJPRES, PROPRES,* and *MAJPAR,* with proportional-parliamentary democracies as the default group. The estimated coefficient of *MAJPRES* thus measures the effect of changing both the electoral rule and the form of government at the same time.

Our empirical findings are discussed in different sections of the chapter, each referring to a specific fiscal policy outcome. In each section and for each policy outcome, we first estimate constitutional effects by means of ordinary (linear) least squares. Then we relax the conditional-independence assumption, using instrumental variables and Heckman's procedure. Finally, we relax the linearity assumption and estimate constitutional effects nonparametrically, using propensity-score matching.

Section 6.2 considers size of government as measured by overall spending or revenue. We find presidential and majoritarian countries to have a smaller size of government, as expected. The effect of presidentialism on size of government is slightly larger and more robust than that of majoritarianism. The effects of both constitutional variables are weaker in the time period before the 1990s and stronger in the 1990s cross section, suggesting that presidential regimes and majoritarian elections have led to smaller governments because they have dampened the growth of governments in the postwar period.

In section 6.3, we evaluate the size of broad welfare state programs. In this case as well, we confirm our priors: presidential regimes and majoritarian elections have a negative effect on the size of welfare state programs, but these effects are weaker than those for the overall size of government. Results from relaxing conditional independence and linearity suggest that the negative effect of majoritarian elections is the more stable finding.

---

1. As discussed in chapter 4, "majoritarian" here refers to strictly majoritarian electoral rules, whereas the alternative state ($MAJ = 0$) aggregates strictly proportional and mixed electoral rules. Allowing for a finer partition of the electoral rule, using our indicator for mixed electoral rules ($MIXED$), does not alter the results reported below, and the estimated coefficient of $MIXED$ is never statistically significant. This difficulty to discriminate between mixed and proportional systems might also reflect the relative scarcity of the mixed electoral systems in our sample.

Section 6.4 extends the analysis of constitutional effects to budget balance. We find one very stable result across time periods and estimation methods, confirming an earlier empirical finding in the literature: majoritarian elections promote smaller budget deficits (or larger surpluses). The form of government has no stable causal effect on the propensity to run unbalanced budgets, even though unconditionally, presidential regimes have larger surpluses than parliamentary regimes.

Section 6.5 concludes by summarizing what we have learned from the results obtained in this chapter. Overall, these empirical results are remarkably in line with the theoretical priors, particularly in the case of the electoral rule.

6.2   Size of Government

Does the type of constitution in a country influence the size of government in that country? To answer this question, we measure the size of government using *central* government spending and revenue as a percentage of GDP (the variables *CGEXP* and *CGREV* introduced in chapter 3). As discussed in chapter 3, data on general government spending do not exist or are much less reliable than those for central government spending. Nevertheless, when we apply the same methods to the smaller sample of countries where some data on general government are available, the results are similar to those reported below. Moreover, a dummy variable for federal countries (*FEDERAL*) is always included in our basic set of control variables.

6.2.1   OLS Estimates
We start by assuming conditional independence and linearity and estimate the constitutional effects using OLS. The results are reported in table 6.1. The most parsimonious specification, presented in column 1, relies on our 1990s cross-section. It holds constant those variables that previous studies or a priori reasoning suggest to be correlated with the size of government spending. As discussed in chapters 3 and 4, we take these variables to be per capita income (*LYH*), openness (*TRADE*), two demographic measures (*PROP1564* and *PROP65*), age and quality of democracy (*AGE* and *GASTIL*, respectively), and dummy variables for federal and OECD countries (*FEDERAL* and *OECD*, respectively). Having a presidential regime

Table 6.1
Size of government and constitutions: Simple regression estimates

	(1)	(2)	(3)	(4)	(5)	(6)	(7)
Dependent variable	CGEXP	CGEXP	CGEXP	CGREV	CGEXP	CGEXP	CGEXP
PRES	-6.08	-5.29		-5.17	-8.29	-3.46	-7.49
	(1.97)***	(1.92)***		(2.44)**	(2.72)***	(3.88)	(2.72)***
MAJ	-3.29	-5.74		-3.03	-5.59	-2.93	-4.81
	(1.73)*	(1.95)***		(1.85)	(2.68)**	(3.09)	(2.75)*
PROPRES			-7.08				
			(2.70)**				
MAJPAR			-7.30				
			(3.02)**				
MAJPRES			-10.36				
			(2.70)***				
Continents	No	Yes	Yes	Yes	Yes	Yes	Yes
Colonies	No	Yes	Yes	Yes	Yes	Yes	Yes
Sample	1990s, broad	1990s, broad	1990s, broad	1990s, broad	1990s, narrow	1960–1990s, broad	1990s, obs as (6)
Number of observations	80	80	80	76	62	60	60
Adjusted R^2	0.58	0.63	0.63	0.58	0.60	0.54	0.63

Note: Robust standard errors in parentheses. All regressions include standard controls: *LYP*, *GASTIL*, *AGE*, *TRADE*, *PROP65*, *PROP1564*, *FEDERAL*, and *OECD*. Narrow sample corresponds to countries where *GASTIL* is less than 3.5.
* significant at 10%; ** significant at 5%; *** significant at 1%.

is found to reduce the size of government by 6% of GDP. The point estimate is not only highly statistically significant, but also economically and politically so. Majoritarian elections also appear to produce smaller governments, but here the effect is smaller, about 3% of GDP, and less precisely estimated.

The next column in the table adds to our specification our indicator variables for geographical location (Africa, Asia, and Latin America) and colonial origin (United Kingdom, Spanish, and other, all discounted to the present from the date of independence). As discussed in chapters 4 and 5, these indicator variables are correlated with constitution selection. Hence the conditional-independence assumption is more credible in this more comprehensive specification. Only the dummy variable for Latin America is found to be significantly different from zero. But the estimated constitutional effect of presidential regimes is remarkably stable, with the estimate dropping just slightly from that in the previous specification and maintaining about the same level of precision. With the addition of the indicator variables, the estimated effect of majoritarian elections now exceeds 5% of GDP. These results are quite robust to more parsimonious specifications of the continental dummy variables and the colonial-origin variables, to dropping one set of dummies but not the other, and to adding other controls such as income inequality, a dummy variable for former socialist countries (not statistically significant), or the age of democracy (AGE) entered both linearly and squared (to allow for different function forms through which the age of democracy influences policy outcomes).

In column 3, we partition the constitutional variables more finely (MAJPRES, MAJPAR, and PROPRES). The effects of the two constitutional features indeed appear to be additive, and introducing both a presidential form of government and majoritarian electoral rules in a parliamentary-proportional country reduces the size of government by a whopping 10% of GDP, according to our results.

In column 4, we measure the size of government in terms of revenue instead of spending (using the variable CGREV rather than CGEXP). The effect of presidential regimes is essentially the same as in the previous specifications, but that of majoritarian elections is weaker. Later in this chapter, we shall see that the difference between government revenue and spending in majoritarian countries has a counterpart in our results for government deficits (which are consistently smaller in majoritarian countries).

The 80 countries in our broad sample for the 1990s for which all variables are available include some whose status as a democracy is dubious. In weak democracies, the formal constitution might play a less important role in shaping policy compared to other informal practices and norms (we will return to a direct test of this idea below). Moreover, weaker democracies tend to be presidential regimes, which might introduce a systematic bias in the estimates. Column 5 thus restricts the estimation to the better democracies in a narrower sample already discussed in chapter 4 (62 countries for which we have data where GASTIL is smaller than 3.5). The effect of presidential regimes on government size now appears to be even stronger, whereas that of majoritarian elections remains stable and significant.

What happens when the average size of government is computed for a longer time period than the 1990s? Column 6 reports on the same specification as column 2 using as the dependent variable the average outcome over time for each of the 60 countries in our 1960–1998 panel. The effect of both presidentialism and majoritarian elections is still negative, as in previous specifications, but neither estimate is significantly different from zero. The weaker results obtained under the specification in column 6 do reflect the different time period, rather than the different sampling of countries. To confirm this, column 7 in the table returns to the 1990s cross section, restricting the regression to those countries that are included in the longer panel. These results strongly suggest that the differences observed in the 1990s data largely result from a faster *growth* of government over the last 40 years in countries with parliamentary regimes and proportional elections than in countries with other regimes and electoral rules. We will return to this important theme in chapter 8.

We also searched for interaction effects between constitutions and our covariates. In particular, we tested whether the share of old people, the quality of democracy, and income inequality have the same effect on spending under different constitutions. We can reject the null in the case of income inequality: higher levels of income inequality seem to produce a larger government, as expected from a simple median-voter model, but only under majoritarian elections and presidential regimes. The estimates involving income inequality are fragile to the sample and how inequality is measured, however, and thus, they are not emphasized here.

In summary, under the assumptions of conditional independence and linearity, the negative constitutional effect of presidential
regimes on government size is large (between -5% and -8% of
GDP) and robust to the specification. The electoral rule also has an
effect on the size of government associated with strictly majoritarian
countries (a negative effect ranging from -3% to -6% of GDP). Both
of these effects conform to prior expectations. They are stronger in
the 1990s than in earlier decades, suggesting that constitutions have
influenced postwar growth in size of government.

6.2.2   Instrumental-Variables and Heckman Estimates

How robust are the above estimates of constitutional effects when
we try to relax conditional independence? The short answer is that
they are quite robust.

Consider first the Heckman procedure. As discussed in chapters 4
and 5, in the first stage, we estimate by means of probit a constitutional selection equation specified as follows. One set of variables
measures the date of origin of the current constitution in a country: the three discretely measured indicators of constitutional origin
(CON2150, CON5180, and CON81) and the continuously measured
age of democracy (AGE). (Recall that the three indicator variables
capture the origin of the current constitution in a particular country
or the date of the country's becoming a democracy, whichever came
later.) A second set of variables measures the cultural influence of
the West, and Great Britain in particular. These are the distance from
the equator (LAT01) (to measure different penetrations of colonization by the West) and the fraction of the country's population
whose mother tongue is English (ENGFRAC) or a European language (EURFRAC). Since countries in Latin America tend to be
presidential systems with proportional legislative elections, we also
include our dummy variable for Latin America (LAAM). Finally,
given the importance of British heritage in explaining the electoral
rule, and since the fraction of the population speaking English is not
highly correlated with colonial origin, we also include a variable for
U.K. colonial origin (COL_UKA). These variables have considerable
explanatory power for both form of government and electoral rule
(see table 5.1).

In the second stage of the Heckman procedure, the policy outcome equation is specified with the usual set of regressors. To
minimize the necessary adjustment for the correlation between

Table 6.2
Size of government and constitutions: Heckman and instrumental-variables estimates

	(1)	(2)	(3)	(4)
Dependent variable	CGEXP	CGEXP	CGEXP	CGEXP
PRES	−10.50	−5.37	−8.65	−4.50
	(3.98)***	(2.19)**	(3.63)**	(3.89)
MAJ	−5.69	−4.92	−3.90	−5.12
	(1.86)***	(2.57)*	(3.46)	(3.61)
Continents and colonies	Yes	Yes	No	COL_UKA, LAAM
Sample	1990s, broad	1990s, broad	1990s, broad	1990s, broad
Endogenous selection	PRES	MAJ	PRES MAJ	PRES MAJ
Method of estimation	Heckman two-step	Heckman two-step	2SLS	2SLS
Rho	0.64	−0.02		
Chi-square: over-id			4.64	3.61
Adjusted R^2			0.59	0.60
Number of observations	75	75	75	75

Note: Standard errors in parentheses. Critical value of $\chi^2(4, 0.05) = 9.49$. Always included in second-stage specification (columns 1–4): *AGE, LYP, TRADE, PROP1564, PROP65, GASTIL, FEDERAL,* and *OECD.* First-stage specification of Heckman (columns 1–2) includes *CON2150, CON5180, CON81, AGE, ENGFRAC, EURFRAC, LAT01,* and *LAAM.* First-stage specification of 2SLS (columns 3–4) includes *CON2150, CON5180, CON81, AGE, ENGFRAC, EURFRAC,* and *LAT01.*
*significant at 10%; **significant at 5%; ***significant at 1%.

unobserved determinants of constitution selection and performance, we also include dummy variables for colonial origin and continental location.[2]

The second-stage estimates for the Heckman procedure are reported in columns 1 and 2 of table 6.2. The estimated constitutional effects on size of government remain negative and strongly significant. Allowing for an endogenous selection of majoritarian elections (column 2), the estimated correlation coefficient between the random parts of constitution selection and performance (rho in the table) is practically zero. Thus the estimate is similar to the OLS estimates. When we allow for endogenous selection of presidential regimes (column 1), the correlation coefficient is instead positive and high (0.64). Thus the OLS estimates are likely to be biased upward, and the Heckman correction produces an even larger negative estimate

2. As noted in chapter 5, we apply the Heckman procedure to one constitutional dimension at a time, treating the other dimension as random.

of the constitutional effect than the OLS estimate. These results are quite robust to alternative specifications of the first-stage equation for constitution selection.

Next, consider instrumental-variables estimation. In such estimation, we exploit the crucial exclusion restriction that some variables entering the first stage do not influence fiscal policy, except through their effect on the constitution, once we hold other determinants of policy constant.

We start with a parsimonious specification for both the first- and the second-stage regression. The second-stage regressors include our standard controls, but no continental and colonial-origin indicator variables. The first stage is kept as in the Heckman estimation, except that we drop the dummy variable for Latin America ($LAAM$) and the variable for U.K. colonial origin (COL_UKA) (i.e., the same specification as reported in table 5.1). Thus, the identifying assumption is that the constitutional dating variables ($CON2150$, $CON5180$, and $CON81$), the language variables ($ENGFRAC$ and $EURFRAC$), and latitude ($LAT01$) are all uncorrelated with the remaining unobserved determinants of fiscal policy. Constitutional effects on size of government are reported in column 3 of table 6.2.[3] The point estimates are similar to and (if anything) larger in absolute value than the OLS estimates of table 6.1. They also closely correspond to those obtained with the Heckman correction in columns 1 and 2.

Our identifying assumption says that any variable omitted from the second-stage is not correlated with our instruments. For instance, if colonial origin or being located in Latin America influences size of government, its effect would appear in the residual of the second-stage equation (because these two variables are omitted in column 3). This would not bias the instrumental-variables estimates, however, as long as our instruments are not correlated with colonial origin or continental location. We consider it reasonable to assume the absence of such correlation in the case of the three dating variables, but we are less certain in the case of the remaining three instruments.

---

3. Thus among the second-stage regressors, only AGE also enters in the first stage. This parsimonious first-stage specification is chosen to avoid having excessively weak instruments for the constitution. Imposing the restriction that only AGE plus the six instruments enter in the first stage, we estimate the first stage using OLS, run the second stage on the predicted values of MAJ and $PRES$, and correct the second-stage residuals as discussed by Maddala (1977, chap. 11) and Wiggins (2000). The point estimates are very similar (or stronger) if all second-stage controls are added to the first-stage regression.

If we assume the dating instruments to be valid, however, the validity of the remaining three can be tested via the implied over-identifying restrictions. As shown in column 3 of the table, we cannot reject these restrictions, which reassures us that the estimates presented in column 3 are consistent, despite the omission of indicators for colonial origin and continental location.

Nevertheless, the overidentification test might have low power, since the dating variables are only weakly correlated with constitution selection. Indeed, if we respecify the first stage by omitting the dubious instruments (*LAT01*, *ENGFRAC*, and *EURFRAC*), the fit of the first stage weakens sufficiently for the estimated constitutional effects to become statistically insignificant (though the point estimate remains negative and, in the case of majoritarian elections, it is even larger in absolute value than previously). For this reason, column 4 reports the results when we add the most likely culprits to the second stage, namely, the variables for British colonial origin and Latin American location. The constitutional effect of presidential regime now drops toward its OLS estimate, but with a larger standard error, whereas the point estimate for majoritarian elections increases in absolute value but remains statistically insignificant.[4] One interpretation of these results is as follows. A parsimonious first stage leaves only a small share of the variation in constitutional arrangements explained by the first-stage regressors. This variation is insufficient to exert a significant influence on size of government, once we have also included all the dummy variables in the second stage (since adding auxiliary controls keeps removing variation from size of government).

6.2.3 Matching Estimates

How robust are the results in section 6.2.1 when we relax the assumption of linearity (but maintain conditional independence) and estimate constitutional effects nonparametrically with matching methods? As discussed at length in chapter 5, these quasi-experimental methods involve pairing up countries with different actual constitutional rules, but similar estimated probabilities (propensity scores) of having selected a particular rule.

---

4. The results are very similar if the first-stage regression associated with the estimates in column 4 is expanded to include the dummy variable for Latin America. If all the colonial-origin and continental variables are added to the second stage, the standard errors increase even further.

The first step in making these estimations is thus to estimate the propensity scores of the countries in our sample for electoral rules and government regimes, respectively. We experimented with different estimation methods for the selection equation: probit versus logit. The differences in the results obtained are minor, and we display only the results for the logit estimates.[5] We also tried different specifications of the variables entering these logits. As explained in chapter 5, our concern here is very different from that in the first stage of the Heckman adjustment for self-selection. To respect conditional independence, we should include the most important determinants of size of government, also correlated with constitution selection. At the same time, we should preserve some randomness in the selection process: if we explain constitution selection too well, the common support becomes empty, and the basis for matching is lost. We report results only for the 1990s cross section, as we want to check whether the main results hold when the strong functional-form assumptions are relaxed.

We report the results for two different logit specifications. Both include four potentially important determinants of size of government, namely, log of per capita income (LYP), share of old people ($PROP65$), quality of democracy ($GASTIL$), and presence of a federal system ($FEDERAL$). In the first specification, we also include the indicators for previous British colonies and Latin American location, which correlate both with size of government and constitution selection (adding other indicators, such as Spanish or Portuguese colonial origin, is not feasible, as we start perfectly predicting some constitutional outcomes if those indicators are added). The second specification instead adds the share of English- and European-language-speaking people in the population ($ENGFRAC$ and $EURFRAC$, respectively), as well as latitude ($LAT01$).

Table 6.3 displays the results. For each method of matching, we report the estimates obtained under both logit specifications. The underlying standard errors have been estimated using a bootstrapping procedure. The kernel estimators (reported in columns 1 and 2) are the most reliable in a small sample such as ours, and the nearest-neighbor matching is the least reliable. As explained in

---

5. Persson and Tabellini (2002) also report estimates of constitutional effects on size of government with these same nonparametric methods and a similar, but not identical, specification of the first (constitutional selection) stage. The results are similar to those reported below.

Table 6.3
Size of government and constitutions: Matching estimates

	(1)	(2)	(3)	(4)	(5)	(6)
Dependent variable	CGEXP	CGEXP	CGEXP	CGEXP	CGEXP	CGEXP
PRES	−7.30	−7.91	−5.87	−7.92	−2.54	−4.00
	(2.30)***	(2.90)***	(4.93)	(5.11)	(2.30)	(3.45)
MAJ	−5.76	−6.55	−4.87	−4.08	−6.59	−8.81
	(2.94)*	(2.82)**	(3.65)	(4.16)	(3.06)**	(3.15)***
Method of estimation	Kernel	Kernel	Stratification	Stratification	Nearest neighbor	Nearest neighbor
Sample	1990s, broad	1990s, broad	1990s, broad	1990s, broad	1990s, broad	1990s, broad
Logit specification	1	2	1	2	1	2
Number of observations	65 PRES	40 PRES	65 PRES	40 PRES	65 PRES	40 PRES
on common support	67 MAJ	57 MAJ	67 MAJ	57 MAJ	67 MAJ	57 MAJ

Note: Standard errors in parentheses obtained by bootstrapping. Kernel, stratification, and nearest-neighbor estimators described in section 5.5.
Logit specifications underlying the propensity score estimates:
1: LYP, PROP65, GASTIL, FEDERAL, COL_UKA, LAAM
2: LYP, PROP65, GASTIL, FEDERAL, ENGFRAC, EURFRAC, LAT01
* significant at 10%; ** significant at 5%; *** significant at 1%.

chapter 5, in a small sample, measurement error or slight changes in the logit specification affect the ranking of countries based on the propensity score. With the nearest-neighbor matching estimator, this can have sizable impacts on our estimates, whereas the kernel estimator is more robust. With the first logit specification, and when the common-support restriction is imposed, we typically discard 10–15 observations from the sample. The second logit formulation (column 2) explains the constitutional features of interest particularly well, and we therefore end up losing more observations, particularly for presidential regimes. We are left with only 40 countries in the sample of the common support of estimated propensity scores for those regimes (see chapter 5).

Despite these changes in the sample of countries and the estimation methods, the estimates reported in table 6.3 confirm the main message of the previous subsections. Given the sample, the results presented in table 6.3 are most directly comparable to those in columns 1 and 2 of tables 6.1 and 6.2. According to the more reliable estimates in columns 1–4 of table 6.3, presidentialism reduces size of government by between 6% and 8% of GDP, and majoritarian elections reduce it by between 4% and 6% of GDP. The nearest-neighbor estimators dampen the effect of presidentialism and increase that of majoritarian elections. The standard errors of the estimates are larger than those of the OLS estimates, but that is to be expected, as we are trading off lower levels of specification bias against larger standard errors in this nonparametric estimation. The most precise estimates are found using the kernel estimator, which is intuitive, as this method is the least sensitive of the three to individual observations.

All in all, allowing for nonlinear constitutional effects does not change the conclusions we draw from these data.

6.2.4 Summary

The three sets of results paint a very consistent picture. If we are willing to assume conditional independence, given a large set of covariates, both constitutional effects are negative for the 1990s cross section. Presidential regimes and majoritarian elections each cut the size of government by about 5% of GDP, perhaps more in the case of presidentialism. These results are robust to relaxing the linearity assumption. Relaxing conditional independence does not change the estimated effect of majoritarian elections, and it appears to increase the effect of presidential regimes. The results for presidential regimes conform with our theoretical prior, obtained from the work discussed in chapter 2. In the case of majoritarian elections, our prior was more fuzzy to begin with, but the empirical results lead us to revise it.

6.3 Composition of Government

Do constitutional effects extend to welfare state spending? As discussed in chapters 2 and 3, pensions and unemployment insurance are normally paid out in broad expenditure programs with many beneficiaries in the population at large. This makes geographic targeting much harder than for other types of discretionary spending, particularly in more developed countries. This is why, based on the theory, we expect the size of welfare spending to be smaller in presidential regimes and under majoritarian electoral rule. In this section, we investigate whether our main constitutional variables ($PRES$ and MAJ) have direct or indirect effects on welfare state spending, relying on the same battery of methods as we used for size of government.

6.3.1 OLS Estimates
Table 6.4 reports on a variety of linear regression estimates. We hold constant the same variables as in the standard specification for size of government. On the whole, the estimated constitutional effects on welfare spending are smaller than those on the overall size of government. But the data reveal important interactions between constitution and other variables also influencing welfare spending.

Column 1 of the table refers to the full sample of countries in the 1990s cross section (SSW, our measure of social transfers, is available for a dozen fewer countries than $CGEXP$, our measure of the size of government). Both presidential regimes and majoritarian elections appear to reduce welfare state spending by about 2% of GDP, quite a large reduction. But neither effect is statistically significant (p-values of 0.14 and 0.11, respectively). The results are similar in other (non-reported) specifications, such as when we drop the dummies for continents and colonial origin or add income inequality or the age of democracy squared.

The absence of a strong constitutional effect on welfare spending may seem puzzling, given that the size of welfare state spending is (unconditionally) much smaller in presidential and majoritarian

Table 6.4
Welfare spending and constitutions: Simple regression estimates

	(1)	(2)	(3)
Dependent variable	SSW	SSW	SSW
PRES	−1.89		−4.42
	(1.27)		(1.84)**
MAJ	−2.01		−2.44
	(1.25)		(1.88)
PROPRES		−2.74	
		(1.58)*	
MAJPAR		−2.72	
		(1.71)	
MAJPRES		−3.51	
		(2.31)	
PRES_OLD			
MAJ_OLD			
AGE	1.14	1.51	1.16
	(2.60)	(2.86)	(3.60)
PRES_BAD			
MAJ_BAD			
GASTIL	−0.55	−0.61	−1.10
	(0.57)	(0.56)	(1.50)
PRES_GIN			
MAJ_GIN			
GINI_8090			
Continents and colonies	Yes	Yes	Yes
Sample	1990s, broad	1990s, broad	1990s, narrow
Number of observations	69	69	56
Adjusted R^2	0.75	0.75	0.73

Note: Robust standard errors in parentheses. All regressions include standard controls: *LYP, PROP65, PROP1564, GASTIL, AGE, TRADE, FEDERAL,* and *OECD.* Narrow sample corresponds to countries where *GASTIL* is less than 3.5.
*significant at 10%; **significant at 5%; ***significant at 1%.

Table 6.4
(continued)

	(4)	(5)	(6)
Dependent variable	*SSW*	*SSW*	*SSW*
PRES	0.22	−8.65	−22.15
	(1.58)	(2.94)***	(6.74)***
MAJ	0.32	−4.96	−4.28
	(1.60)	(2.70)*	(5.41)
PROPRES			
MAJPAR			
MAJPRES			
PRES_OLD	−8.54		
	(3.81)**		
MAJ_OLD	−7.69		
	(2.99)**		
AGE	9.60	3.62	−0.84
	(4.14)**	(3.09)	(2.90)
PRES_BAD		2.67	
		(1.09)**	
MAJ_BAD		1.50	
		(0.86)*	
GASTIL	−0.67	−2.43	−1.39
	(0.58)	(0.96)**	(0.75)*
PRES_GIN			0.57
			(0.16)***
MAJ_GIN			0.06
			(0.13)
GINI_8090			−0.33
			(0.12)***
Continents and colonies	Yes	Yes	Yes
Sample	1990s, broad	1990s, broad	1990s, broad
Number of observations	69	69	58
Adjusted R^2	0.78	0.78	0.81

countries than in parliamentary and proportional ones (cf. table 4.5). The key socioeconomic covariate driving the result is the proportion of elderly in the population (as measured by *PROP65*). When this variable is held constant, the estimated constitutional effects are about −2% of GDP in magnitude, but statistically insignificant; when the variable is omitted, these effects are much larger in absolute value and statistically significant. In other words, presidential and majoritarian countries do have smaller welfare spending on average than their parliamentary and proportional counterparts, but for the most this reflects their younger populations.

In column 2, constitution is further subdivided into four separate groups. As expected, switching both electoral rule and form of government is estimated to have the strongest effect (the point estimate of the dummy variable *MAJPRES* has the largest point estimate in absolute value). But only the estimated coefficient of the dummy variable *PROPRES* (corresponding to a change in the form of government in proportional countries) is statistically significant.

As discussed in chapter 5, constitutional features may shape policy outcomes with different strengths at different stages of democracy. If such interactions exist, they may be particularly important here, as welfare state spending may be precisely triggered by broad political participation. Columns 3–5 of table 6.4 show that the quality and age of a democracy indeed interact with alternative constitutional features.

In column 3, we confine the sample of countries to better democracies (56 countries in which *GASTIL* is, on average, lower than 3.5 in the 1990s). Now the estimated effect of a presidential regime is much stronger (more than −4% of GDP) and significant, as predicted. The effect of majoritarian elections is also stronger, but remains imprecisely estimated.[6]

Columns 4 and 5 return to the full sample of democracies but interact electoral rule and form of government with age and quality of democracy (measured by *AGE* and *GASTIL*, respectively). Vari-

---

6. These results on electoral rule are weaker than the findings by Milesi-Ferretti, Perotti, and Rostagno (2002), who estimate a negative and significant effect of less-proportional electoral rules on social transfers in the OECD countries from 1960 to 1995 (they disregard form of government). Restricting the regressions for the longer cross section to the 23 OECD countries in our sample (including the same covariates except the continental and colonial-origin dummies), we obtain an insignificant effect close to zero, however.

ables PRES_OLD and MAJ_OLD in column 4 are defined as the product of PRES and AGE and MAJ and AGE, respectively; the suffix OLD reminds us that higher values of AGE correspond to older democracies. Similarly, the variables PRES_BAD and MAJ_BAD in column 5 are defined as the product of PRES and GASTIL and MAJ and GASTIL, respectively; the suffix BAD reminds us that higher values of GASTIL correspond to worse democracies.

The estimates yield two results. First, and confirming the results in column 3, presidentialism and majoritarian elections restrain welfare spending only among older and better democracies (i.e., those with higher values of AGE and lower values of GASTIL). We infer this from the negative estimated coefficients of PRES_OLD and MAJ_OLD in column 4 and the negative estimated coefficients of PRES and MAJ in column 5, together with the positive and significant estimated coefficients of PRES_BAD and MAJ_BAD.

The significant estimated coefficients of variables AGE and GASTIL in columns 4 and 5, respectively, also suggest a second inference. Older and better democracies (higher values of AGE and lower values of GASTIL) have significantly higher welfare state spending only if they are parliamentary and proportional (the default constitutional state).[7] This finding is consistent with the common view among political scientists that proportional elections and parliamentary systems allow for a better representation of disadvantaged groups, that is, the likely beneficiaries of welfare state spending. In other words, these political institutions might better aggregate the policy preferences of disadvantaged groups into an actual influence on policy. As democracies become older and allow greater opportunities for political participation, the size of the welfare state increases. This effect of democratization is observed only in proportional and parliamentary democracies, however, and not among presidential and majoritarian democracies.[8]

---

7. Summing the coefficients of AGE and PRES_OLD, we obtain a point estimate of 1.06 with a standard error of 2.04 (transformed to take the linear combination of estimated coefficients into account). Thus we cannot reject the null hypothesis that the effect of AGE on welfare spending is zero among presidential regimes. The same results are obtained for the set of majoritarian (parliamentary) countries, or for the effects of GASTIL.

8. These interactions between quality and age of democracy and constitution are found only when the dependent variable is welfare spending and not when it is the overall size of government. This further supports the interpretation of the results proposed in the text.

What do the estimates tell us about the overall constitutional effect of presidential regimes or majoritarian elections under the maintained assumption of conditional independence? In chapter 5, we defined the constitutional effect as the average effect of constitutional reform in a country drawn at random, a definition that might also include interaction terms. Recalling the definition of constitutional effect in equation (5.9), in column 5 of table 6.4 we should add the estimated intercept (the coefficient on *PRES* or *MAJ*) to the estimated interaction effect (the coefficient on *PRES_BAD* or *MAJ_BAD*) times the average quality of democracy (the average value of *GASTIL*)—or equivalently for the age of democracy in column 4. These calculations for the estimates in columns 4 and 5 produce a point estimate of the full constitutional effect close to that in column 1 (i.e., both presidential regimes and majoritarian elections reduce welfare state spending by about 2% of GDP).

Finally, in column 6 of table 6.4 we interact our constitutional variables with income inequality (measured by the Gini coefficient in the 1980s and 1990s). One a priori reason why this should be of interest to us has already been mentioned. The central prediction from the simple median-voter model—that income inequality boosts redistributive transfer payments—is most relevant when elections have fewer candidates, which is more likely under majoritarian elections or presidential forms of government. Higher levels of inequality (higher values of *GINI_8090*) affect welfare spending in opposite directions under different forms of government. The significant negative coefficient on inequality (*GINI_8090*) in column 6 shows that higher levels of *inequality* are associated with a smaller welfare state in parliamentary democracies, contrary to expectations and irrespective of the electoral rule (the estimated coefficient of *MAJ_GIN* is close to zero). Since inequality is measured here in the 1980s and 1990s, whereas these welfare programs have existed in their current form for a longer time span, the finding might also reflect some reverse causation (larger transfers might reduce inequality). In presidential regimes, inequality is instead associated with higher levels of welfare spending (the sum of the coefficients on *GINI_8090* and *PRES_GIN* is positive and significant). Reverse causation might be less of a problem in Latin America (the home of many presidential regimes), since welfare programs in Latin American countries are more recent and more likely to target urban workers rather than the poor in the countryside.

Do the conditional results on quality of democracy and income inequality reflect different channels of influence, or are they two sides of the same coin? After all, bad democracies are more likely to have higher levels of income inequality than good democracies (the simple correlation between *GINI_8090* and *GASTIL* in our 1990s cross section is 0.38). Furthermore, both variables are strongly correlated with presidential regime (correlation coefficients around 0.5). To answer this question, we allowed both interactions to appear simultaneously in the same specification. The results (not reported) are surprisingly stable, despite having relatively few degrees of freedom.

We also estimated the same set of equations appearing in table 6.4 in the longer panel of 60 countries for which data are also available from the early 1970s onward (unlike data for the overall size of government, social security and other transfer data are not available for the 1960s). The results are very similar to all the results reported in table 6.4, including the interaction effects, suggesting that the results are not a peculiarity of the 1990s.

6.3.2 Instrumental-Variables and Heckman Estimates

Next, we relax the conditional-independence assumption, using instrumental variables and the Heckman two-step procedure in the broad 1990s cross section, in which we have the largest number of countries. Despite the interaction results just reported, we retain the restriction of a linear model with constant slope coefficients. It would just be too demanding on the data to also allow for endogenous constitution selection in this more complex specification; moreover, we do not have reliable instruments for measuring quality of democracy (as measured by *GASTIL*) or income inequality. Thus, the estimates reported in table 6.5 should be compared to the OLS estimates in column 1 of table 6.4.

The specification of the first- and second-stage regressions for both the Heckman and the instrumental variables estimates is identical to those used for the size of government in section 6.2.2.[9] In particular, when we estimate using instrumental variables, we report two specifications for the second-stage estimates, one inclusive of the dummy variables for British colonial origin and Latin America (column 4),

---

9. Except in the first stage of the Heckman estimation when *MAJ* is treated as endogenous, where we drop the variable *CON2150* to avoid a perfect prediction of nine observations.

Table 6.5
Welfare spending and constitutions: Heckman and instrumental variables estimates

	(1)	(2)	(3)	(4)
Dependent variable	SSW	SSW	SSW	SSW
PRES	−1.99	−1.62	0.30	−0.39
	(2.06)	(1.37)	(1.96)	(2.34)
MAJ	−1.76	−3.21	−3.63	−4.13
	(1.13)	(1.64)**	(1.82)**	(2.12)*
Continents and colonies	Yes	Yes	No	COL_UKA LAAM
Sample	1990s, broad	1990s, broad	1990s, broad	1990s, broad
Endogenous selection	PRES	MAJ	PRES MAJ	PRES MAJ
Method of estimation	Heckman two-step	Heckman two-step	2SLS	2SLS
Rho	0.08	0.47		
Chi-square: over-id			5.73*	9.81**
Number of observations	64	64	64	64
Adjusted R^2			0.78	0.78

Note: Standard errors in parentheses. Critical value of $\chi^2(4, 0.05) = 9.49$. Always included in SSW equation: *AGE, LYP, TRADE, PROP1564, PROP65, GASTIL, FEDERAL,* and *OECD.* 2SLS first-stage specification includes *CON2150, CON5180, CON81, AGE, EURFRAC, ENGFRAC,* and *LAT01.* Heckman first-step probit specification includes *CON2150, CON5180, CON81, LAT01, ENGFRAC, EURFRAC, AGE, COL_UKA,* and *LAAM* (*CON2150* dropped from probit for *MAJ* to avoid perfect predictions).
*significant at 10%; **significant at 5%; ***significant at 1%.

the other not (column 3). (Our previous concerns about the validity of the instruments remain, but we do not repeat them here.) Now the overidentifying restrictions can indeed be rejected at the 10% level for the more parsimonious second-stage specifications (column 3) and at the 5% level for the less parsimonious ones. Recalling the interaction effects identified in the previous section 6.3.1, the fragility of the Heckman correction to possible functional-form misspecification is also an issue.

Despite these concerns, the pattern of constitutional effects is consistent across the estimates reported in table 6.5, although somewhat different from that in the OLS estimates in table 6.4. The presidential effect is not significantly different from zero. In the Heckman estimates, it is about the same size as in the OLS regressions, namely, about −2% of GDP (cf. column 1), consistent with the finding that the estimated correlation coefficient between the unobserved determinants of constitution selection and performance (rho) is close to zero. In the instrumental-variables estimates, it is practically zero. Overall, relaxing conditional independence weakens the estimated effect of presidentialism.

The effect of majoritarian elections, on the other hand, is reinforced by relaxing conditional independence. The estimated coefficient of *MAJ* is now negative and statistically significant according to both procedures. Column 2 of table 6.5 suggests errors with a strong positive correlation (a rho of +0.47), implying an upward bias in the OLS estimate of constitutional effect in table 6.4. When this bias is corrected, the constitutional effect of majoritarian elections becomes negative and statistically significant (column 2), a result confirmed by each of the instrumental-variables estimates (columns 3 and 4).

The consistency of these results under two different estimation methods is an indication that accounting for deviations from conditional independence might be important. Once such deviations have been accounted for, there is stronger evidence that majoritarian elections induce a smaller welfare state, whereas the form of government appears to be less important.

6.3.3 Matching Estimates

Finally, we turn to matching methods and relax the assumption that the equation determining the size of the welfare state is linear in the covariates. In light of the interactions reported in the OLS regressions, this relaxation seems quite important for assessing the robustness of our inferences. Once more, we proceed as for the overall size of government, by estimating two alternative logit specifications of the propensity score: the same as those already discussed for the size of government. The second specification entails a loss of a larger number of countries, particularly when we estimate the presidential effect.

Table 6.6 displays the results for these specifications and our three matching methods. As noted in section 6.2.3, the kernel estimators are the most reliable in such a small sample. Despite the different estimators and first-stage specifications for the propensity scores, most estimates are quite similar to those reported in tables 6.4 and 6.5, if not larger in absolute value: both presidential regimes and majoritarian elections have a negative effect on welfare state spending of about −2–3% of GDP, although the estimates are rarely statistically significant. As larger standard errors are to be expected,

Table 6.6
Welfare spending and constitutions: Matching estimates

	(1)	(2)	(3)	(4)	(5)	(6)
Dependent variable	SSW	SSW	SSW	SSW	SSW	SSW
PRES	-3.75	-3.11	-3.15	-1.83	-0.45	-2.02
	(2.43)	(1.89)	(3.38)	(2.78)	(1.77)	(1.54)
MAJ	-3.29	-4.62	-1.84	-1.89	-2.47	-3.70
	(1.74)*	(1.61)***	(1.92)	(2.09)	(1.96)	(2.01)*
Method of estimation	Kernel	Kernel	Stratification	Stratification	Nearest neighbor	Nearest neighbor
Sample	1990s, broad	1990s, broad	1990s, broad	1990s, broad	1990s, broad	1990s, broad
Logit specification	1	2	1	2	1	2
Number of observations on common support	56 PRES 58 MAJ	35 PRES 50 MAJ	56 PRES 58 MAJ	35 PRES 50 MAJ	56 PRES 58 MAJ	35 PRES 50 MAJ

Note: Standard errors in parentheses obtained by bootstrapping. Kernel, stratification, and nearest-neighbor estimators described in section 5.5.
Logit specifications underlying the propensity score estimates:
   1: *LYP, PROP65, GASTIL, FEDERAL, COL_UKA, LAAM*
   2: *LYP, PROP65, GASTIL, FEDERAL, ENGFRAC, EURFRAC, LAT01*
* significant at 10%; ** significant at 5%; *** significant at 1%.

these consistently negative and stable estimates strengthen our belief that both constitutional effects on welfare spending are indeed negative, despite the interaction effects discussed in connection with the OLS regressions.

6.3.4 Summary
Our findings suggest interesting constitutional effects on welfare state spending. Majoritarian elections cut welfare spending, as predicted by theory, and by as much as 2–3% of GDP. For presidential regimes, the evidence points in the same direction, although the estimates are somewhat less robust. Furthermore, there are interaction effects. Both constitutional effects are much stronger among better and older democracies. Moreover, better democracies have larger welfare states, but only if they are parliamentary-proportional. Selection bias seems to be a more severe problem in the estimations for welfare spending than in those for the size of government. Correcting for this bias reinforces the negative constitutional effect of majoritarian elections but weakens the effect of form of government.

6.4 Budget Surplus

Is there a constitutional effect on government deficits? Earlier informal work and empirical results suggest that proportional electoral rules may be conducive to government debts and deficits, since such rules are often associated with unstable governments and coalition governments. Is this also the case in the broad data sets used in this book? To investigate this question in a reduced-form manner, we apply the same approach as in sections 6.2 and 6.3, using government surplus as a percentage of GDP (SPL) as our dependent variable.

As noted in chapters 3 and 4, a country cannot keep running a budget deficit forever. The 1990s stand out as a somewhat special decade in this respect. Many countries began running large budget deficits in the 1970s and 1980s, whereas the 1990s was a period of budgetary consolidation, particularly for some of the countries that had accumulated large debts in earlier decades. To avoid basing our conclusions on data from a decade when several countries were trying to recover from large public debts, we study only the 60-country panel, for which we can take averages for the whole period 1960–

1998. Most of the results reported below are very similar, however, for the 1990s cross section.

6.4.1 OLS Estimates

Columns 1–4 of table 6.7 report the OLS estimates. Column 1 runs the same specification as our basic regressions in sections 6.2 and 6.3. Countries with majoritarian elections have larger surpluses (smaller deficits) than those with proportional elections; the effect is precisely estimated and quite large, about 2% of GDP. Note that the regression in column 1 includes a set of continental dummies on top of our standard controls, so that the results do not reflect, say, larger deficits and a greater incidence of proportional countries in Latin America. There is no significant effect of governmental regime.

To address the possibility that larger or smaller deficits simply reflect initial debt levels, in column 2 (and in all remaining columns in the table), we also control for the level of debt in a country in the first year when deficit data become available for that country. The estimated coefficient on initial debt (not reported) is negative and highly significant, meaning that a larger initial debt indeed leads to a smaller surplus, presumably because of higher interest payments.[10] The majoritarian effect decreases only marginally over that in column 1, however, and remains significant. Similarly, the result is robust to excluding the worst democracies (column 4).

Column 3 reports on the results from the finer disaggregation of the sample into four constitutional states. Clearly, the main result in the other columns derives from differences within the group of parliamentary countries. This gives some indirect support to the idea that coalition or minority governments, which are much more common under proportional elections, may suffer from a status quo bias or a dynamic common-pool problem and find it harder to get their fiscal house in order, compared to majority governments.

Finally, as noted in chapter 3, we do not succeed in explaining any considerable fraction of the cross-country variation in the surplus: the adjusted R^2 is low, between 20% and 30%, despite the inclusion of dummy variables for colonial origin and continental location. Other important determinants of budget deficits are unaccounted for by our standard controls. Nevertheless, the results are stable

---

10. Note, however, that in this kind of cross-country regressions, the initial-debt variable could be negatively correlated with the error term, leading to a possible downward bias in the estimated debt coefficient (the dependent variable is the surplus).

Table 6.7
Government surplus and constitutions: Simple regressions and Heckman estimates

	(1)	(2)	(3)	(4)	(5)	(6)
Dependent variable	SPL	SPL	SPL	SPL	SPL	SPL
PRES	1.31	1.00		1.05	0.18	1.01
	(1.24)	(1.26)		(1.34)	(1.69)	(.99)
MAJ	2.11	1.79		2.06	1.65	1.19
	(0.68)***	(0.71)**		(0.79)**	(0.75)**	(1.13)
PROPRES			2.36			
			(1.21)*			
MAJPAR			2.81			
			(0.91)***			
MAJPRES			2.51			
			(1.74)			
Endogenous selection					PRES	MAJ
Method of estimation	OLS	OLS	OLS	OLS	Heckman two-step	Heckman two-step
Rho					0.31	0.28
Continents and colonies	Yes	Yes	Yes	Yes	Yes	Yes
Sample	1960–1990s, broad	1960–1990s, broad	1960–1990s, broad	1960–1990s, narrow	1960–1990s, broad	1960–1990s, broad
Number of observations	60	59	59	53	59	59
Adjusted R^2	0.17	0.28	0.30	0.31		

Note: Robust standard errors in parentheses. All regressions include standard controls: *AGE, LYP, TRADE, PROP1564, PROP65, GASTIL, FEDERAL,* and *OECD;* in columns 2–6 initial debt is also included. Heckman first-step probit specifications (columns 5–6) include *LAT01, ENGFRAC, EURFRAC, AGE, COL_UKA,* and *LAAM.* Narrow sample corresponds to countries where *GASTIL* is less than 3.5.
* significant at 10%; ** significant at 5%; *** significant at 1%.

to alternative specifications or the sample of the 1990s. Experiments with various interaction effects yield no stable results but do not change the effect of majoritarian elections reported above.

6.4.2 Heckman Estimates

The last two columns of table 6.7 relax conditional dependence. Instrumental-variables estimation is problematic in the longer period 1960–1998: in that period, the variables dating constitutional origin are no longer reliable instruments, because the sample includes some constitutional reforms and some countries becoming democracies for the first time (recall from chapter 4 that the constitutional-origin instruments reflect the year when the country's current constitutional feature was first selected or the year when the country became a "democracy," whichever came later). Hence, these instruments should be more carefully redefined for the longer period, which we have not done. Since we are left with only the less reliable instruments ($LAT01$, $ENGFRAC$, and $EURFRAC$), we do not report on instrumental-variables results. For the same reason, the first stage of the Heckman model does not rely on the variables dating constitutional origin (the auxiliary instruments are less of a problem in the Heckman procedure, as we can still achieve identification through the functional-form assumption, as discussed in chapter 5).

Consider the constitutional effect of majoritarian elections (column 6 of table 6.7). The OLS estimates place this effect at around 2% of GDP (lower deficits under majoritarian elections). The Heckman procedure estimates the correlation coefficient between the unobserved parts of the electoral rule and performance to be 0.28. This implies a small positive bias in the OLS estimates; when this bias is corrected, the constitutional effect of majoritarian elections drop toward 1% of GDP and becomes statistically insignificant. A similar result is obtained for presidentialism (column 5), the constitutional effect of which is estimated under the Heckman procedure to be very close to zero.

Overall, relaxing conditional independence suggests weaker constitutional effects. This result partly depends on the sample, however. In the cross section of the 1990s (not reported), the constitutional effect of majoritarian elections remains about 2% and is statistically significant according to the Heckman estimates, just as it is under the OLS estimates.

6.4.3 Matching Estimates

As in sections 6.2 and 6.3, we complement our parametric estimates of constitutional effect with nonparametric estimates obtained using matching methods. Once again, the results rely on two logit specifications of the propensity score estimates. These are identical to the specifications used for government size in section 6.2.3, except that we also include the initial debt level (*CCG_NET_0*). Table 6.8 shows the results for these two specifications and our three matching methods. In the case of presidential regimes, the second (more comprehensive) logit specification predicts too well in our smaller sample of 60 countries, and the remaining observations on the common support are too few for reliable inference. Hence, for this second specification, we report only the estimates of constitutional effects for electoral rule.

The estimates presented in table 6.8 are most directly comparable to those in columns 2, 5, and 6 of table 6.7. Once again, majoritarian elections seem to promote larger surpluses (smaller deficits). The effect is estimated to be between 1% and 2% of GDP, although the effect is not always statistically significant; as already noted, large standard errors are not surprising with this nonparametric method. The estimated effect of presidential regimes fluctuates between being positive and negative and is not in any instance statistically significant.

6.4.4 Summary

All in all, our finding that majoritarian elections lead to smaller government deficits is quite robust to statistical pitfalls. The effect is also economically large: about 2% of GDP. No robust effect on government deficits seems to be present when we compare presidential versus parliamentary forms of government.

6.5 Concluding Remarks

What have we learned in this chapter about the differences between alternative electoral rules and alternative forms of government and their impact on fiscal policy? One important conclusion is that electoral rules exert a strong influence on fiscal policy. Majoritarian elections induce smaller governments, smaller welfare states, and smaller deficits. Estimates of these constitutional effects are not only

Table 6.8
Budget surplus and constitutions: Matching estimates

	(1)	(2)	(3)	(4)	(5)	(6)
Dependent variable	SPL	SPL	SPL	SPL	SPL	SPL
PRES	−0.21		−0.26		0.20	
	(1.17)		(1.43)		(1.01)	
MAJ	1.16	0.78	1.80	1.12	2.11	1.91
	(0.56)**	(0.71)	(0.76)**	(1.28)	(0.82)**	(0.90)**
Method of estimation	Kernel	Kernel	Stratification	Stratification	Nearest neighbor	Nearest neighbor
Sample	1960–1990s,	1960–1990s,	1960–1990s,	1960–1990s,	1960–1990s,	1960–1990s,
	broad	broad	broad	broad	broad	broad
Logit specification	1	2	1	2	1	2
Number of observations	37 PRES	44 MAJ	37 PRES	44 MAJ	37 PRES	44 MAJ
on common support	55 MAJ		55 MAJ		55 MAJ	

Note: Standard errors in parentheses obtained by bootstrapping. Kernel, stratification, and nearest-neighbor estimators described in section 5.5.
Logit specifications underlying the propensity score estimates:
1: LYP, PROP65, GASTIL, FEDERAL, COL_UKA, LAAM, CCG_NET_0
2: LYP, PROP65, GASTIL, FEDERAL, ENGFRAC, EURFRAC, LATO1, CCG_NET_0
* significant at 10%; ** significant at 5%; *** significant at 1%.

statistically significant and robust. They are also quantitatively relevant. For a country drawn at random from our sample—and over a sufficiently long period to neglect transitory effects—a constitutional reform from proportional to majoritarian elections reduces the size of central government spending by 4–5% of GDP, the size of welfare and social security programs by 2–3% of GDP, and the budget deficit by 1–2% of GDP.

These findings are remarkably consistent with the qualitative predictions of existing theory. As discussed in chapter 2, there is no single unified theoretical model of how electoral rules shape fiscal policy. Different authors have emphasized different aspects and implications of electoral rules. But several existing models predict that broad programs with many beneficiaries are larger under proportional elections than under majoritarian elections, and some also predict that proportional elections are associated with larger overall spending and less disciplined fiscal and financial policies. The cross-country evidence uncovered here suggests these theoretical ideas to be on the right track. We have not attempted to discriminate among alternative theories, however, nor have we sought to identify the precise channel through which electoral rules shape fiscal policy. Does the constitutional effect operate through the electoral incentives in two-party electoral competition, as some recent theories have suggested? Or is the electoral rule of importance because it influences party structure and thus the incidence of coalition governments or the average duration of governments? Discriminating among these alternative hypotheses is the next important step in this research program.

Turning to forms of government, our central empirical result is that presidential regimes create considerably smaller governments than parliamentary regimes. A negative constitutional effect of presidential regimes on welfare spending is also present, but it is less robust. Once more, these constitutional effects are quantitatively large and about the same size as those for electoral rules. A reform from parliamentary to presidential regime shrinks the size of overall spending by about 5% of GDP and the size of welfare programs by about 2% of GDP. The effect of such a reform on welfare spending is less precisely estimated, however, perhaps because many presidential regimes have younger populations and it is difficult to separate the effect of the constitution from that of demographics in cross-country comparisons. These fiscal policy effects are in line with our theoretical priors, though the theory of how forms of government shape fiscal policy is less advanced than that for electoral rules. No effect of the form of government on budget deficits is apparent from the data, nor did we expect to find one a priori.

The robustness of some of these findings is remarkable, given the variety of estimation techniques employed in this chapter. Cross-country comparisons are often associated with ambiguous and frag-ile inference. We expected this to be particularly true in our case, given the nonrandom pattern of constitutional forms in our sample and the extensive differences among countries belonging to different constitutional groups. Nevertheless, when it comes to the broad features of fiscal policy investigated in this chapter, constitutional effects do seem robust to the most common econometric pitfalls in cross-sectional analysis. One reason for this robustness might be that the unconditional differences in fiscal policy across constitutional groups are indeed very large. As pointed out in chapter 4, govern-ments in parliamentary countries are larger than in presidential countries by about 11% of GDP; the unconditional difference in government size between proportional and majoritarian countries amounts to about 5% of GDP. The unconditional means of the other fiscal policy variables are also very different across constitutional groups. It is difficult to explain away such large differences on the basis of omitted variables, misspecified functional forms, or other possible econometric pitfalls.

Finally, the cross-country comparisons presented in this chapter have revealed some interesting interactions between formal consti-tutional rules and stages of democracy. The effect of constitutions on welfare spending is stronger in older and better democracies. Con-versely, older and better democracies are associated with larger welfare states, but only under parliamentary-proportional constitu-tions. This effect of stage of democracy on policy outcomes, and its interaction with different constitutional rules, is a theme recurring in the next chapter, where we focus on political rents and economic development. Although they are plausible ex post, we did not expect these findings on the basis of existing theory. They deserve more attention in future research.

7

Political Rents and Productivity: Variation across Countries

7.1 Introduction

In this chapter, we study the effect of constitutions on the size of political rents, on policies promoting economic development, and economic development itself. As explained in chapter 3, political rents are measured in terms of perceptions of corruption and abuse of power by public officials and in terms of perceptions of (in)effectiveness in provision of public services. Economic development is measured by output per worker or total factor productivity and policies toward development by a broad policy indicator of protection of property rights. Since these variables are available only in the second half of the 1990s, or, in the case of labor productivity and policies toward development, from the mid-1980s, we confine our analysis of these variables to comparisons in our 1990s cross section.[1] Throughout, we employ the same battery of estimation methods as in the previous chapter's study of fiscal policy.

The theoretical work reviewed in chapter 2 identifies several channels through which a country's constitution can influence the incidence of corruption and the abuse of power by public officials. Presidential regimes often have greater separation of powers than parliamentary regimes. Moreover, the executive is directly accountable to voters in a presidential regime, and the dilution of responsibility that often plagues coalition governments is not an issue. On these grounds, the theory suggests lower levels of rent extraction

---

1. Our analysis of perceptions of corruption and the electoral rule draws on Persson, Tabellini, and Trebbi 2003, which also studies a short panel of data on perceptions of corruption for which yearly data are available from the mid-1980s until the late 1990s (the source is ICRG). The results of the panel data study confirm the cross-sectional findings reported in this chapter.

and less corruption under presidential regimes as compared to parliamentary forms of government.

When it comes to the electoral rule, the predictions are more subtle. A few papers on rent extraction have focused on the simple distinction between strictly majoritarian and purely proportional electoral systems. Since the outcome of an election is generally more sensitive to the incumbent's performance in the former than in the latter, the prediction is that majoritarian elections are more effective in deterring political rents. But other theoretical studies have emphasized details of electoral rules: ballot structure and number of legislators elected in each district (i.e., district magnitude). Electing politicians from party lists (rather than individually) weakens their incentives for good behavior, because it creates a free-rider problem and a more indirect chain of delegation, from voters to parties to politicians rather than from voters to politicians. Thus ballots on which voters directly choose individual incumbents are predicted to reduce the incidence of corruption, relative to those on which citizens vote on party lists. Smaller electoral districts raise higher barriers to entry, which is predicted to increase corruption by reducing the choice set available to voters. With small districts, a smaller number of parties (or ideological types) are represented in the legislature, leaving voters with fewer alternatives to corrupt politicians or parties. What do these detailed predictions imply for the simple distinction between majoritarian and proportional elections? The answer is ambiguous, since the two effects tend to offset one another: proportional electoral systems typically combine large districts (which decrease corruption) and party list ballots (which increase corruption), whereas majoritarian elections (single-member districts with plurality rule) typically combine small districts (which increase corruption) and voting for individual candidates (which decreases corruption).

In section 7.2, we seek to discriminate among these different hypotheses. Presidential regimes are found to have lower levels of corruption, as expected, but this is a fragile result: it appears only among better democracies or if we relax conditional independence. Turning to electoral rule, we find that what is of importance are the details, not the raw distinction between majoritarian and proportional systems. Large districts and voting over individuals under plurality rule both reduce corruption, as expected. But levels of corruption are roughly the same when we compare across our broad classification into proportional versus majoritarian systems. Evidently, the opposite effects of the ballot structure and district magnitude offset one another, with no robust net effect.

The rest of the chapter tries to identify the effect of constitutions on two ultimate measures of good economic performance, namely, labor and total factor productivity. As discussed in chapter 3, previous studies have found productivity to be well explained by a broad policy indicator of protection of property rights and anti-diversion policies (*GADP*). In this chapter, we ask whether electoral rules or forms of government have an effect on productivity, directly or through this broad policy indicator.

A priori, a country's constitution could influence productivity and policies toward development in that country in several ways. Naturally, one channel for such influence is corruption. Whenever corruption redistributes rents from producers to politicians, it hurts economic development. Hence any constitutional feature that has an impact on corruption is also likely to influence productivity. This suggests that presidentialism, large electoral districts, and ballots for individuals should be associated with better economic policies and higher productivity. There are other possible channels, however, through which these effects may be offset. Small governments and low levels of tax distortion in presidential and majoritarian political systems could induce high productivity by means of inducing high investment. But as discussed in chapters 2 and 6, presidentialism and majoritarian elections could also lead to targeted redistribution and low public-goods provision. Such policies are likely to involve poor general protection of property rights and distortions in the allocation of economic activity, with negative effects on productivity. Overall, constitutional effects on productivity and policies toward development have an ambiguous sign. Hence our empirical work in this chapter is really more of a preliminary search for interesting patterns in the data than a test of specific hypotheses.

In conducting that search, we also try to determine the link between productivity and age of democracy (as measured by *AGE*). The variable *AGE* could also influence performance in two opposite ways. On the one hand, older democratic institutions might perform better, as citizens will have learned to use them effectively in fighting government abuse and corruption. Indeed, a recent empirical "event study" by Roll and Talbott (2002) shows economic growth taking off once a country becomes democratic. On the other hand, according to

Olson (1982), older and more stable democracies are more easily captured by organized special interests, which might hurt their long-run economic performance.

Our empirical results on economic performance are reported in section 7.3. Majoritarian elections at large do not have a robust causal effect on policy or productivity, but the finer details of electoral systems do: voting over individuals and large district magnitude promote productivity-enhancing policy in much the same way as they deter rent extraction. We also find parliamentary regimes and older democracies to select better policies toward economic development, and for this reason, they have higher productivity. But our results also indicate that the negative effect of presidentialism on productivity is mainly due to the worse democracies in our sample. Combining these results with those on corruption, we tentatively conclude that presidentialism reduces rent extraction under better democratic conditions, but it hurts economic performance under worse democratic conditions.

Section 7.4 summarizes the results obtained in the chapter and presents some concluding remarks.

7.2   Political Rents

As discussed in chapter 3, we gauge political rents by means of three alternative measures concerning perceptions of rent extraction. Two of these refer to the perception of corruption by public officials (*GRAFT* and *CPI9500*), the third to (in)effectiveness in the provision of government services (*GOVEF*). As we have the most observations for *GRAFT*, and this variable is probably most closely related to the theoretical construct of political rents, we focus mainly on this indicator, but we show that the results we obtain also extend to the other measures. Our goal in this section is to describe how alternative constitutional features influence the perceptions of rent extraction.

The form of government is measured by our binary indicator for presidentialism (*PRES*). The simple distinction between majoritarian and proportional or mixed electoral systems is measured by the binary variable *MAJ*. In this chapter, however, we also measure more detailed aspects of a country's electoral rule. The continuous variable *MAGN* measures *inverse* average district magnitude (see chapter 4). It captures barriers to entry in electoral races, as it assigns higher values to fewer candidates elected per district, and we expect this variable to be associated with more corruption. The continuous variables *PIND* and *PINDO* measure the percentage of legislators *not* elected from party lists or open party lists (again, chapter 4 gives an exact definition). Thus, they are predicted to induce less corruption. Since the definition of these two variables is similar, we mainly report the results where the ballot structure is measured by *PIND*. But we also discuss what happens when we replace *PIND* with *PINDO* (recall that the main difference between the two is that *PIND* adopts a stricter definition and classifies as individually elected only those legislators elected via an individual ballot under plurality rule, whereas *PINDO* classifies as individually elected also legislators elected via open party lists in proportional elections).

We follow the same empirical strategy in this chapter as in chapter 6: first we estimate some simple regressions, then we relax conditional independence, and finally we relax linearity. The more general estimation methods apply only to the effects of the binary constitutional variables (*MAJ* and *PRES*), however. Hence the analysis of how the details of electoral rule influence rent extraction is confined to the simple linear regressions reported in section 7.2.1.

7.2.1   OLS Estimates

Table 7.1 reports the results of simple regressions estimated under the assumptions of linearity and conditional independence. To help reduce the noise from measurement error, the estimation method is always weighted least squares, where the weights are given by the (inverse) standard deviation of the dependent variable (see chapter 3 for more details). Estimating by means of OLS and correcting the standard errors for heteroscedasticty produces very similar results. Throughout this section, we hold constant a dozen variables that other studies have found to influence perception of corruption, such as per capita income, religious beliefs, and education (see chapter 3 for discussion and references, and the notes to table 7.1 for a complete list of the controls). We also hold constant continental location and colonial origin. Controlling for legal origin instead of colonial origin leads to similar or stronger estimated constitutional effects, meaning that we report the specification that is least favorable for the theory discussed in chapter 2.

We consider first the effect of form of government on rent extraction. In column 1 of the table, rent extraction is measured by *GRAFT*, and constitutional features are measured by the binary

Table 7.1
Political rents and constitutions: Simple regression estimates

	(1)	(2)	(3)	(4)	(5)
Dependent variable	GRAFT	GRAFT	GRAFT	GRAFT	GRAFT
PRES	−0.52	−0.79	−1.41	−0.27	−0.53
	(0.30)*	(0.38)**	(0.68)**	(0.30)	(0.31)*
PRES_BAD			0.35		
			(0.24)		
MAJ					−0.24
					(0.62)
PIND	−2.12	−2.88	−2.10		−1.83
	(0.76)***	(0.85)***	(0.75)***		(1.06)*
PINDO				−0.57	
				(0.29)**	
MAGN	2.72	3.53	2.61	0.86	2.63
	(0.87)***	(0.95)***	(0.86)***	(0.41)**	(0.90)***
SPROPN					
SDM					
Continents and colonies	Yes	Yes	Yes	Yes	Yes
Sample	1990s, broad	1990s, narrow	1990s, broad	1990s, broad	1990s, broad
Number of observations	78	59	78	78	78
Adjusted R^2	0.84	0.87	0.84	0.83	0.84

Note: Standard errors in parentheses. Estimation: by weighted least squares. Weights for dependent variable is $1/\text{std(depvar)}$. All regressions include the following controls: GASTIL, AGE, LYP, LPOP, EDUGER, TRADE, OECD, FEDERAL, AVELF, PROT80, CATHO80, and CONFU. Narrow sample consists of countries where GASTIL is less than 3.5.
*significant at 10%; **significant at 5%; ***significant at 1%.

variable for presidentialism (PRES) and two continuous measures for the electoral rule (PIND and MAGN). Presidentialism has a negative estimated effect on rent extraction, as expected. But its estimated coefficient is significant only at the 10% level and is small in absolute value (recall that all our measures of corruption vary from 0 to 10). Disregarding columns 2 and 3 for a moment, the estimated coefficient of presidentialism is insignificant in all the other columns of table 7.1, in which rent extraction is measured by the other two perception variables, CPI9500 and GOVEF, or the electoral rule is measured by other indicators such as SPROPN, SDM, or MAJ.

Table 7.1
(continued)

	(6)	(7)	(8)	(9)	(10)
Dependent variable	GRAFT	CPI9500	GOVEF	GRAFT	GRAFT
PRES	−0.42	−0.27	−0.30	−0.04	−0.28
	(0.31)	(0.43)	(0.35)	(0.30)	(0.32)
PRES_BAD					
MAJ	−0.81				−0.14
	(0.46)*				(0.31)
PIND		−2.88	−2.01		
		(1.02)***	(0.87)**		
PINDO	−0.45				
	(0.29)				
MAGN	1.51	3.39	2.14		
	(0.54)***	(1.14)***	(1.01)**		
SPROPN				1.25	
				(0.47)**	
SDM				−0.01	
				(0.00)**	
Continents and colonies	Yes	Yes	Yes	Yes	Yes
Sample	1990s, broad	1990s, broad	1990s, broad	1990s, broad	1990s, broad
Number of observations	78	68	78	72	78
Adjusted R^2	0.83	0.88	0.75	0.87	0.81

A possible interpretation of this inconclusive finding on the effect of form of government on rent extraction is that our measure of presidentialism does not square well with the theory. As discussed in chapter 4, our distinction between different forms of government relies on the confidence requirement, and not on the separation of powers. Yet according to the theories reviewed in chapter 2, presidential governments reduce political rents mainly because they have greater separation of powers than parliamentary governments.

But columns 2 and 3 of the table suggest another possibility: an interaction between form of government and quality of democracy. Presidential regimes are often found in worse and younger democracies, where formal constitutional rules might be less important and the stronger checks and balances associated with presidentialism might not exert their full effect. Indeed, as shown in column 2, presidentialism has a negative and significant effect on corruption, once

we restrict the sample to better democracies. In column 3, we interact the *PRES* indicator with quality of democracy (as measured
by *GASTIL*) in the full sample. The estimated coefficient of presidentialism increases further and acquires a stronger statistical significance, but its effect is dampened in worse democracies (recall that
higher values of *GASTIL* correspond to worse democracies).

A third possibility is a combination of the other two. It may be that
separation of powers is lacking precisely in the worst democracies.
Indeed, as discussed in chapter 4, the *GASTIL* measure partly reflects
whether there are effective checks on the behavior of the executive.

Next, we consider the effect of electoral rules on rent extraction.
The data strongly support the idea that the details of the electoral
rule in a particular country are important determinants of rent
extraction in that country. As shown in the first two columns of table
7.1, inverse district magnitude and ballots with individuals elected
under plurality rule are statistically significant with the expected
sign: more individual voting by plurality rule (higher values of
PIND) reduces corruption, whereas higher barriers to entry associated with smaller districts (higher values of *MAGN*) increase corruption. This result is robust to the sample of better democracies
(column 2, i.e., those with a *GASTIL* score smaller than 3.5). Moreover, the estimated coefficients of *PIND* and *MAGN* are large (both
variables are defined so that they lie between 0 and 1), and their
standardized beta coefficients are, by far, the largest of all the regressors. For example, switching from a system in which all legislators
are elected on party lists ($PIND = 0$) to one in which all are elected as
individuals ($PIND = 1$) is estimated to reduce perceptions of corruption by well over 20% (2 points out of 10) in the sample of good
democracies, which is about twice the effect on corruption of *not*
being a Latin American country. The estimated effect of inverse district magnitude (also taking positive values below 1) is even larger,
though it is somewhat less stable with regard to the specification.
Omitting the dummy variables for continental location and colonial
origin does not affect the coefficient of *PIND* in any important way,
though the coefficient of *MAGN* becomes somewhat smaller when
these variables are omitted and remains statistically significant only
at the 10% level. Finally, these variables are not only individually,
but also jointly, significant. Given the high correlation between these
two variables and their opposite effect on corruption, this is a further
sign that we are not just picking up a statistical artifact.

Column 4 replaces *PIND* with *PINDO* as an alternative measure of individual voting. With this substitution, the estimated coefficient drops a great deal in absolute value, although it remains significantly different from 0. This suggests that it is really plurality rule (and the associated absence of a free-rider problem) that strengthens individual incentives for good behavior, rather than the possibility of holding politicians individually accountable via open party lists. Note that the estimated coefficient of district magnitude (*MAGN*) is also affected by this different specification, although it remains statistically significant.

To shed further light on how the details of electoral rules influence corruption, columns 5 and 6 add to the specification the dummy variable for majoritarian elections, *MAJ*. As discussed in chapter 4, this variable is coded as 1 for countries that rely exclusively on plurality rule and 0 otherwise. Thus, the variable *MAJ* is a binary variable for the electoral formula. As such, it is highly correlated with the ballot structure as measured by *PIND* (the correlation coefficient is 0.93) as well as with district magnitude, *MAGN*, since most countries with strictly majoritarian elections also have single member districts (the correlation coefficient between *MAJ* and *MAGN* is 0.87). The correlation between *MAJ* and *PINDO* is lower (0.68), however, because the variable *PINDO* not only classifies countries on the basis of plurality rule, but also on the basis of open versus closed lists. When the continuous indicators of individual voting under plurality rule (*PIND*) and of district magnitude (*MAGN*) are included (the specification in column 5), the binary variable for majoritarian elections (*MAJ*) does not have any additional explanatory power. But if the ballot structure is instead measured by *PINDO*, which measures individual accountability irrespective of the electoral formula, then (cf. column 6) the binary indicator *MAJ* gains significance, presumably picking up the effect on corruption due to the electoral formula; on the other hand, the estimated coefficient of *PINDO* drops further in value and becomes statistically insignificant. Similarly, when both *PIND* and *PINDO* are included in the same regression, only the coefficient of *PIND* is significantly different from zero (results not reported). As our alternative measures of electoral rules are highly correlated with each other, we cannot be too demanding of these cross-sectional data. Nevertheless, columns 5 and 6 confirm the interpretation that it is really the combination of the ballot structure and the electoral formula that deters corruption. The possibility of holding individual politicians accountable through open lists seems a less powerful deterrent than individual ballots associated with plurality rule. (Persson, Tabellini, and Trebbi [2003] contains a further investigation of how different aspects of the electoral system affect the incidence of corruption and [in]effectiveness and also exploits the time variation in the data associated with electoral reforms in the 1990s.)

Because it is a survey of surveys, the dependent variable is clearly measured with error. This is the rationale for our weighted least squares estimation, which attaches lower weights to observations in which the different components of the perception index are more divergent. In columns 7–10 of table 7.1, we carry out additional sensitivity analyses, with alternative measures for our dependent and independent variables. Columns 7 and 8 report on the same specification as in column 1, but with either *CPI9500* or *GOVEF* as the dependent variable. The results are even stronger than those in column 1 when we measure corruption using *CPI9500*, and they are almost as strong as those in column 1 when we instead consider *GOVEF*, measuring ineffectiveness in government (recall from section 3.3 that we have rescaled all these measures to run on a scale from 0 to 10). Column 9 replaces our own two measures of the electoral system with the alternatives from the data set constructed by Seddon et al. (2001) and defined in chapter 4. Recall that *SDM* is Seddon et al.'s measure of district size, defined so that higher values mean larger districts, not smaller as with our variable *MAGN*. Similarly, *SPROPN*, their measure of legislators elected at the national level, is an inverted measure of individual accountability, and not a direct measure like our *PIND* variable. Thus, the expected sign of these two variables is the opposite of *MAGN* and *PIND*. As shown in column 9, the main results hold up equally well with these alternative measures.

Overall, these simple regressions strongly suggest that the details of electoral rules influence corruption as expected. Countries predominantly voting over individuals tend to have less corruption than those predominantly voting over parties. Countries with smaller electoral districts also tend to have more corruption. According to these results, a comprehensive electoral reform, going from a Dutch-style electoral system with party lists in a single national constituency to a U.K.-style system with first past the post in one-member districts (i.e., moving both *MAGN* and *PIND* from approximately 0 to approximately 1), would have two counteracting effects on corruption, producing a net result close to zero. A better reform from the viewpoint of reducing rent extraction would be to switch to plurality rule voting for individuals, but retaining districts with more than one member as in Chile (two-member districts and $MAGN = 0.5$) or Mauritius (three-member districts and $MAGN = 0.33$). Indeed, these countries, especially Chile, turn out to have very low corruption levels as compared to neighboring countries.[2]

Another way of determining the effects of a comprehensive electoral reform from proportional to majoritarian elections is to infer the constitutional effect from the estimated coefficient of our binary indicator for electoral rule, MAJ. This issue is of independent interest, since according to some models reviewed in chapter 2, majoritarian electoral systems enhance electoral accountability and thus deter corruption. The result is shown in column 10 of table 7.1, where the specification includes only the variable MAJ, but drops all other continuous measures of electoral rules. Since the binary variable MAJ is highly correlated with both district magnitude and voting on individuals under plurality rule, a specification that includes only this variable estimates the effect of switching from a purely majoritarian system with plurality voting in single-member districts to a proportional (or mixed) electoral system with large districts. The distinction between mixed and proportional systems, and the corresponding details of electoral rules, are thus assumed to be irrelevant. Of course, to the extent that this assumption is false, the equation with only the binary indicator MAJ is misspecified, and its estimated coefficient could reflect an omitted-variable bias. The estimated MAJ coefficient is negative, but small and statistically insignificant. The estimated MAJ coefficient increases somewhat in absolute value and becomes marginally significant if we do not control for colonial origin (results not reported). As noted in chapter 4, majoritarian electoral rules are often found in former British colonies, and it is difficult to tell the influence of electoral rules and colonial history

---

2. There is however a caveat, due to an important fragility in the estimates reported in table 7.1. As noted in chapter 4, Chile's electoral system is hard to classify. Unfortunately, this single observation and our classification matter for our results. If we drop Chile from the sample, or reclassify its electoral system so that $PIND = 0$ (rather than 1), the estimated effects of the electoral variables on corruption become less precisely estimated and lose significance. Chile is not the only outlier observation, however, and dropping Chile together with other influential observations does not significantly affect the results reported in table 7.1.

apart (when we control for continents or legal origin, the constitutional effect remains negative and statistically significant, so it is really colonial origin that makes a difference). But to interpret the estimate of a regression that does not control for British colonial origin as a causal constitutional effect, we would need to assume that colonial origin has no effect on perceptions of corruption, which is not very plausible.

7.2.2 Instrumental-Variables and Heckman Estimates

We attempt to relax conditional independence only for the binary constitutional indicators (MAJ and $PRES$). In principle, continuous measures of electoral rules (such as $PIND$ and $MAGN$) might also be correlated with the random component of rent extraction, which would bias OLS estimates. But the Heckman procedure cannot be applied to continuous variables. Instrumental-variables estimates are also problematic, because our instruments for constitutional origin are unlikely to be appropriate for such estimates. The finer measures of electoral system change more frequently than the simpler classification into majoritarian and presidential constitutions, so it would be more difficult to date them back to specific historical periods. Thus, in this section, we apply instrumental variable estimation and the Heckman procedure only to the binary variables MAJ and $PRES$. The caveat in section 7.2.1, about possible specification bias due to the omission of our continuous measures of electoral rules, should be kept in mind.

With our standard specification (colonies and continents included in the second stage), the two-step Heckman procedures yield estimates of the correlation coefficient (rho) of $+1$ or -1, suggesting a perfect correlation between the error terms for constitution selection and performance. As this is implausible, we instead perform the Heckman correction with a maximum-likelihood estimator. To achieve convergence of the maximization algorithm, however, we must impose more parsimonious first-step and second-step specifications for both constitutional variables, as compared to the specification adopted in chapter 6. Specifically, when estimating the first-step (probit) regressions, we drop the indicator variables for constitutional origin ($CON2150$, $CON5180$, and $CON81$); the remainder of the specification is as in chapter 6 (see also the discussion in chapter 5). In the second step, we include only the dummy variables for U.K. colonial origin and Latin America, in addition to all the standard controls, omitting the other continental and colonial-origin indicators.

Instrumental-variables estimation is also performed in a slightly different way compared to chapter 6. Our instruments are still the same as those discussed in chapter 5 and used in chapter 6: the three indicators for constitutional origin (CON2150, CON5180, and CON81), latitude (LAT01), and the fractions of the population whose mother tongue is English or a European language (ENGFRAC and EURFRAC, respectively). But in this chapter we move in the opposite direction and adopt a less parsimonious first-stage specification than in chapter 6: we now run the first-stage regression of the two-stage least squares estimates on the full set of the six instruments plus all controls entering the second-stage regression (see table 7.2 for a

Table 7.2
Political rents and constitutions: Instrumental-variable and Heckman estimates

	(1)	(2)	(3)	(4)	(5)
Dependent variable	GRAFT	GRAFT	GRAFT	GOVEF	CPI9500
PRES	−1.28	−0.50	−1.89	−1.47	−2.16
	(0.44)***	(0.28)*	(0.83)**	(0.83)*	(1.32)
MAJ	−0.18	0.30	0.31	−0.26	0.46
	(0.26)	(0.66)	(0.61)	(0.64)	(0.98)
Endogenous selection	PRES	MAJ	PRES MAJ	PRES MAJ	PRES MAJ
Method of estimation	Heckman ML	Heckman ML	2SLS	2SLS	2SLS
Rho	0.57***	−0.49			
	(0.17)	(0.58)			
Chi-square: over-id			3.08	2.97	2.49
Sample	1990s, broad	1990s, broad	1990s, broad	1990s, broad	1990s, broad
Number of observations	73	73	73	73	63
Adjusted R^2			0.75	0.68	0.75

Note: Standard errors in parentheses. Always included in performance equations: GASTIL, AGE, LYP, LPOP, EDUGER, TRADE, OECD, FEDERAL, AVELF, PROT80, CATHO80, CONFU, LAAM, and COL_UKA. 2SLS first-stage specification includes CON2150, CON5180, CON81, LAT01, ENGFRAC, and EURFRAC, plus all controls in performance equations. "Chi-square over-id" refers to the test statistic for the over-identifying restriction that the instruments in the first-stage regressions underlying columns 1 and 2 do not enter the performance equations. Critical value of $\chi^2(4, 0.05)$ is 9.49. Heckman probit specification includes LAAM, COL_UKA, LAT01, ENGFRAC, EURFRAC, and AGE.
*significant at 10%; **significant at 5%; ***significant at 1%.

complete list). Several of the second-stage controls now measure historical and social variables, such as religious beliefs or ethnic fractionalization, which could also influence constitutional selection. Excluding such controls from the first stage, if they belong there, might bias the two-stage least squares estimates of constitutional effect. Furthermore, adding the full set of controls to the first stage now *increases* the explanatory power of the dummy variables dating constitutional origin and thus reduces our concern about weak instruments.[3] For both these reasons, the inference is more reliable with a less parsimonious first-stage specification.

Consider the constitutional effect for presidentialism. The Heckman procedure (column 1) produces a positive and highly significant estimate (rho = 0.57) of the correlation between selection of a presidential regime and corruption. Correcting the upward bias in the OLS estimates, the constitutional effect is a reduction in corruption/rent extraction by about 1 point (out of 10), a statistically significant and nontrivial effect. The two-stage least squares estimates (column 3) yield the same result, namely, a large and statistically significant effect of presidentialism on corruption. The fact that both estimators produce similar results, despite the different identification assumptions, suggests that a violation of conditional independence could indeed bias the OLS estimates toward zero. As shown by columns 4 and 5, there is a negative effect when we replace *GRAFT* with the two alternative measures of rent extraction (*GOVEF* and *CPI9500*, respectively).

For majoritarian elections, we reach the opposite conclusion with regard to bias. The estimated correlation coefficient in column 2 is negative (rho = −0.47), though imprecisely estimated, and the constitutional effect is now positive, although insignificant (i.e., a sign reversal relative to the OLS estimates). Once more, the instrumental-variables estimation in columns 3–5 reinforces the conclusion about bias.

Thus, addressing conditional independence does make a difference in the case of estimating constitutional effects on corruption. The OLS estimates suggested no effect (or a negative but small and fragile effect) of government regimes and majoritarian elections on corruption. The conclusion regarding the form of government is reversed

---

3. The *F*-tests of the null hypothesis that all instruments dating constitutional origin have a zero coefficient in the first-stage regressions for presidentialism and majoritarian elections yield the test statistics $F = 3.06$ and $F = 2.26$, respectively.

Table 7.3
Political rents and constitutions: Matching estimates

	(1)	(2)	(3)	(4)	(5)	(6)
Dependent variable	GRAFT	GRAFT	GRAFT	CPI9500	GOVEF	GRAFT
PRES	0.52	0.06	0.02	0.19	0.63	0.73
	(0.44)	(1.94)	(0.41)	(0.63)	(0.47)	(0.59)
MAJ	−0.23	−0.46	−0.25	−0.39	−0.23	−0.26
	(0.49)	(0.54)	(0.38)	(0.74)	(0.48)	(0.43)
Method of estimation	Kernel	Stratification	Nearest neighbor	Kernel	Kernel	Kernel
Sample	1990s, broad	1990s, broad	1990s, broad	1990s, broad	1990s, broad	1990s, broad
Logit specification	1	1	1	1	1	2
Number of observations on common support	64 PRES 69 MAJ	64 PRES 69 MAJ	64 PRES 69 MAJ	46 PRES 57 MAJ	64 PRES 69 MAJ	48 PRES 58 MAJ

Note: Standard errors in parentheses obtained by bootstrapping. Kernel, stratification, and nearest-neighbor estimators described in section 5.5. Logit specifications underlying estimated propensity scores:
    1: LYP, GASTIL, AVELF, PROT80, COL_UKA, LAAM
    2: LYP, GASTIL, AVELF, PROT80, ENGFRAC, EURFRAC, LAT01

when allowance is made for conditional independence. Presidential regimes are found to reduce corruption, and for majoritarian elections, the inference of no constitutional effect is reinforced.

7.2.3 Matching Estimates

We end our discussion with the nonparametric estimates, reimposing the conditional independence assumption. Because our matching methodology requires a binary variable, we report only results for the two simple constitutional indicators (MAJ and PRES). Columns 1–3 of table 7.3 show the constitutional effects on rent extraction as measured by GRAFT, according to our three matching estimators. The specification of the propensity score includes a basic set of six covariates (LYP, GASTIL, AVELF, PROT80, COL_UKA and LAAM). In columns 4 and 5, GRAFT is replaced by the two alternative measures (CPI9500 and GOVEF, respectively) for the same logit specification and the kernel estimator. Column 6, finally, maintains GRAFT as the dependent variable but relies on a different propensity score specification.

The results can be stated briefly. The presidential effect now becomes positive, though it is in all cases statistically insignificant and small. The effect of majoritarian elections is in all cases negative but not significant. In neither case is the estimate very stable, and in other (nonreported) specifications, the sign of both effects changes, though it in all cases remains small and insignificant. Overall, these estimates suggest that neither constitutional feature has a robust effect on corruption. Our conjecture that the linear OLS estimates of presidential effect were hiding a potentially relevant interaction between form of government and quality of democracy does not seem supported by this more general estimation method, which allows for nonlinear functional forms. Note, however, that we do impose conditional independence.

7.2.4 Summary
The overall picture emerging from this section is multidimensional. Presidential regimes do not have a stable effect on political rents under the maintained assumption of conditional independence (required by OLS and matching), except in better democracies. Relaxing conditional independence seems empirically important, however, and produces a negative constitutional effect.

With regard to the electoral rule, the central empirical result is that the devil is in the details. Larger electoral districts seem to cut rent extraction, as do elections in which voters cast their ballots for individual politicians under plurality rule rather than party lists under PR. From the perspective of a radical reform from proportional to majoritarian elections, these two aspects of the electoral system tend to offset one another, with no net effect on corruption, a result confirmed by the estimates associated with our binary indicator for plurality rule.

7.3 Productivity

In this section, we search for constitutional effects on two ultimate measures of economic performance, namely, labor productivity (i.e., output per worker, *LOGYL*) and total factor productivity (*LOGA*). The main difference between these two measures is that labor productivity largely reflects underlying capital intensity and thus previous capital accumulation, whereas total factor productivity does not. We first estimate a *direct* constitutional effect on these two variables, using a reduced form similar to that in the existing literature on cross-country productivity differences. It is important to probe beyond any reduced-form findings, however. Specifically, do our constitutional variables explain a broad policy indicator of protection of property rights and antidiversion policies (*GADP*) that previous studies have found to be an important determinant of productivity? (See chapter 3 and Hall and Jones 1999 for a precise definition and discussion.) Do such *indirect* constitutional effects on productivity operate through the policies studied earlier in this chapter and the previous one, namely, size and composition of government spending or corruption? Are higher productivity and better economic policies related to age of democracy? Are the estimates robust to endogenous selection of the constitution and nonlinearities in the outcome relation?

7.3.1   Reduced-Form Estimates

We begin by estimating a simple reduced form using OLS, with the two productivity measures as our dependent variables. The underlying specification is the same as in chapter 3, which, in turn, follows Hall and Jones 1999 closely. Thus, we control for latitude (*LAT01*), the fractions of the population speaking English or a European language (*ENGFRAC* and *EURFRAC*, respectively), a measure of comparative advantage in international trade (*FRANKROM*), and our indicator for federalism (*FEDERAL*). To these regressors we add our usual constitutional variables plus the age of democracy (*AGE*). We always hold constant continental location and colonial origin to lend more credibility to the conditional-independence assumption (when we omit these indicator variables, we obtain stronger estimated constitutional effects, with the same signs as those described below).

Columns 1 and 2 of table 7.4 show that both presidential regimes and majoritarian elections have a negative coefficient: according to the reduced-form estimates presented in these two columns, both constitutional features harm economic performance. Their effect on total factor productivity is smaller and not statistically significant, suggesting that the negative effects might operate through disincentives for capital deepening (i.e., investments in physical or human capital). The variation in total factor productivity is also harder to explain (the regression in column 2 explains about 50% of the variation in productivity, as opposed to about 70% in column 1),

Table 7.4
Productivity and constitutions: Reduced-form estimates

	(1)	(2)	(3)	(4)	(5)	(6)
Dependent variable	LOGYL	LOGA	LOGYL	LOGA	LOGYL	LOGYL
PRES	−0.29 (0.16)*	−0.21 (0.15)	−0.09 (0.17)	−0.09 (0.14)	−0.08 (0.18)	0.08 (0.20)
MAJ	−0.29 (0.15)*	−0.15 (0.11)			−0.13 (0.20)	
PIND			0.78 (0.28)***	0.47 (0.29)		0.60 (0.25)**
MAGN			−1.18 (0.34)***	−0.74 (0.36)**		−0.62 (0.35)*
AGE	1.05 (0.38)***	0.68 (0.34)**	0.83 (0.35)**	0.54 (0.32)	0.51 (0.26)*	0.42 (0.24)*
Continents and colonies	Yes	Yes	Yes	Yes	Yes	Yes
Method of estimation	OLS	OLS	OLS	OLS	OLS	OLS
Sample	1990s, broad	1990s, broad	1990s, broad	1990s, broad	1990s, narrow	1990s, narrow
Number of observations	74	73	73	72	56	55
Adjusted R^2	0.73	0.50	0.76	0.52	0.69	0.73

Note: Robust standard errors in parentheses. Other controls always included: *FEDERAL, LAT01, ENGFRAC, EURFRAC,* and *FRANKROM.* Narrow sample consists of countries where *GASTIL* is less than 3.5.
* significant at 10%; ** significant at 5%; *** significant at 1%.

probably because of larger measurement error. To gauge the size of the constitutional effect, recall that labor productivity is expressed in logarithms and ranges from a maximum of about 10.5 for the United States to a minimum of about 7 for Malawi. According to the estimates in column 1, switching from parliamentarism to presidentialism or from proportional to majoritarian elections reduces labor productivity by about 0.3, a nontrivial effect close to the difference between the United States and the United Kingdom, or between Spain and Greece, in the mid-1980s.

Columns 3 and 4 decompose the effect of electoral rules in the same two dimensions as in the previous section, namely, the fractions of legislators elected with an individual vote under plurality rule (*PIND*) and (the inverse of) district magnitude (*MAGN*). Our previous results for rent extraction lead us to expect positive and

negative effects on productivity, respectively, from these two variables. Effects with these signs are indeed what we find. Moreover, the
estimated coefficients are statistically significant and quite large. In
these regressions, however, the effect of the form of government
seems to vanish.

The constitutional effect on labor productivity of presidential
regimes and majoritarian elections is sensitive to the sample of
countries: a significant estimate is obtained in the broader sample,
but not among the better democracies (column 5). This sensitivity
does not extend to the finer measures of the electoral system (*PIND*
and *MAGN*), however, which remain statistically significant when
we restrict the sample to the better democracies (column 6). In the
case of total factor productivity, none of the constitutional variables
is statistically significant in the narrow sample, and the fit of the
regression is generally rather poor.

If the measure of ballot structure *PIND* is replaced by our alternative measure based on the distinction between open and closed lists,
PINDO, the results are much weaker. The variable *PINDO* is never
statistically significant, and the estimated coefficient of district magnitude (*MAGN*) drops (although it generally remains statistically
significant). This is consistent with the earlier results on corruption,
where we also found to be stronger with *PIND* than with *PINDO*. If
the ballot structure really shapes individual incentives of politicians,
the effect seems to be associated with the free-rider problem under
PR, rather than with voters not being able to rank candidates on
closed party lists.

As shown in all columns of the table, age of democracy (*AGE*) is
strongly correlated with economic performance. Older democracies
are more productive, and the effect is statistically significant for all
measures of productivity, all specifications, and almost all samples.

The reduced-form estimates presented in table 7.4 indicate some
intriguing constitutional effects on productivity, over and beyond
the historical, geographic, and cultural variables held constant in
these regressions. Presidential and majoritarian countries seem to
have lower levels of productivity, particularly in worse democracies,
and the specific form of the electoral system also seems to be of
importance for productivity. To gain more insights into the channels
through which these constitutional effects operate, we need to estimate a more structural model, one that maps our constitutional

measures onto observable policies and these policies onto productivity. Section 7.3.2 attempts to make some progress on this nontrivial task.

7.3.2 Structural-Form Estimates

Do constitutional effects on productivity operate exclusively through the comprehensive policy indicator of antidiversion policies (*GADP*)? Answering this question requires that we break it up into two parts: (1) is there a constitutional effect on this broad policy indicator? (2) are there direct constitutional effects not going through this indicator, thus reflecting other policy channels?[4]

Column 1 of table 7.5 addresses subquestion (1) using OLS estimation (retaining the assumption of conditional independence) and a specification that follows the reduced form of table 7.4. Thus we control for the age of democracy and our indicators for federalism, colonial origin, and continental location, plus the four Hall-Jones variables mentioned in section 7.3.1. Recall that higher values of the policy indicator (*GADP*) equate to better policies and that the values range from about 0.3 (for Bangladesh) to 1 (for Switzerland). As expected from the reduced-form estimates, parliamentary regimes have better policies, with the effect being quite substantial. Age of democracy is also statistically significant, with older democracies having much better policies. But in the current specification, the broad form of the electoral rule does not seem to be of importance.

Next we ask whether the antidiversion policy indicator has an effect on productivity. The effect is estimated using two-stage least squares; policy is endogenized in the first stage with the specification underlying column 1. The second-stage productivity equations reported in columns 2 and 3 still include colonial-origin and continental variables, but no other variables. Thus the instruments for *GADP* are the same as those used by Hall and Jones (1999), plus our four constitutional variables: the dummy variables for presidentialism, majoritarian elections, federalism, and age of democracy.

---

4. As discussed in chapter 3, Hall and Jones (1999) argue that two policy variables could account for cross-country differences in productivity. One is the indicator of antidiversion policies (*GADP*), the other an indicator of commercial policy (*YRSOPEN*). The effect of commercial policy on productivity is not robust, however, and disappears when we include dummy variables for continents and colonial origin. We omit it from the analysis of this chapter, since it is almost never statistically significant.

Table 7.5
Productivity and constitutions: Structural-form estimates

	(1)	(2)	(3)	(4)	(5)	(6)	(7)
Dependent variable	GADP	LOGYL	LOGA	LOGYL	LOGA	GADP	LOGYL
GADP		3.51 (0.50)***	2.35 (0.58)***	3.24 (0.54)***	2.00 (0.58)***		3.65 (0.55)***
PRES	−0.10 (0.03)***					−0.06 (0.03)*	
MAJ	0.02 (0.04)			−0.38 (0.13)***	−0.22 (0.15)		−0.40 (0.13)***
AGE	0.33 (0.06)***					0.32 (0.05)***	
PIND						0.21 (0.07)***	
MAGN						−0.20 (0.09)**	
Continents and colonies	Yes	Yes	Yes	Yes	Yes	Yes	Yes
Method of estimation	OLS	2SLS	2SLS	2SLS	2SLS	OLS	2SLS
Chi-square: over-id		10.51	7.46	1.04	1.95		4.65
Sample	1990s, broad	1990s, broad	1990s, broad	1990s, broad	1990s, broad	1990s, broad	1990s, broad
Number of observations	73	73	73	73	73	72	72
Adjusted R^2	0.74	0.81	0.49	0.83	0.53	0.79	0.83

Note: Robust standard errors in parentheses. Other first-stage regressors (columns 1 and 5): *LAT01, ENGFRAC, EURFRAC, FRANKROM,* and *FEDERAL.* Other second-stage regressors (columns 4, 5, and 7 only): *ENGFRAC* and *EURFRAC.* "Chi-square over-id" refers to the test statistic for the overidentifying restriction that the instruments in the first-stage regressions do not enter the performance equations in columns 2–5 and 7. The critical value (at the 10% level) in the specification underlying columns 2 and 3 is 10.64.
* significant at 10%; ** significant at 5%; *** significant at 1%.

The identifying assumption is that these instruments affect productivity only through the policy indicator *GADP*. According to the results in columns 2 and 3, policy has a positive and significant effect on both productivity measures. The coefficients are roughly the same as those obtained in Hall and Jones 1999 and chapter 3, with a larger impact on labor productivity than on total factor productivity. Together with the first-stage estimates, this result suggests that parliamentary regimes and older democracies have higher levels of productivity, because they promote better policies, as summarized by the *GADP* indicator.

As can be seen from columns 2 and 3, however, the overidentification restrictions for the instruments are almost rejected at the 10% level of significance. Some of the variables entering in the first-stage regressions of column 1 may thus have a direct effect on productivity that is not captured by our policy indicator, answering subquestion (2) above. It turns out that three instruments are responsible for this behavior. The main culprit is the dummy variable for majoritarian elections (*MAJ*), but the fractions of the population whose mother tongue is English or a European language (*ENGFRAC* and *EURFRAC*, respectively) also play some role. When these three variables are added to the second-stage regressions reported in columns 4 and 5, the test statistic for the overidentifying restrictions stay very comfortably within the acceptance range. Moreover, the direct effect of majoritarian elections on productivity is negative and, in the case of labor productivity, significantly different from zero. Majoritarian elections thus seem to diminish productivity through some other policy channel that is not captured by the indicator of antidiversion policies.

To shed some further light on the role played by the electoral system, we respecify the first-stage equation for the antidiversion policy indicator, *GADP*, replacing the binary indicator for majoritarian elections with our two continuous measures. Both influence policy choice as expected: a greater number of individually elected legislators leads to better policies (*PIND* has a positive coefficient in column 6), as does a larger district size (*MAGN* has a negative coefficient). Thus electoral system seems to influence policy choices, but only through its finer details, a result entirely in line with the rent extraction results obtained in section 7.2. Nonetheless, the second-stage regressions reported in column 7 reveal that even with this alternative first-stage specification, majoritarian elections still have a direct effect on productivity.

In light of these last results, it is natural to ask whether the policies discussed in the previous section and the previous chapter—rent extraction and the size and composition of government spending— affect economic performance, and whether such an effect could explain the direct impact of majoritarian elections on productivity. The short answer is probably not. None of the other policy measures is significant in the second-stage regression for labor productivity as long as the comprehensive policy indicator $GADP$ is included, whereas the coefficient on $GADP$ is basically immune to the inclusion of these other policy measures.

But the long answer may be worth spelling out. The other policy measures do have an impact on productivity if we omit antidiversion policies ($GADP$) from the productivity regression.[5] First, as might be expected, corruption (measured by $GRAFT$) has a negative effect on labor productivity. But majoritarian elections still have a direct effect, and it is even stronger and more precisely estimated than that in table 7.5. Moreover, the measures of corruption and antidiversion policies are highly correlated (a correlation coefficient of -0.87) and thus probably measure similar aspects of policy-making. Second, size of government ($CGEXP$) and welfare spending (SSW) also appear as determinants of productivity, with a positive and significant estimated coefficient. This effect is particularly robust for welfare spending. It is difficult to see why welfare spending should improve productivity, and the fragility of the result to the inclusion of the policy indicator $GADP$ also suggests that we should play it down. But when both antidiversion policies and welfare spending are included as determinants of productivity, the direct effect of majoritarian elections on productivity disappears, and the overidentifying restrictions can no longer be rejected. This suggests a possible interpretation. According to the theories reviewed in chapter 2, majoritarian regimes have less welfare spending but also less public-goods provision, and the latter hurts productivity. If welfare spending and public-goods provision are indeed positively correlated across countries, evidence of a direct constitutional effect of

---

5. Naturally, these variables like the indicator $GADP$, are treated as endogenous. In the case of the fiscal policy variables, the first-stage regressors include the same specification for $GADP$, plus the proportion of elderly in the population ($PROP65$).

majoritarian elections on productivity should be dampened when we also control for welfare spending.

Before we claim too much, however, we should follow the approach of the earlier sections and ask whether the results are robust to relaxing conditional independence.

7.3.3 Endogenous Selection

Relaxing conditional independence is somewhat more difficult here than in earlier sections, as we have added another level of relations: endogenously selected institutions influence policies that, in turn, influence productivity. We therefore break our estimation problem into three parts.

First, we want to estimate the constitutional effect on the policy indicator *GADP*, allowing for endogenous constitutional selection. In section 7.2 we used six instruments for the constitution: the three dummy variables dating constitutional origin, plus three of Hall and Jones's (1999) variables (latitude and the fractions of the population with English or European language as their mother tongue). As discussed in chapters 4 and 5, the last three instruments have more power in explaining constitution selection than the timing instruments. But in the present context, these variables have a direct impact on the policy indicator *GADP* and perhaps also on productivity, so we cannot credibly assume that they affect outcomes only through their effect on constitution selection. In fact, such a restriction is strongly rejected by the data. We are thus left with the three weaker instruments dating constitutional origin. The data, however, also reject the overidentifying restriction that these three dummy variables affect constitution selection, but not policy.[6] Whatever the reason behind this rejection, we lack reliable instruments correlated with constitutional selection, but we do have reliable instruments correlated with policy.

We can still relax conditional independence using the Heckman procedure, however, basing our identification entirely on the functional-form assumption. The results are shown in column 1 of table 7.6. The first-stage probit for constitution selection is the same as that used in section 7.2. The second-stage regression for antidiversion policies controls for age of democracy, federalism, the four Hall-

---

6. The first stage for constitution selection is specified exactly as in earlier sections, and the test of the overidentifying restrictions is performed on the residuals of the *GADP* equation.

Table 7.6
Productivity and constitutions: Endogenous selection

	(1)	(2)	(3)	(4)	(5)
Dependent variable	GADP	LOGYL	LOGA	LOGYL	LOGA
GADP		3.56 (0.56)***	2.37 (0.65)***	3.48 (0.68)***	2.35 (0.62)***
PRES	−0.10 (0.06)*				
AGE	0.33 (0.07)***				
MAJ				0.14 (0.37)	0.22 (0.34)
Continents and colonies	COL_UKA and continents	Yes	Yes	COL_UKA and continents	COL_UKA and continents
Other controls	1	2	2	3	3
Endogenous selection	PRES	PRES	PRES	MAJ	MAJ
Method of estimation	Heckman two-step	Generated regressors	Generated regressors	Heckman two-step and generated regressors	Heckman two-step and generated regressors
Rho	0.01			−0.67	−0.67
Sample	1990s, broad	1990s, broad	1990s, broad	1990s, broad	1990s, broad
Number of observations	73	73	73	73	73
Adjusted R^2		0.74	0.52		

Note: Standard errors in parentheses. Other controls included:
    1: FEDERAL, AGE, LAT01, ENGFRAC, EURFRAC, FRANKROM
    2: none
    3: ENGFRAC, EURFRAC
First-stage probit specifications for selection in Heckman always include CON2150, CON5180, CON81, LAT01, ENGFRAC, EURFRAC, AGE, COL_UKA, and LAAM. Precise specifications underlying columns 2–5 described in the text.
*significant at 10%; **significant at 5%; ***significant at 1%.

Jones variables, continental origin, and British colonial origin (other colonial-origin variables are omitted to facilitate convergence of the maximum-likelihood estimation). Since majoritarian elections seem to have no influence on antidiversion policies, according to the OLS estimates, we omit their indicator (MAJ).[7] The previous results (column 1 of table 7.5) continue to hold. Conditional independence cannot be rejected (the estimated value of rho is almost zero), presidentialism still has a negative and significant effect on antidiversion policies, and older democracies have better policies.

Second, we want to estimate the effect of policy on productivity, allowing both constitutional selection and policy choices to be endogenous. Columns 2 and 3 of table 7.6 perform this estimation for labor and total factor productivity. Predicted antidiversion policies $(GADP)$ are generated from the two-step Heckman procedure described above. They are used as a regressor in the productivity equations, in which the standard errors are corrected, taking into account that $GADP$ is a generated regressor. The results are very similar to the two-stage least squares estimates reported in table 7.5, columns 2 and 3, confirming that the prior estimates are robust to endogenously selected forms of government. Combining the results in columns 1–3 of table 7.6, we can safely conclude that parliamentary regimes are good for productivity, because they promote better antidiversion policies.

Third, we would also like to know if the direct negative effect of majoritarian elections on productivity is robust to relaxing conditional independence. This is a very difficult question: to address it in full, we would need to allow for a joint endogenous selection of government regimes and electoral rules. Instead, we take the same kind of shortcut as in section 7.2, allowing the selection of only one constitutional dimension at a time. More precisely, we first estimate the equation for antidiversion policies with Heckman's two-step procedure, as in column 1 of table 7.6, allowing for endogenous selection of forms of government but imposing the restriction that electoral rules do not enter this equation. Then we once more apply the two-step procedure, estimating our productivity equation with

---

7. The results are identical if the dummy variable MAJ is also included in the $GADP$ equation but treated as exogenous, and the estimated MAJ coefficient does not differ significantly from zero. Moreover, estimating the effect of majoritarian elections on $GADP$ with the Heckman procedure (and treating presidentialism as exogenous) still leads to an estimated MAJ coefficient not significantly different from zero.

the predicted value of *GADP* as a regressor and allowing for endogenous selection of electoral rule. In the latter estimation, we neglect the fact that *GADP* is a generated regressor and do not correct the estimated standard errors.[8]

For a comparison with the two-stage least squares estimates in columns 4 and 5 of table 7.5, we also add to the productivity equation the fractions of the population speaking English or a European language (recall that testing the overidentifying restrictions suggested that these variables have a direct impact on productivity). The results appear in columns 4 and 5 of table 7.6. Now the direct constitutional effect of majoritarian elections on productivity vanishes: the estimated coefficient is positive (rather than negative as in table 7.5), but not significantly different from zero. This is consistent with the estimated correlation coefficient (rho), which is negative and large, suggesting that the earlier estimates were indeed downward biased.

Thus once we allow for endogenous constitution selection, we are led to the conclusion that the indirect negative effect of presidentialism on productivity through worse antidiversion policies is robust, but the direct negative effect of majoritarian elections on productivity is not. A broad reform from proportional to majoritarian electoral rules would therefore not have a robust effect on productivity, either directly or indirectly through better antidiversion policies.

7.3.4 Matching Estimates

Finally, we report two sets of nonparametric estimates: the constitutional effect on antidiversion policy (*GADP*) and the reduced-form constitutional effect on productivity (*LOGYL* and *LOGA*). Our different findings for samples of good and bad democracies (cf. table 7.4) suggest that nonlinearities may be important. The matching is based on propensity scores estimated using a logit specification that includes the four Hall and Jones variables (*LAT01*, *EURFRAC*, *ENGFRAC*, and *FRANKROM*). Given the strong effect of age of democracy on productivity and antidiversion policies reported in section 7.3.3, the age of democracy (*AGE*) is always included in the logit regressions as well.

---

8. We can still test the null hypothesis that *GADP* does not enter the productivity equation without correcting the standard errors, because under the null, the standard errors are correctly estimated. But this does not apply to the other estimated coefficients and, in particular, to those of *MAJ*.

Table 7.7
Productivity and constitutions: Matching estimates

	(1)	(2)	(3)	(4)	(5)	(6)
Dependent variable	GADP	GADP	GADP	LOGYL	LOGYL	LOGYL
PRES	−0.16	−0.13	−0.14	−0.63	−0.53	−0.32
	(0.05)***	(0.07)*	(0.05)***	(0.29)**	(0.76)	(0.22)
MAJ	−0.02	0.04	0.03	−0.61	−0.30	−0.32
	(0.05)	(0.10)	(0.07)	(0.23)***	(0.77)	(0.32)
Method of estimation	Kernel	Stratification	Nearest neighbor	Kernel	Stratification	Nearest neighbor
Sample	1990s, broad	1990s, broad	1990s, broad	1990s, broad	1990s, broad	1990s, broad
Number of observations on common support	42 PRES 61 MAJ	42 PRES 61 MAJ	42 PRES 61 MAJ	43 PRES 61 MAJ	43 PRES 61 MAJ	43 PRES 61 MAJ

Note: Standard errors in parentheses obtained by bootstrapping. Kernel, stratification, and nearest-neighbor estimators described in section 5.5. Logit specification underlying estimated propensity score includes AGE, LAT01, ENGFRAC, EURFRAC, and FRANKROM.
* significant at 10%; ** significant at 5%; *** significant at 1%.

Table 7.7 shows the main results. Columns 1–3 confirm that presidentialism leads to significantly worse antidiversion policies. In fact, the estimated effect under matching is even larger than the OLS estimate reported in column 1 of table 7.5. As in the linear estimates, the electoral rule has no effect on antidiversion policies.

Columns 4–6 report the estimated effects on output per worker, which correspond to the reduced-form OLS estimates in table 7.4. Both presidential regimes and majoritarian elections are associated with lower levels of labor productivity, for all three of our matching methods. The point estimates are slightly higher than in table 7.4 and, as usual, the standard errors are larger than those in table 7.4. The more reliable kernel estimator produces statistically significant effects for both the form of government and the electoral rule. The estimates for total factor productivity (not shown) are similar, although the effects they reveal are less pronounced.

Overall, maintaining the assumption of conditional independence but relaxing linearity reinforces the earlier conclusions from the linear regressions. Proportional and parliamentary regimes have higher levels of productivity. The effect of forms of government operates through antidiversion policies, whereas the effects of electoral rules are direct (or operate through some other policy channels than antidiversion policy).

7.3.5 Summary

Sorting out the causal relations among institutions, policies, and productivity is not straightforward. Nevertheless, the results in this section can be summarized as follows.

The form of government and age of democracy have strong constitutional effects. In particular, parliamentary regimes and older democracies pursue better antidiversion policies (as measured by *GADP*) and thus promote productivity. These results are robust to endogenous selection of government regimes and possible nonlinearities, although the negative effect of presidentialism seems confined to worse democracies.

Once more, the details of the electoral rule are of great importance, in a way consistent with the earlier results on rent extraction: larger electoral districts and more direct voting over individuals under plurality rule promote better policies. A radical reform from proportional to majoritarian elections has no effect on antidiversion policies; it does have a negative direct effect on productivity, but this effect is not robust. Specifically, under the assumption of conditional independence, majoritarian elections are associated with lower levels of productivity, but the effect disappears when this assumption is relaxed.

7.4 Concluding Remarks

The primary goals of any democratic constitution include limiting the abuse of power by political leaders, protecting private property rights, and thus promoting economic development. In this chapter, we have seen that some constitutional features are more effective in achieving these goals than others.

One robust lesson from the estimations presented in this chapter is that the fine details of the electoral rule are more important than the crude distinction between majoritarian and proportional elections. Individual accountability in plurality-rule elections reduces corruption and is associated with policies more respectful of property rights. But small electoral districts are associated with more corruption and worse policies toward economic development, in line with the idea that barriers to entry are higher in single-member districts. Since these two dimensions of the electoral rule tend to covary, the net effect of our binary election indicator of corruption and growth-promoting policies is ambiguous.

A second lesson from the chapter is that the effects of the form of government interact in subtle ways with the overall quality of democratic institutions. Under good and well-established democratic traditions, levels of corruption are lower under presidentialism than under a parliamentary government, which is what we expected, given existing theories. But in worse democracies, the positive effect of presidentialism on corruption seems to be lost. On the contrary, in these worse democratic environments, presidentialism is associated with less protection of property rights and overall, worse policies toward economic development. These results may be due partly to our definition of presidential government, which is based on the confidence requirement's neglecting the separation-of-powers dimension, and due partly to our quality-of-democracy measure's picking up constraints on executive power. But it may not be too surprising that institutions vesting a great deal of power in the executive branch of government fare well only or mainly in countries with strong democratic traditions.

A robust empirical result of the estimations presented in the chapter is that older democracies are more productive, with economic policies more favorable to growth. Olson's (1982) conjecture that older democracies are more easily captured by organized special interests and hence perform worse than younger ones is not supported by our data.

In many ways, the empirical findings in this chapter are more preliminary than those in the chapter on fiscal policy. One problem with the findings is that the measures of performance we have tried to explain (perceptions of corruption, perceptions of antidiversion policies) have larger amounts of error and are more loosely related to theory than those for fiscal policy.

A second problem with the findings, particularly in our analysis of productivity, is that theory offers little guidance on which variables to hold constant and on the primary mechanisms through which constitutions affect economic development. There are many possible channels for this influence, some of which are likely to produce offsetting effects. For instance, in chapter 6, we saw that presidentialism leads to a smaller government and less taxation, which is probably good for economic performance, but also to less universalistic programs and less public-goods provision, which might have the opposite effect. Given these possibilities and the lack of a well-specified theory, drawing inferences from the data is much more difficult.

Finally, we have neglected a third important issue throughout this chapter: the reverse link from economic development to quality of democratic institutions.[9] This link could partly account for our finding that older democracies have better economic policies than newer democracies. Sorting out these difficult issues, with better measurement and more precisely formulated theoretical hypotheses, is a difficult but challenging task for future research.

---

9. See, however, the recent paper by Kaufmann and Kraay (2002), which finds the feedback effect from development to corruption to be weak or even positive.

8

Fiscal Policy: Variation across Time

8.1 Introduction

Whereas the previous two chapters relied exclusively on cross-country variation to estimate constitutional effects, we now turn to analysis of the time variation in the data. Since we want to go as far back in time as possible, we confine the analysis to fiscal policy in the 60-country panel, for which we have data since the 1960s or 1970s. Throughout the chapter, we limit the analysis to a few variables: overall (central) government spending or revenue, welfare state spending, and budget surplus, all expressed as a percentage of GDP.[1] As described in chapter 3, these policy measures are available from the 1960s for most OECD countries and many countries in Latin America and from the 1970s for most of the remaining countries (though welfare spending is available for all countries only since the 1970s). Thus we study an unbalanced panel, with considerable variation in the length of the time series available for different countries, but with quite long time series for the average country.

To repeat a point made earlier in the book, deep constitutional reforms are so rare that they cannot be meaningfully exploited for statistical inference. Instead, we exploit the interaction between the constitution and other time-varying variables. In chapter 3, we showed that fiscal policy exhibits considerable time variation. This variation to some degree shows up in unexplained common time trends. In the 1970s and the first part of the 1980s, the size of government, welfare state spending, and budget deficits increased everywhere, a common time variation that is difficult to attribute

---

1. The work in this chapter builds heavily on an earlier study by Persson and Tabellini (2000b) but extends the analysis of that study both methodologically and substantively.

to observable determinants of policy. Moreover, fiscal policy fluctuates over time in response to observable shocks and events, like income fluctuations and elections. In this chapter, we ask whether these patterns are common across different constitutional groups, or whether they take different forms in presidential versus parliamentary regimes, or under proportional versus majoritarian elections.

In most of chapter 6, our investigation of fiscal policy was guided by specific predictions derived from the theory summarized in chapter 2. But to date, the formal modeling of fiscal policy and political institutions has typically dealt with static environments and does not entail predictions concerning the interaction between institutions and other events. Hence our goal in this chapter is somewhat different and more modest than in chapter 6. Rather than testing specific hypotheses, we aim at establishing some stylized facts that can be used in the next stage of theorizing. We also aim at gaining a somewhat better understanding of what mechanisms might underlie the constitutional differences in fiscal policy uncovered in chapter 6. In particular, what has led to the larger overall size of government and welfare spending in parliamentary-proportional countries? As noted in chapter 6, these differences among constitutional groups were more pronounced in the 1990s than in the earlier part of the postwar period. Thus, they must at least partly be related to the dynamics of spending between the early 1960s and the late 1990s.

Compared to chapters 6 and 7, we pay less attention in this chapter to the endogeneity (selection) of the constitution. The reason is twofold. For one thing, it is difficult. As we will be estimating dynamic interaction effects between the constitution and other variables, allowing for endogenous constitution selection would raise a number of new econometric subtleties. For another thing, selection bias is arguably less of a concern here. We always allow for country fixed effects' picking up any time-invariant but country-specific unobserved determinants of fiscal policy, such as any *direct* effects of the constitution itself or of history, geography, or culture. We instead focus on *indirect* constitutional effects, which are captured by interactions between the constitution and other variables. The possibility that historical or cultural determinants of the constitution would also influence these interactions seems more remote than the likelihood of a direct influence of the constitution on fiscal policy. In section 8.2, we present our empirical methodology, clarifying the questions we pose to the data and the estimation strategy we employ.

Section 8.3 then considers the response of fiscal policy to common unexplained events and compares policy persistence in different constitutional groups. In presidential regimes, spending (and particularly welfare spending) displays a more dampened response than in parliamentary regimes to whatever common events led to the expansion of government spending from the 1960s to the mid-1980s. Fiscal policy variables are also less persistent in presidential than in parliamentary regimes. Moreover, majoritarian electoral rules have a dampening effect on persistence and reaction to common events, but this effect is weaker and less robust than for presidentialism.

In section 8.4, we turn to the cyclical behavior of fiscal policy. In that section, we find a second mechanism that can partly account for a more rapid growth of government in the postwar period in parliamentary-proportional countries than in other political systems. This group of countries (and only this group) displays a ratchet effect in government spending, with an expansion of size of government and welfare programs during economic downturns that is not undone in subsequent upturns. We also encounter some evidence of a procyclical fiscal policy in presidential regimes.

Finally, section 8.5 contrasts electoral cycles under different constitutions. All types of governments are found to cut taxes during election years. Presidential regimes also postpone fiscal adjustments until after elections. Governments in majoritarian countries cut not only taxes, but also spending, in election years, whereas governments in proportional countries raise welfare-state spending on both sides of the election. Section 8.6 concludes and summarizes the chapter.

8.2 Methodology

Does the constitution influence how fiscal policy reacts to economic or political events or to other time-varying determinants of policy? This is the general question addressed in this chapter. In this section, we discuss how to formulate it more precisely and how to structure our strategy of estimation.

8.2.1 The Question

Retaining the same notation as in chapter 5, let Y_{it}^S denote the *potential* policy outcome in country i, year t, and constitutional state S, and let $\mathbf{X}_{it}$ be a vector of time-varying controls (i.e., of policy determinants). The constitution is measured by a *time-invariant* dummy variable, $S_i = 0, 1$, reflecting the distinction between majoritarian and proportional electoral rules or between presidential and parliamentary forms of government. As in previous chapters, we observe only actual policy outcomes, $Y_{it} = S_i Y_{it}^1 + (1 - S_i) Y_{it}^0$.

Suppose that potential policy outcomes are determined by the following stochastic process, which is a reformulation of (5.8) allowing for time variation and interaction effects:

$$Y_{it}^S = \alpha_i^S + \lambda^S Y_{it-1} + \boldsymbol{\beta}^S \mathbf{X}_{it} + \varepsilon_{it}^S. \tag{8.1}$$

Here, α_i^S captures the effect of *all* time-invariant policy determinants, including the constitution, colonial history, and geography, λ^S and $\boldsymbol{\beta}^S$ are unknown coefficients, and ε_{it}^S is an unobserved error term uncorrelated with the controls $\mathbf{X}_{it}$. As suggested by the results in chapter 3, we assume some persistence: potential policy outcomes in the current period depend on actual policy outcomes in the previous period. But now the serial-correlation parameter λ^S is allowed to depend on the constitutional state. We can rewrite (8.1) in terms of observed policy outcomes:

$$Y_{it} = \alpha_i + \lambda^0 Y_{it-1} + S_i(\lambda^1 - \lambda^0) Y_{it-1}$$
$$+ \boldsymbol{\beta}^0 \mathbf{X}_{it} + S_i(\boldsymbol{\beta}^1 - \boldsymbol{\beta}^0) \mathbf{X}_{it} + e_{it}, \tag{8.2}$$

where $\alpha_i = \alpha_i^0 + S_i(\alpha_i^1 - \alpha_i^0)$ and $e_{it} = \varepsilon_{it}^0 + S_i(\varepsilon_{it}^1 - \varepsilon_{it}^0)$. Chapters 6 and 7 sought to determine direct constitutional effects: how the intercept α_i^S varies with S for a country drawn at random. We can now formally see an obvious point made earlier: since both S_i and α_i^S are time invariant, this direct effect can be estimated only from the cross-country variation in the data, as is done in chapters 6 and 7.[2] In this chapter, our goal is instead to quantify differences in coefficients λ^S and $\boldsymbol{\beta}^S$ across constitutional groups, exploiting both time and country variation. The differences $(\lambda^1 - \lambda^0)$ or $(\boldsymbol{\beta}^1 - \boldsymbol{\beta}^0)$ capture what might be called "indirect constitutional effects" on fiscal policy, namely, interactions between the constitution and other policy determinants.[3] If these differences are zero, the reaction of fiscal policy to

---

2. The intercept α_i^S can be written as $\alpha_i^S = \alpha^S + \gamma \mathbf{R}_i$, where $\mathbf{R}_i$ is a vector of constant policy determinants, such as colonial origin or geography, γ is a vector of unknown parameters, and α^S is a coefficient reflecting the direct constitutional effects on policy. If $\mathbf{R}_i$ is observed, parameters γ and α^S can be identified separately, but only by exploiting the cross-country variation in the data, which is what we did in chapters 6 and 7.

3. These indirect effects are similar to the constitution-dependent slope coefficients discussed at the end of section 5.3 and the interaction effects estimated for welfare spending in section 6.3, although these were identified from the cross-sectional variation, rather than the time variation in policy.

events or other time-varying variables is not systematically related to the constitution. Our general purpose is thus to identify relevant interactions between the constitution and other policy determinants.

Specifically, we focus on three sets of interactions. In section 8.3, we ask whether the constitution modifies the influence of *unobserved* determinants of policy that are *common* across countries. An example of such common unobserved events would be the worldwide rise of left-wing ideologies in the late 1960s and early 1970s and of more conservative political movements in the mid-1980s. These common events are unobserved, however, or—at least—are very hard for the econometrician to measure. We therefore capture their effect through time dummy variables, asking whether the estimated coefficients of these variables differ across constitutional groups. In section 8.4, we focus on cyclical fluctuations, asking whether deviations of GDP from its long-run trend have an impact on fiscal policy that depends on the constitution. We also ask in that section whether fiscal policy responds in different ways to positive and negative output gaps. Finally, in section 8.5, we turn to electoral cycles, measuring election dates by means of indicator variables for election or postelection years. We begin by looking for unconditional electoral cycles in fiscal policy but focus our search on fiscal policy behavior in proximity to elections systematically related to the constitution.

8.2.2 Estimation

Throughout this chapter, we take the selection bias problems that occupy center stage in chapters 5–7 more lightly; most often we assume that $\varepsilon_{it}^1 = \varepsilon_{it}^0 = e_{it}$ for all is and ts and that this error term is uncorrelated with constitutional state, S_i. Under this assumption, equation (8.2) is reduced to a standard dynamic panel (dynamic because it contains a lagged dependent variable) where the parameters of interest can be estimated using a variety of techniques, depending on the assumed properties of the error term (see, e.g., Hsiao 1986, Baltagi 1995, or Wooldridge 2002 for overviews).

It is useful to decompose the error term e_{it} in (8.2) into three components: $e_{it} = \eta_i + v_t + u_{it}$, one varying across countries (η_i), one varying only across time (v_t), and one varying across both countries and time (u_{it}). A general equation to be estimated can then be written as

$$Y_{it} = \lambda^0 Y_{it-1} + S_i(\lambda^1 - \lambda^0)Y_{it-1} + \boldsymbol{\beta}^0 \mathbf{X}_{it} + S_i(\boldsymbol{\beta}^1 - \boldsymbol{\beta}^0)\mathbf{X}_{it} + \alpha_i^* + v_t + u_{it},$$

$$(8.3)$$

where $\alpha_i^* = \alpha_i + \eta_i$ captures all (observed and unobserved) country-specific and time-invariant policy determinants, including any direct constitutional effect. Such a decomposition was already used (although not formally explained) when we obtained our basic estimates in chapter 3.

First, consider the time-specific component of the error term, v_t. We deal with this component in two ways. In one specification, all controls X_{it} vary across both countries and time; we then always include year-specific indicator variables (a set of time dummies) as additional regressors, thus removing the yearly mean from all observations. Even if v_t is random, this procedure ensures that the time component of the error term does not (asymptotically) bias our estimates of λ^S and β^S. Moreover, as discussed in chapter 3, the estimated coefficients of the time dummy variables are of independent interest, since they capture the effects of unobserved determinants of policy outcomes common to all countries, such as common ideological trends. A second specification includes the dollar price of oil as a regressor (allowed to enter differently for oil exporters and importers) instead of the year dummies. Since the oil price is common for all countries, we cannot separately estimate its coefficient and those of the year indicator variables. In this specification, we thus omit the year dummy variables, imposing the restriction that $v_t = 0$ for all t, which essentially assumes that the oil price is the only time-varying policy determinant common for all countries. If that assumption is violated, the estimated coefficient of the oil price might be biased, because of an omitted-variables problem: this bias would reflect the correlation of the oil price with the omitted common policy determinants.

Next, consider the country-specific component of the error term, α_i^*. Once more, we deal with this component in two ways. Our preferred specification is to estimate (8.3) in levels. In this specification, we always include country fixed effects (i.e., country-specific indicator variables), thus removing the country means from all observations. If the coefficients on the lagged dependent variables are zero $(\lambda^1 = \lambda^0 = 0)$, this method removes any bias due to this component of the error term as the number of countries increases. But if, as is plausible, $\lambda^1, \lambda^0 > 0$, an asymptotic bias remains in our estimate of λ^S, even as the number of countries tends to infinity. The reason for this remaining bias is that the initial condition, Y_{i0}, is correlated with the component α_i^* of the error term, which creates a correlation of order $1/T$ between the lagged dependent variable (in the deviation from country means) and the remaining component of the error term, u_{it} (see, for instance, Hsiao 1986, chap. 4, or Baltagi 1995, chap. 8). The direction of the bias in our estimate of λ^S has the opposite sign of the true λ^S; if, as likely, $\lambda^S > 0$, we thus tend to underestimate the persistence of policy. Note, however, that this bias decreases as the length of the panel (T) increases. When the policy under consideration is the size of government or the budget surplus, the average country panel in our 60-country data set is 26 years, and the bias is probably negligible. In the case of welfare state spending, we have 16 years per country on average, and the bias problem could be more relevant. A second way of dealing with this component of the error term is to estimate equation (8.3) in first differences. This removes the α_i^* component but introduces a moving-average component in the remainder of the error term, $u_{it} - u_{it-1}$. To cope with this possible pattern of serial correlation, when (8.3) is specified in first differences, we impose the restriction that $\lambda^S = 0$ and estimate using Generalized Least Squares (GLS), allowing for country-specific autocorrelation coefficients in the residuals.[4]

The remaining component of the error term, u_{it}, does not pose any specific challenges beyond the usual pitfalls that it may be correlated with the controls ($\mathbf{X}_{it}$) and the lagged dependent variable (Y_{it}) because of omitted variables, reverse causation, selection bias, or serial correlation. (Some of these issues are discussed below in the context in which they arise.)

8.3   Unobserved Common Events

As discussed in chapters 3 and 4, several of our fiscal policy measures display a similar qualitative development over time in most countries. A plausible conjecture is that these common trends reflect some common economic and political events, such as the worldwide rise of left-wing ideologies in the late 1960s and 1970s, the turn to the right in the mid-1980s, or the productivity slowdown and the oil

---

4. When estimating in first differences, we have also used the Arellano and Bond (1991) Generalized Methods of Moments (GMM) method, which uses earlier lags as instruments for the lagged dependent variable. This method is sensitive to the choice of instruments and can be biased in small samples, especially when the number of panels is low. The results when applying the Arellano-Bond estimator are similar to those reported below, but the overidentifying restrictions for validity of the instruments are always rejected. Hence we do not report those estimates.

shocks in the 1970s and 1980s. Our goal in this section is to find out whether and how the impact of such common events on fiscal policy depends on the constitution. Our main interest is the constitution, so we do not seek to identify and measure the common events. Instead, we treat them as unobserved and proxy for them using a set of year-specific indicator variables, focusing on the interaction between this set and the constitution. This method was suggested by Blanchard and Wolfers (2000) to study how labor market institutions influence the reaction of unemployment to common unobservable shocks and was also used by Milesi-Ferretti, Perotti, and Rostagno (2002) to compare the reaction of fiscal policy to common shocks under different electoral systems in the OECD countries.

Let us rewrite equation (8.3) slightly to get

$$Y_{it} = \lambda^0 Y_{it-1} + S_i(\lambda^1 - \lambda^0)Y_{it-1} + \boldsymbol{\beta}\mathbf{X}_{it} + (1 + \gamma S_i)\boldsymbol{\delta}\mathbf{Q}_t + \alpha_i^* + u_{it}, \qquad (8.4)$$

where we have assumed that all observable controls $\mathbf{X}_{it}$ have the same vector of coefficients, irrespective of the constitution, and $\mathbf{Q}_t$ is the time-t value of a vector $\mathbf{Q}$ of year indicators (i.e., a set of dummies, one of which takes the value of 1 in year t, and the others of which take the value of 0). Our interest is in the γ-coefficients (one for each constitutional rule). If these are zero, the unobserved common events have the same impact in all countries, irrespective of the constitution; conversely, if γ is different from zero, the policy impact of unobserved common events systematically depends on the constitution. A positive value of γ implies that the constitutional feature measured by $S_i = 1$ inflates the impact of common events relative to the default constitutional feature $S_i = 0$, whereas a negative value implies a dampening effect. Note that the time-varying component of the error term, v_t, has been dropped from (8.4), since its effect is now fully captured by the vector of time dummy variables. The country-specific component, α_i^*, is still included, however.

Given the form of (8.4), we estimate the parameters of interest using nonlinear least squares, also including country dummy variables.[5] Throughout this section, the vector of controls $(\mathbf{X}_{it})$ always includes the variables introduced in chapter 3 and used in chapter 6, namely per capita income (*LYP*), demographics (*PROP65* and *PROP1564*) and openness (*TRADE*). All these variables vary across

---

5. In the estimation, we use a set of time dummies from 1961 to 1998, plus an intercept.

Table 8.1
Unobserved common events and size of government

	(1)	(2)	(3)	(4)
Dependent variable	CGEXP	CGEXP	CGEXP	CGEXP
LCGEXP		0.79	0.84	0.86
		(0.02)***	(0.02)***	(0.02)***
PRES * LCGEXP			−0.19	−0.19
			(0.04)***	(0.05)***
MAJ * LCGEXP			−0.09	−0.04
			(0.03)***	(0.02)
PRES	−0.59	−0.42	−0.19	
	(0.04)***	(0.13)***	(0.18)	
MAJ	−0.37	−0.23	0.03	
	(0.04)***	(0.12)*	(0.18)	
LAAM * LCGEXP				0.01
				(0.04)
COL_UK * LCGEXP				−0.05
				(0.03)*
Method of estimation	NLS FE	NLS FE	NLS FE	OLS FE
Number of observations	1,594	1,550	1,550	1,550
Adjusted R^2	0.86	0.95	0.95	0.82

Note: Standard errors in parentheses. Other controls always included: *TRADE, LYP, PROP65, PROP1564,* and country fixed effects. In column (4), "Adjusted R^2" refers to within-R^2.
*significant at 10%, **significant at 5%, ***significant at 1%.

both countries and time. But we omit time-invariant variables, such as the indicators for federalism, OECD membership, geography, or colonial origin, because their effects on policy are already subsumed in the country fixed effect, together with the direct effect of the constitution.

8.3.1   Size of Government

Table 8.1 considers the size of government spending and reports the estimates of the coefficient γ for presidential regimes and majoritarian elections (in the rows for the indicators *PRES* and *MAJ*). Since both constitutional dummy variables are included in the same regression, the default group consists of parliamentary-proportional countries. Thus, the vector of estimated coefficients $\delta = (\delta_t)$ (one per year, not reported in the table) reflects the impact of the vector of unobserved common events **Q** in this default group. The estimated coefficient of presidentialism (*PRES*) in table 8.1 captures the difference between presidential-proportional and parliamentary-proportional countries, or alternatively (due to additivity) between majoritarian-presidential and majoritarian-parliamentary countries. The estimated coefficient of majoritarian elections (MAJ) in table 8.1 instead captures, say, the difference between majoritarian-parliamentary and proportional-parliamentary countries.

In column 1 of the table, we impose the restriction that $\lambda^0 = \lambda^1 = 0$, thereby excluding the lagged dependent variable from the regression. This specification thus forces all the dynamics to be captured either by the included controls or by the time dummies. Since the controls included in X_{it} exhibit a limited time variation, we attribute a large fraction of the dynamics in government spending to the unobserved common events. The estimated values of γ for $PRES$ and MAJ in column 1 are both negative and highly significant. The estimated coefficient of -0.59 for presidential regimes can be interpreted as follows: an unobserved event in period t that raises government spending by 1% of GDP in proportional-parliamentary countries (formally, a year when $\delta_t - \delta_{t-1} = 1$) raises spending only by about 0.4% of GDP ($\approx 1 - 0.59$) in presidential-proportional countries. This is a very large difference in the effect of the event between the two types of countries. The dampening effect of majoritarian elections is smaller, with a coefficient of -0.37, but also sizeable.

Figure 8.1 depicts the estimated effect of unobserved common events in our four groups of countries when their starting point for spending is normalized to the same level in 1960. The uppermost line (marked with diamonds) refers to the default group of proportional-parliamentary countries (in each year, the line depicts the estimated coefficient δ_t, premultiplying the dummy variable of that year in the regression of column 1). The lines marked with square, triangular, and circular shapes indicate majoritarian-parliamentary, presidential-proportional, and majoritarian-presidential countries, respectively (i.e., each point on these lines depicts the same estimated coefficient δ_t, multiplied by the corresponding $(1 + \gamma)$ expression).[6] Until the early 1980s, spending reacted in a very different way in each of these constitutional groups to whatever generated the common upward movement in spending. But from the early 1980s

6. The levels of these curves have all been normalized to zero in 1960 to illustrate the relative growth paths of government spending in the four constitutional groups during the last 40 years, but not the relative levels of these paths. (To illustrate the latter, we would also have to take into account the average estimated fixed effect in each group.)

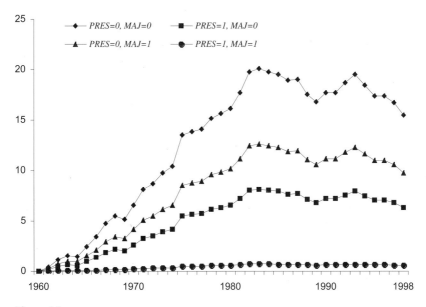

Figure 8.1
Unobserved common events and the size of government.

onward, the time pattern of spending in each constitutional group looks much more similar to that in all the other groups.

These time patterns across constitutional groups might seem surprising. The early 1980s coincide with the rise of conservative governments in a number of countries. It is natural to conjecture that different constitutions would imply different reactions of spending to such an ideological swing to the right. But this is not what we observe. The time trend of government spending stabilizes at about the same time in all countries in the mid 1980s (except in the group of majoritarian-presidential countries, in which the time trend was already absent even before the 1980s). But the common slope of these time patterns is really imposed through the constraint in our specification that the differences across constitutional groups remain constant over time. To relax this constraint, we respecify equation (8.4), allowing the γ coefficients interacted with *MAJ* and *PRES* (separately) to take on different values before 1982 (the period of an average upward trend) and after 1982 (the period without an average upward trend). But the estimates for these constitution-dependent γ coefficients (not shown) are very similar across the two subperiods we have defined, both for electoral rules and for forms of government. The interaction between the constitution and the common unobserved events is thus the same before and after the 1980s. In the early half of the sample, however, something drove up government spending everywhere, although much more so in parliamentary and proportional countries. The differences in the size of government across constitutional groups observed today (and documented in chapter 6) thus, to a large extent, seem due to events that occurred between 1960 and 1980.

As government spending is highly persistent over time, it would be a mistake to attribute all unexplained variation in spending in a particular year to unobserved common events in that same year. Some of the observed variation could simply reflect a delayed response to previous events. To allow for such persistence in government spending, the specification in column 2 of table 8.1 adds the lagged dependent variable ($LCGEXP$) to the regression while retaining the restriction that its coefficient be common across constitutions (i.e., we assume that $\lambda^1 = \lambda^0$). The common events captured by the time dummy variables now play a smaller role: their estimated coefficients δ are much smaller than in the regression of column 1 and precisely estimated. The estimated constitutional effects associated with the year effects also change somewhat with the addition of $LCGEXP$: although the estimate of γ for presidential regimes remains quite stable and highly significant, the estimated effect of majoritarian elections drops to -0.23 and is now significantly different from zero only at the 10% level.

In column 3 of the table, we also allow the coefficient for the lagged dependent variable to take on a different value across constitutional groups. (The estimated coefficient in the $PRES * LCGEXP$ row of column 3 corresponds to the difference in persistence between presidential-proportional and parliamentary-proportional countries $(\lambda^1 - \lambda^0)$; similarly, the estimated coefficient of $MAJ * LCGEXP$ corresponds to the difference between majoritarian-parliamentary and proportional-parliamentary countries.) Proportional and parliamentary democracies display more persistence (the estimate of λ^0 rises from 0.8 in column 2 to 0.85 in column 3), whereas presidential regimes and (to a smaller extent) countries with majoritarian elections display less. Both constitutional effects on persistence are statistically significant, though the effect of presidentialism is larger. But the evidence for a constitutional interaction with the unobserved common events is now much weaker: the estimate of the γ coefficient for presidentialism is smaller and no longer statistically different from zero; in the case of majoritarian elections, the estimated value of γ is close to zero.

Finally, column 4 asks whether these results are robust if the degree of persistence is allowed also to vary with colonial origin or geographic location. In terms of equation (8.4), we are thus concerning ourselves with nonrandom selection in the form of a correlation between the error term u_{it} and the constitutional indicators S_i. In light of the results reported in column 3 and to simplify the estimation problem, we remove the nonlinear interaction between the constitution and the time dummy variables, constraining the γ coefficients to zero. We thus estimate with linear fixed effects, including both time dummy and country dummy variables. Presidential regimes continue to have significantly less persistence than parliamentary regimes, with a point estimate identical to the earlier one, even though we interact the lagged dependent variable with a dummy variable for Latin America ($LAAM * LCGEXP$), the continent where presidential regimes are most overrepresented. The effect of electoral rules on persistence is not as robust, however; it disappears when the lagged dependent variable is interacted with U.K. colonial origin ($COLUK * LCGEXP$), the historical origin for which majoritarian elections are most overrepresented.

From these results, we infer that presidential democracies indeed have less persistent dynamics in overall spending than parliamentary democracies. This reflects less inertia in spending, as well as a more dampened reaction to common unobserved events. Majoritarian democracies have less persistent dynamics than proportional democracies, but electoral rules seem to affect the dynamics of spending less than forms of government.

In other words, government spending increased in many countries from the postwar period until the mid-1980s. It increased more in parliamentary countries, because the (generally upward) movements in spending had a larger permanent component in those countries than in presidential countries and because the reaction of spending to unobserved common events was greater in this group than in the presidential group.

8.3.2 Welfare Spending
We already know from chapters 4 and 6 that proportional and parliamentary democracies have larger welfare states than other

constitutional groups. As welfare state spending typically stems
from entitlement programs, it is likely to be highly persistent. Thus if
we find a higher persistence of total government spending in proportional or parliamentary democracies, it is natural to attribute this
to their larger welfare states. With this motivation in mind, we now
turn to the interaction between the constitution and the dynamics of
welfare state spending, repeating the analysis of the previous section
8.3.1. Note that our panel is shorter in this case, as data on welfare
spending are available only from the early 1970s onward for most
countries.

Table 8.2 presents the results we obtain for the effect of unobserved common events with social security and welfare spending
(as a percentage of GDP, SSW) as the dependent variable. In column 1, we do not include the lagged dependent variable. The year-
specific indicator variables proxying for common events now span
the period 1973–1998. The estimated coefficients on these variables
peak in the early 1990s and remain roughly constant thereafter. At

Table 8.2
Unobserved common events and welfare spending

	(1)	(2)	(3)	(4)
Dependent variable	SSW	SSW	SSW	SSW
LSSW		0.82	0.81	0.81
		(0.02)***	(0.02)***	(0.02)***
PRES * LSSW			0.04	
			(0.04)	
MAJ * LSSW			−0.01	
			(0.03)	
PRES	−0.52	−0.33	−0.36	−0.45
	(0.05)***	(0.18)**	(0.17)**	(0.16)***
MAJ	−0.17	−0.37	−0.35	−0.05
	(0.05)***	(0.15)**	(0.16)**	(0.13)
LAAM				−0.13
				(0.18)
COL_UK				−0.03
				(0.00)***
Method of estimation	NLS FE	NLS FE	NLS FE	NLS FE
Number of observations	1,000	942	942	942
Adjusted R^2	0.96	0.99	0.99	0.99

Note: Standard errors in parentheses. Other controls always included: *TRADE, LYP,*
PROP65, PROP1564, and country fixed effects.
*significant at 10%; **significant at 5%; ***significant at 1%.

the peak, the difference between the estimated coefficient and the coefficient of the 1973 year dummy is about 5. This result suggests that unobserved common events account for a rise in welfare spending of about 5% of GDP in the default group of proportional-parliamentary countries throughout this period. But the impact on the other constitutional groups is much smaller, as revealed by the estimated γ coefficients: -0.52 for presidential regimes and -0.17 for majoritarian elections. These estimates are quite similar to those for total government spending, reported in column 1 of table 8.1. In words, the unobserved common events that raised welfare spending by 5% of GDP in the default group raised it by 4% of GDP in majoritarian-parliamentary countries, only by 2.5% of GDP in proportional-presidential countries, and only by 1.5% of GDP in majoritarian-presidential countries.

When we add the lagged dependent variable ($LSSW$) in column 2, the estimated interaction between the time dummy variables and presidentialism drops to -0.33 and remains significantly different from zero; the interaction term with majoritarian elections increases to -0.37 and also retains its significance. These estimated interaction effects remain stable around the same values (and stay significantly different from zero) when we allow the coefficient on the lagged dependent variable to vary across constitutional groups in column 3. Contrary to the findings for total government spending, we cannot reject the hypothesis that the lagged dependent variable has the same coefficient irrespective of the constitution. This last result remains true even if we interact the lagged dependent variable with the constitution as well as with dummy variables for Latin America and British colonial origin (results not shown). As a final piece of sensitivity analysis, we let the nonlinear response to unobserved common events depend not only on constitutional indicators, but also on indicators for Latin America and British colonial origin.[7] In column 4, the dampening effect of presidential regimes remains at its level in the previous columns, whereas the dampening effect of majoritarian elections appears less robust than in the previous specifications.

To summarize, the data reveal important indirect constitutional effects on welfare spending. The effects are similar to those uncov-

7. In terms of equation (8.4), we thus allow for four gamma coefficients: one each for presidential regimes ($PRES$), majoritarian elections (MAJ), Latin American location ($LAAM$), and British colonial origin (COL_UK).

ered for total government spending but show some subtle differences from those effects. The dynamics of both total spending and welfare spending are more dampened in presidential than in parliamentary regimes. But although total spending is less persistent in presidential countries, the constitution does not seem to affect the persistence of welfare spending. Instead, the constitutional effect on welfare spending stems from a different reaction in the two regimes to common unobserved events: the common events that increase welfare spending in parliamentary countries have a much smaller impact in presidential regimes. Finally, electoral rules also affect the dynamics of welfare spending, with majoritarian countries reacting less to unobserved common events, although this finding is somewhat less robust. Naturally, the different constitutional effects for the two types of spending could, to some degree, reflect the different time periods of available data: 1973–1998 for welfare spending and 1961–1998 for total government spending.

8.3.3   Budget Surplus

As noted in chapters 3, 4, and 6, most countries have, on average, been running deficits over the period since 1960; that is, they have negative values of our dependent variable (SPL). For this variable, yearly data are available for the full sample period of 1960–1998 in many countries. Column 1 of table 8.3 shows the results when we estimate the response to unobserved common events in the form of time dummy variables, but without the lagged dependent variable. In the default group of parliamentary-proportional countries, unobserved common events increased the deficit by a whopping 8% of GDP from 1961 to a peak reached in the early 1980s (the coefficient on the year indicators is close to 0 in the early 1960s and about −8 in the early 1980s, results not shown in table). From then onward, unobserved common events reduce the deficit in the default group by 4–5% of GDP, with a gradual and monotonic decline continuing until 1998. But in presidential democracies, unobserved common events had a considerably more muted impact than in parliamentary democracies: as shown in column 1, the estimated γ coefficient for presidentialism is −0.44. The electoral rule, in contrast, seems to have a weaker and less precisely estimated effect on the response to unobserved common events.

Columns 2 and 3 of the table show these results to be robust to including the lagged dependent variable ($LSPL$), with or without

Table 8.3
Unobserved common events and budget surplus

	(1)	(2)	(3)	(4)	(5)
Dependent variable	SPL	SPL	SPL	SPL	SPL
LSPL		0.70	0.77	0.70	0.79
		(0.02)***	(0.03)***	(0.02)***	(0.03)***
PRES * LSPL			−0.29		−0.18
			(0.05)***		(0.06)***
MAJ * LSPL			−0.03		0.01
			(0.04)		(0.04)
PRES	−0.44	−0.53	−0.40	−0.08	
	(0.09)***	(0.19)***	(0.21)*	(0.39)	
MAJ	−0.17	0.33	0.48	0.23	
	(0.09)*	(0.23)	(0.27)*	(0.31)	
LAAM				−0.25	
				(0.41)	
COL_UK				0.04	
				(0.01)**	
LAAM * LSPL					−0.19
					(0.06)***
COL_UK * LSPL					−0.03
					(0.04)
Method of estimation	NLS FE	NLS FE	NLS FE	NLS FE	OLS FE
Number of observations	1,561	1,515	1,515	1,474	1,515
Adjusted R^2	0.45	0.72	0.73	0.72	0.58

Note: Standard errors in parentheses. Other controls always included: *TRADE, LYP, PROP65, PROP1564,* and country fixed effects. "Adjusted R^2" in column 5 refers to within-R^2.
* significant at 10%; ** significant at 5%; *** significant at 1%.

the constraint of common coefficients across constitutional groups. A further result now emerges, however: budget deficits also display less persistence in presidential regimes than in parliamentary regimes. Electoral rules do not affect degree of persistence.

Finally, columns 4 and 5 show the results of further sensitivity analysis. In these columns, we include the interaction of the indicator variables for Latin America and U.K. colonial origin with the unobserved common events (column 4) and the lagged dependent variables (column 5). These specifications demand a great deal from the data, perhaps too much. In any case, they show that differences in persistence between presidential and parliamentary countries are robust, whereas the dampening effect of presidentialism is not.

8.3.4 Summary

This section uncovers several indirect constitutional effects on fiscal policy dynamics. Presidential countries in particular stand out as quite different from the others.

Overall government spending grew in all countries from the early 1960s to the early 1980s as a result of some common (but unobserved) events. Whatever the reasons for this common increase, it had a much larger impact among proportional and parliamentary democracies. Generally, presidential regimes were much less affected, with some dampening also in majoritarian democracies. Similarly, common events increased welfare spending in all countries before the 1990s; a majoritarian electoral rule and a presidential form of government dampened this pattern, with a particularly strong effect of presidentialism. The differences in these time trends are large enough to account quantitatively for a good portion of the constitutional effects documented in the cross-sectional analysis of chapter 6.

A second and related finding concerns degree of persistence: overall spending is less persistent in presidential than in parliamentary countries. Since the persistence of welfare state spending does not differ across constitutions, other components of government spending (such as public employment and health spending) must be more persistent in parliamentary democracies.

Finally, budget deficits in presidential countries display a unique time pattern: they are less persistent and respond less (than in parliamentary countries) to the common events that raised deficits worldwide in the 1970s and 1980s.

8.4 Output Gaps

Part of the time variation in fiscal policy reflects responses to changes in other variables, such as shocks to aggregate output and income. These responses might be the result of automatic stabilizers—for given tax schedules or remuneration rates in entitlement programs— or of deliberate policy decisions triggered by the business cycle. In this section, we focus on such cyclical fluctuations in fiscal policy and their interaction with the constitution. As in the previous section, we are not led by sharp theoretical priors but seek to describe systematic patterns in the data. Nevertheless, the finding in chapter 6 that there are direct constitutional effects on all aspects of fiscal policy leads us to expect that cyclical policy responses might also be systematically influenced by the constitution.

Throughout this section, we estimate the following version of equation (8.3):

$$Y_{it} = \lambda^0 Y_{it-1} + S_i(\lambda^1 - \lambda^0)Y_{it-1} + \phi^0 YGAP_{it}$$
$$+ S_i(\phi^1 - \phi^0)YGAP_{it} + \boldsymbol{\beta}\mathbf{X}_{it} + \alpha_i^* + u_{it}. \tag{8.5}$$

The variable $YGAP$ is the output gap, the percentage by which income deviates from a country-specific trend, as defined in chapter 3. We want to know whether the effect of this variable on fiscal policy depends on the constitutional state (i.e., whether the coefficients ϕ^1 and ϕ^0 are the same). The other controls in $\mathbf{X}$ are the same as in the section 8.3 (the two demographic variables, openness to trade, and per capita income). As in chapter 3, we also include the price of oil (OIL) as a proxy for economic shocks common to most countries, while allowing for these shocks to have a different effect in oil-exporting and oil-importing countries. The constitution is measured by our two indicators for majoritarian elections and presidential regimes (MAJ and $PRES$, respectively), with proportional and parliamentary countries as the default group ($MAJ = PRES = 0$).

In principle, all controls in $\mathbf{X}$ could interact with the constitution, and their $\boldsymbol{\beta}$ coefficients could vary with the constitutional state. In practice, this does not occur, however: for most variables and most specifications, we cannot reject the null hypothesis that the $\boldsymbol{\beta}$ coefficients are the same irrespective of the constitutional state. Although the results vary across specification and estimation methods, we find no robust and clear pattern of interactions with the constitution. Therefore, we impose the constraint that all controls in $\mathbf{X}$ have the same $\boldsymbol{\beta}$ coefficients irrespective of the constitution, and we focus exclusively on output gaps.

To take into account the country-specific component of the error term, α_i^*, we estimate equation (8.5) in levels with country fixed effects. We also check that the results are robust to estimating in first differences and allowing for country-specific autocorrelation in the error term. Since one of the regressors (oil price) is common to all countries, we drop the year dummies to avoid colinearity.

As noted in chapter 3, the output gaps take on very large values (as large as 10% or more) for some observations. To avoid basing our inferences on a few outlying observations, we restrict the sample to observations for which the gaps are strictly less than 5% in absolute value. (Including the full sample with the outlying observations for output gaps strengthens the results reported below.) Finally, we ignore a possibly important estimation problem: a component of the output gap could be endogenous and reflect an exogenous variation in fiscal policy itself. This might bias the estimated coefficient ϕ downward when the dependent variable is government revenue or the budget surplus and upward when the dependent variable is government spending. The bias is unlikely to affect inferences about constitutional interactions, however, unless the endogenous component of output varies with the constitution.

8.4.1   Size of Government

We begin with overall government spending (*CGEXP*). Consider the first three columns of table 8.4. Column 1 estimates equation (8.5) for the full sample of democracies, excluding those with output gaps that exceed 5% in absolute value. Columns 2 and 3 restrict the sample to countries with smaller output gaps (less than 3% in absolute value) and to better democracies (those with values of the variable *POLITY_GT* less than 1.1). The results are very similar across all samples. First, we confirm the finding in the previous section that government spending is much more persistent in parliamentary than in presidential democracies, whereas the indirect constitutional effect of the electoral rule on persistence is more frail.

Second, the contemporaneous response of government spending (as a percentage of GDP) to output gaps varies with the constitution. In the default group of parliamentary-proportional countries, the estimated coefficient of output gaps (*YGAP*) is consistently negative, with a value of about −0.2, meaning that a 5% drop in real income induces an increase in the spending ratio of nearly one percentage point. Since spending is highly serially correlated, this effect persists over time. But in presidential regimes, the spending-to-GDP ratio reacts in a different way to output gaps (*PRES* ∗ *YGAP* has a coefficient significantly different from zero). In these countries, government spending as a share of GDP is acyclical (the sum of the coefficients of *YGAP* and *PRES* ∗ *YGAP* is not significantly different from zero). Note, however, that this constitutional effect on the cyclical response of spending is much weaker in good democracies (the variable *PRES* ∗ *YGAP* is not statistically significant in column 3). In majoritarian countries, the estimated contemporaneous impact of income fluctuations is smaller than in proportional countries, but this difference is neither robust nor statistically significant.

The estimated policy responses to output gaps under different constitutions are depicted in figure 8.2. This figure pushes the results somewhat by portraying the spending responses in the four constitutional subgroups in the wake of a one-year positive 1% output gap, according to the point estimates in column 1 of table 8.4.[8] The labeling of the groups is the same as in figure 8.1. Whereas a positive boost to income has virtually no effect in presidential-proportional countries (marked by squares), it leads to a marked and protracted drop in the spending-to-GDP ratio in proportional-parliamentary countries (marked by diamonds), a small drop in that ratio in majoritarian-parliamentary countries (marked by triangles), and a small hike in that ratio in majoritarian-presidential countries (marked by circles).

To gain a better understanding of the results, column 4 of the table disaggregates output gaps into positive ($POSYG$) and negative ($NEGYG$), still interacting them with our two constitutional dummy variables. Figure 8.3 depicts the responses of spending to positive and negative deviations of income from the trend. The two panels of this figure reveal an interesting asymmetry, in that the main action is associated with negative rather than positive output gaps. In proportional-parliamentary countries, only negative output gaps significantly change the spending ratio, and the estimated coefficient is much larger in absolute value than for positive output gaps. This asymmetry suggests a ratchet effect: a drop in income induces a lasting expansion in the size of government in proportional-parliamentary countries that is not undone when income grows above its potential. But this ratchet effect is not present in proportional-presidential countries, and if anything appears to occur but with the reverse sign (that is, a drop in income induces a lasting contraction) in majoritarian-presidential countries (though the difference between the effect in countries with proportional and majoritarian elections is not statistically significant).

Columns 5 and 6 of table 8.4 assess the robustness of these results to alternative specifications and estimation methods. In both

---

8. Note that here we are neglecting possible delayed effects of fiscal policy on the $YGAP$ variable itself. To take those fully into account, we would need to estimate a panel VAR.

Table 8.4
Cyclical response of government spending to output gaps

	(1)	(2)	(3)
Dependent variable	CGEXP	CGEXP	CGEXP
LCGEXP	0.83	0.83	0.83
	(0.02)***	(0.02)***	(0.02)***
PRES * LCGEXP	−0.22	−0.22	−0.30
	(0.04)***	(0.04)***	(0.04)***
MAJ * LCGEXP	−0.06	−0.04	−0.05
	(0.02)**	(0.03)	(0.02)*
YGAP	−0.19	−0.17	−0.19
	(0.06)***	(0.08)**	(0.06)***
PRES * YGAP	0.17	0.21	0.11
	(0.08)**	(0.12)*	(0.10)
MAJ * YGAP	0.11	0.02	0.12
	(0.08)	(0.11)	(0.09)
POSYG			
PRES * POSYG			
MAJ * POSYG			
NEGYG			
PRES * NEGYG			
MAJ * NEGYG			
LAAM * YGAP			
COL_UK * YGAP			
Sample	$|YGAP| < 5$	$|YGAP| < 3$	$|YGAP| < 5$, narrow
Method of estimation	CTRY FE	CTRY FE	CTRY FE
Number of observations	1,452	1,283	1,201
Number of countries	60	60	54
Adjusted R^2	0.83	0.83	0.84

Note: Standard errors in parentheses. Other controls always included: *LYP, TRADE, PROP1564, PROP65, OIL_IM,* and *OIL_EX.* Narrow sample corresponds to countries where *POLITY_GT* is less than 1.1. "Adjusted R^2" refers to within-R^2.
*significant at 10%; **significant at 5%; ***significant at 1%.

Table 8.4
(continued)

	(4)	(5)	(6)
Dependent variable	CGEXP	CGEXP	DCGEXP
LCGEXP	0.83	0.83	
	(0.02)***	(0.02)***	
PRES * LCGEXP	−0.22	−0.22	
	(0.03)***	(0.04)***	
MAJ * LCGEXP	−0.06	−0.06	
	(0.02)**	(0.02)**	
YGAP		−0.27	−0.33
		(0.07)***	(0.04)***
PRES * YGAP		0.13	0.31
		(0.11)	(0.05)***
MAJ * YGAP		0.03	0.02
		(0.09)	(0.04)
POSYG	−0.06		
	(0.11)		
PRES * POSYG	-0.03		
	(0.16)		
MAJ * POSYG	0.08		
	(0.15)		
NEGYG	−0.31		
	(0.11)***		
PRES * NEGYG	0.37		
	(0.16)**		
MAJ * NEGYG	0.14		
	(0.15)		
LAAM * YGAP		0.15	0.12
		(0.10)	(0.04)***
COL_UK * YGAP		0.18	0.19
		(0.09)**	(0.05)***
Sample	$|YGAP| < 5$	$|YGAP| < 5$	$|YGAP| < 5$
Method of estimation	CTRY FE	CTRY FE	DIFF, GLS
Number of observations	1,452	1,452	1,448
Number of countries	60	60	59
Adjusted R^2	0.83	0.83	

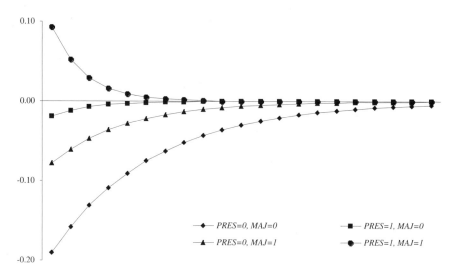

Figure 8.2
Response of government spending to a +1% output gap.

columns, we try to address the nonrandom pattern of constitution selection by interacting the output gap not only with our two constitutional dummy variables, but also with the dummy variables for Latin American location $(LAAM * YGAP)$ and British colonial origin $(COL\_UK * YGAP)$. Thus, we allow the effect of output gaps to vary not only with the constitution, but also with history and geography. We estimate both in levels (column 5) and in differences with country-specific serial correlation in the residuals (column 6). Each set of estimates should be compared with those in column 1. In column 5, the estimated γ coefficient on the output gap for presidential democracies remains large (0.13) but is no longer statistically significant. In column 6, however, the contrast between parliamentary and presidential countries reappears strongly and with statistical significance, even though the interaction of output gaps with the Latin American and the British colonial-origin dummy variables is also significant. In both specifications, the indirect effect of different electoral rules vanishes, however, and is picked up by the colonial-origin variable.

How can these constitutional effects be explained? The larger cyclical response of the spending-to-GDP ratio in proportional-parliamentary democracies could reflect their larger welfare states:

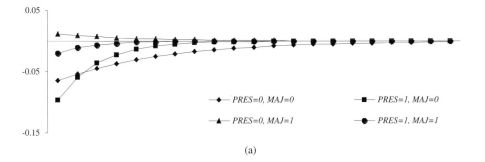

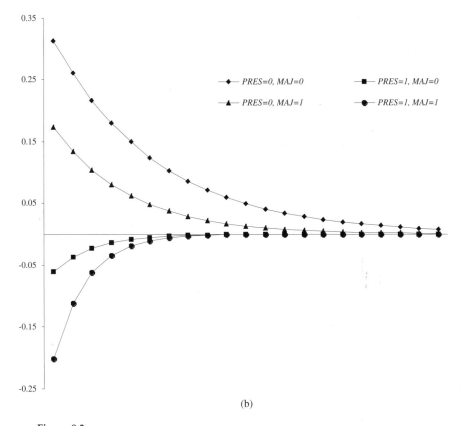

Figure 8.3
(a) Response of government spending to a +1% output gap. (b) Response of government spending to a −1% output gap.

outlays for such entitlement programs are fixed in cash terms or might even be inversely related to income. But the presence of a ratchet effect only among proportional-parliamentary countries is harder to explain and suggests that the constitution might also have a direct effect on the discretionary policy reaction to exogenous events. One possible explanation for this phenomenon is related to the theoretical discussion in chapter 2 and the empirical findings in chapter 6. If countries with proportional elections and parliamentary regimes indeed both have a bias toward larger overall spending, politicians in those countries may be less prepared to cut spending when the economy is doing badly. Another possible explanation may lie in the incidence of coalition governments. As discussed in chapters 2 and 4, such governments are common in proportional-parliamentary countries. And they may induce a greater status quo bias, particularly in bad times, because of the difficulties involved in bargaining over policy, highlighted by economists such as Alesina and Drazen (1991) and political scientists as Tsebelis (2002).

Yet another possible explanation is that some democracies are more likely than others to face binding borrowing constraints. If presidential democracies are more likely to experience political crises, as some political scientists hold (cf. chapter 2), they may also have more frequent debt or currency crises. Borrowing constraints would impart a procyclical bias to fiscal policy: governments must cut spending or raise revenues when hit by a recession or by a financial crisis, since they cannot let the deficit absorb the shock. Indeed, many presidential regimes are located in Latin America or Africa, where financial crises have been more frequent, and earlier studies have shown fiscal policy in Latin America to be more pro-cyclical than elsewhere (see, in particular, Gavin and Perotti 1997). The estimates in columns 5 and 6 of table 8.4 are consistent with this notion, yet we find that the indirect effect of presidential regimes remains in those columns. Whatever its interpretation, the asymmetric ratcheting upward of government spending contributes to the differential size of governments in different political systems that was uncovered by our cross-sectional analysis.

To shed further light on these alternative interpretations of the asymmetric ratcheting of government spending, we now turn to the analysis of the cyclical response of welfare state spending and budget deficits.

8.4.2 Welfare Spending

In this section, we consider regressions for welfare state spending similar to those for size of government presented in section 8.4.1. Columns 1 and 2 of table 8.5 report the estimated response to output gaps smaller than 5% (column 1) and 3% in absolute value (column 2) in the default sample of democracies. Column 3 restricts the sample to better democracies ($POLITY\_GT < 1.1$). The results are similar to those for overall government spending, although there are some discrepancies between the two. Like total spending, welfare spending is most countercyclical among proportional-parliamentary democracies and least countercyclical among majoritarian-presidential ones, with the other two groups falling in between. Electoral rules also play a role, however, with majoritarian countries responding significantly less to the cycle than proportional countries (particularly when the sample is restricted to good democracies). Moreover, in proportional-parliamentary countries, the cyclical response of welfare spending to output gaps is somewhat smaller than that of total government spending (cf. the first three columns in table 8.4), meaning that other components of overall spending besides welfare spending are also strongly countercyclical. But the difference between presidential and parliamentary governments is not so marked: while *total* government spending as a fraction of GDP is constant over the cycle in presidential democracies, welfare spending remains somewhat countercyclical even in presidential countries. Finally, in contrast to that in total government spending, inertia in welfare spending is never affected by the constitution (thus confirming what we found in the nonlinear estimation in section 8.3).

Column 4 of the table decomposes output gaps into positive and negative ones. Once more, there is a ratchet effect in proportional-parliamentary countries, with positive gaps having no effect on welfare spending relative to GDP, but negative gaps expanding the welfare state. As was the case for total government spending, the ratchet effect does not exist in proportional-presidential democracies. Here the electoral rule also makes a significant difference (as in columns 1–3 of table 8.5 but unlike in column 4 of table 8.4), however. Once more, the estimated coefficients reported in table 8.5 are somewhat smaller than those in table 8.4. This suggests that the ratchet effect mainly concerns the welfare state, but that other spending items must also exhibit an asymmetric response to output gaps.

Table 8.5
Cyclical response of welfare spending to output gaps

	(1)	(2)	(3)
Dependent variable	SSW	SSW	SSW
LSSW	0.79	0.75	0.79
	(0.02)***	(0.02)***	(0.02)***
PRES * LSSW	0.03	0.05	0.02
	(0.04)	(0.05)	(0.05)
MAJ * LSSW	−0.03	−0.01	−0.03
	(0.03)	(0.03)	(0.03)
YGAP	−0.13	−0.13	−0.15
	(0.02)***	(0.03)***	(0.02)***
PRES * YGAP	0.07	0.11	0.05
	(0.03)**	(0.04)**	(0.04)
MAJ * YGAP	0.07	0.03	0.09
	(0.03)**	(0.04)	(0.03)***
POSYG			
PRES * POSYG			
MAJ * POSYG			
NEGYG			
PRES * NEGYG			
MAJ * NEGYG			
LAAM * YGAP			
COL_UK * YGAP			
Sample	|YGAP| < 5	|YGAP| < 3	|YGAP| < 5, narrow
Method of estimation	CTRY FE	CTRY FE	CTRY FE
Number of observations	890	779	752
Number of countries	56	56	49
Adjusted R^2	0.77	0.77	0.78

Note: Standard errors in parentheses. Other controls always included: *LYP, TRADE, PROP1564, PROP65, OIL_IM, OIL_EX*, and country fixed effects. Narrow sample corresponds to countries where *POLITY_GT* is less than 1.1. "Adjusted R^2" refers to within-R^2.
*significant at 10%; **significant at 5%; ***significant at 1%.

Table 8.5
(continued)

	(4)	(5)	(6)
Dependent variable	*SSW*	*SSW*	*DSSW*
LSSW	0.80	0.79	
	(0.02)***	(0.02)***	
*PRES * LSSW*	0.03	0.03	
	(0.04)	(0.04)	
*MAJ * LSSW*	−0.03	−0.03	
	(0.03)	(0.03)	
YGAP		−0.16	−0.11
		(0.03)***	(0.01)***
*PRES * YGAP*		0.06	0.07
		(0.04)	(0.01)***
*MAJ * YGAP*		0.04	0.03
		(0.03)	(0.01)***
POSYG	−0.05		
	(0.04)		
*PRES * POSYG*	−0.02		
	(0.06)		
*MAJ * POSYG*	0.02		
	(0.05)		
NEGYG	−0.20		
	(0.04)***		
*PRES * NEGYG*	0.15		
	(0.06)**		
*MAJ * NEGYG*	0.12		
	(0.06)**		
*LAAM * YGAP*		0.05	0.05
		(0.04)	(0.01)***
*COL_UK * YGAP*		0.07	0.07
		(0.03)**	(0.01)***
Sample	$|YGAP| < 5$	$|YGAP| < 5$	$|YGAP| < 5$
Method of estimation	CTRY FE	CTRY FE	DIFF, GLS
Number of observations	890	890	830
Number of countries	56	56	55
Adjusted R^2	0.77	0.77	

Finally, columns 5 and 6 of the table add the interaction of the output gap with the dummy variables for Latin American location and British colonial origin, estimating in levels and first differences, respectively. The results for levels are fragile, and the constitutional interactions lose statistical significance, but they reappear as significant in the results for first differences. In both cases, Latin American location and British colonial origin make the response to output gaps less countercyclical.

These estimates shed some light on the possible interpretations offered at the end of section 8.4.1 of the asymmetric ratcheting of government spending. They suggest that the larger welfare states in proportional-parliamentary democracies indeed make automatic stabilizers more important in this constitutional group. But the somewhat different results obtained for total spending and welfare spending suggest that the welfare state is not the whole story and that other spending items also respond differently to the cycle under different constitutions.

8.4.3 Budget Surplus and Government Revenue

If a deviation of income from trend expands government spending, the expansion can be financed either by taxation or by borrowing. In this section, we try to infer whether the choice between these two financing alternatives also depends on the constitution. Table 8.6 estimates the cyclical response of the budget surplus and government revenue (both scaled to GDP) to output gaps. (To save space, we report only the results for the default sample of democracies and output gaps not exceeding 5% in absolute value.)

Columns 1 and 2 of table 8.6 are estimated using seemingly unrelated regressions (SURs), in levels and with fixed country effects, for government spending, government revenue, and budget surplus. The results for spending are not reported, since they are similar to those in table 8.4; those for revenues are reported in columns 5 and 6.[9] Column 1 reports the results for output gaps in the basic specification, and column 2 decomposes the output gaps into different signs. In columns 3 and 4, we add output gaps interacted with the dummy variables for Latin America and British colonial origin to

---

9. In table 8.4, we estimated the spending equation in isolation, rather than using SUR, because we have more observations on spending than on tax revenue and surpluses; hence the joint estimation using SUR increases efficiency for the last two dependent variables but implies a loss of observations for government spending.

allow for nonrandom constitutional selection, estimating in levels with country fixed effects and in differences with GLS.

What do we find? First of all, budget deficits are less persistent in presidential regimes than in parliamentary regimes, confirming the findings of the nonlinear estimation in table 8.3. As in that table, persistence is not significantly related to electoral rules. Second, the constitution also affects the cyclical response of the budget surplus to output gaps. In the default group of proportional-parliamentary democracies, the budget surplus increases in booms and shrinks in recessions, as expected. The cyclical response of the surplus in this constitutional group of countries is particularly evident and large in columns 3 and 4, in which we also interact output gaps with Latin American location and British colonial origin. But the cyclical response seems to emanate mainly from recessions (column 2), conforming to the earlier findings of asymmetric spending responses to positive and negative output gaps. Majoritarian-parliamentary countries behave in the same qualitative way as proportional-parliamentary countries, but the procyclical response of the surplus is more accentuated in the former, particularly when British colonial origin is controlled for (columns 3 and 4). In proportional-presidential countries, we find an acyclical rather than a procyclical response of the surplus to output gaps, consistent with the acyclical spending response found in table 8.4. The absence of a systematically cyclical budget surplus in presidential democracies is due to large, negative responses to positive output gaps (column 4): in a boom, presidential governments shrink the surplus (or expand the budget deficit). A possible interpretation for this finding was mentioned above: presidential regimes may face binding borrowing constraints that are relaxed in good economic times. Another possible interpretation is reverse causation: an expansionary fiscal policy leads to a boom, rather than vice versa.

The last two columns of table 8.6 estimate the cyclical response of government revenue to output gaps. In these two columns, we do not detect many constitutional interactions, except for a strong response of government revenues to negative output gaps in majoritarian countries. The positive estimated coefficients of output gaps interacted with majoritarian electoral rule show that only majoritarian countries cut taxes during recessions, perhaps because they engage in Keynesian stabilization policies.

Table 8.6
Cyclical response of budget surplus and government revenue to output gaps

	(1)	(2)	(3)
Dependent variable	SPL	SPL	SPL
LDEPVAR	0.72	0.73	0.75
	(0.02)***	(0.02)***	(0.03)***
PRES * LDEPVAR	−0.32	−0.33	−0.34
	(0.04)***	(0.04)***	(0.05)***
MAJ * LDEPVAR	0.05	0.05	0.03
	(0.03)	(0.03)	(0.04)
YGAP	0.08		0.21
	(0.05)		(0.06)***
PRES * YGAP	−0.13		−0.11
	(0.07)*		(0.10)
MAJ * YGAP	0.05		0.19
	(0.07)		(0.08)**
POSYG		−0.03	
		(0.10)	
PRES * POSYG		−0.21	
		(0.15)	
MAJ * POSYG		0.09	
		(0.13)	
NEGYG		0.18	
		(0.10)*	
PRES * NEGYG		−0.03	
		(0.15)	
MAJ * NEGYG		0.03	
		(0.14)	
LAAM * YGAP			−0.18
			(0.09)**
COL_UK * YGAP			−0.32
			(0.08)***
Sample	|YGAP| < 5	|YGAP| < 5	|YGAP| < 5
Method of estimation	SUR, CTRY FE	SUR, CTRY FE	CTRY FE
Number of observations	1,352	1,352	1,427
Number of countries	59	59	60
Adjusted R^2	0.74	0.74	0.56

Note: Standard errors in parentheses. SUR run on system of three equations (*CGREV*, *SPL* and [not shown] *CGEXP*). Other controls always included: *LYP*, *TRADE*, *PROP1564*, *PROP65*, *OIL_IM*, *OIL_EX*, and country fixed effects. "Adjusted R^2" is unadjusted for columns 1–2 and 5–6, within-R^2 for column 3. *LDEPVAR* denotes the lagged dependent variable.
*significant at 10%; **significant at 5%; ***significant at 1%.

Table 8.6
(continued)

	(4)	(5)	(6)
Dependent variable	*DSPL*	*CGREV*	*CGREV*
LDEPVAR		0.81	0.80
		(0.01)***	(0.01)***
*PRES * LDEPVAR*		−0.21	−0.20
		(0.03)***	(0.03)***
*MAJ * LDEPVAR*		−0.03	−0.02
		(0.02)	(0.02)
YGAP	0.20	−0.11	
	(0.04)***	(0.05)**	
*PRES * YGAP*	−0.16	0.02	
	(0.04)***	(0.07)	
*MAJ * YGAP*	0.14	0.13	
	(0.04)***	(0.07)**	
POSYG			−0.02
			(0.10)
*PRES * POSYG*			−0.05
			(0.14)
*MAJ * POSYG*			0.00
			(0.12)
NEGYG			−0.19
			(0.09)**
*PRES * NEGYG*			0.08
			(0.14)
*MAJ * NEGYG*			0.27
			(0.13)**
*LAAM * YGAP*	−0.01		
	(0.04)		
*COL_UK * YGAP*	−0.25		
	(0.05)***		
Sample	$|YGAP| < 5$	$|YGAP| < 5$	$|YGAP| < 5$
Method of estimation	DIFF, GLS	SUR, CTRY FE	SUR, CTRY FE
Number of observations	1,422	1,352	1,352
Number of countries	59	59	59
Adjusted R^2		0.96	0.96

8.4.4 Summary

The cyclical response of fiscal policy to output gaps is indeed affected by the constitution. Proportional-parliamentary countries display strong ratchet effects in total and welfare spending: spending as a percentage of GDP increases in cyclical troughs but does not decrease in booms. This ratchet effect is absent in presidential regimes, in which spending relative to GDP varies much less over the business cycle, whatever the electoral rule. Larger welfare states in proportional-parliamentary countries account for some of these patterns, but not for all of them. In other words, the ratchet effect in parliamentary-proportional countries extends also to other spending items.

Finally, the cyclical pattern of the budget surplus (and, to some extent, overall spending) suggests that presidential democracies—and not only those found in Latin America—pursue fiscal policies in which the budget deficit strongly expands in economic upturns. Such a procyclicity is not found, however, in parliamentary democracies. On the contrary, majoritarian-parliamentary countries appear to cut taxes during recessions.

8.5 Elections

Not only economic, but also political, events are likely to induce variations in a country's fiscal policy. Elections of the legislature and the executive are recurrent political events in any democracy. (Naturally, executive elections are separately held only in systems with a popularly elected president.) In this section, we study the behavior of fiscal policy in the proximity of elections, again trying to identify interactions with the constitution.

A sizable empirical literature deals with electoral policy cycles. Most of this literature has focused on monetary policy in OECD countries, however, with somewhat inconclusive results. Empirical work on fiscal policy is more recent and less systematic, and many studies rely on data sets from a small number of political jurisdictions. Recent research suggests that politicians systematically manipulate fiscal policy *before* elections. Moreover, some studies find these preelection cycles to be more pronounced in developing countries ruled by worse democratic institutions or to be affected by other constitutional provisions. Little is known about the systematic pattern of fiscal policy *after* elections, as existing research on postelection cycles has focused almost exclusively on "partisan" (i.e., left or right) cycles.[10]

Why is it reasonable to expect the nature of electoral cycles to vary with the constitution? In chapter 2, we discussed the career concern model of electoral cycles due to Persson and Tabellini (2000a, chap. 9), in which majoritarian elections are associated with stronger individual accountability—and therefore lower taxes and wasteful spending—than proportional elections, in which politicians are more collectively accountable. Sharper incentives under majoritarian elections should result in larger tax and spending fluctuations around the elections. Moreover, we have emphasized the prediction that proportional electoral rules give politicians stronger incentives to garner votes via broad policy programs, such as welfare state spending. It is not far-fetched to expect these incentives to be at their strongest at election time, resulting in different electoral cycles in the composition of spending, depending on the electoral rule in effect.

In regard to forms of government, we have stressed how policy-making incentives differ in presidential and parliamentary democracies, both for the size and for the composition of government spending. Once more, it is reasonable to expect these effects to show up more strongly at election time. Another difference between presidential and parliamentary forms of government is the individual versus collective nature of the executive in the two. By analogy with the career concern argument presented above that individual political accountability gives stronger incentives than collective accountability, we might expect stronger electoral cycles under presidential regimes.[11]

---

10. Among the more recent studies on international data, Shi and Svensson 2001 analyzes a large panel of developed and developing countries, focusing on how electoral cycles interact with voters' access to information and incumbents' access to rents. Schuknecht 1996 and Block 2000 study different samples of developing countries, as does Gonzalez 1999, which also focuses on the interaction of cycles with the quality of democratic institutions. Among the papers using regional data, Besley and Case 1995 and Lowry, Alt, and Ferree 1998 focus on the U.S. states, the former asking whether cycles are stronger when governors are not up against a term limit and the latter conditioning on the form of election and the party in power. Pettersson-Lidbom 2002 studies a panel of almost 300 Swedish municipalities. All of these papers find evidence of preelection cycles in fiscal policy. Alesina, Roubini, and Cohen 1997, Drazen 2000a and 2000b, and Persson and Tabellini 2000a review the theoretical and empirical literature.

11. Lowry, Alt, and Ferree (1998) make a similar point when arguing—and showing empirically—that voters respond more vigorously to policy in gubernatorial elections than in legislative elections in the U.S. states.

Based on the above motivation, we search for evidence of different electoral cycles in fiscal variables under different electoral rules and forms of government. To carry out this search, we adapt the empirical methodology used in section 8.4. As we want to find evidence of electoral cycles, it is important that we allow for reasonably rich dynamics in the policy variables we consider. As we have seen in earlier sections, all of our fiscal instruments display a great deal of inertia. Therefore, we always include the lagged dependent variable on the right-hand side of our regressions. Since fiscal instruments tend to be highly cyclical, we also include our measure of cyclical deviations from trend ($YGAP$). On top of this, we allow the dynamics to differ across constitutional groups; specifically, we include in the regression terms of interaction between both constitutional indicators (MAJ and $PRES$) and the lagged dependent variable, as well as the output gap. Doing this is important to avoid confounding different general policy dynamics with different electoral cycles in different constitutional groups. A natural starting point is thus equation (8.5), in which the lagged dependent variable and the output gaps are allowed to have different coefficients across constitutional groups, but the other variables included in the control vector $\mathbf{X}$ are constrained to have the same coefficients. Throughout this section, we make our estimations in levels, adding country fixed effects. To better separate the effect of elections from other common events in a given year, we replace the oil price with a vector of time dummy variables constrained to have the same coefficients in all countries.

To search for constitution-dependent electoral cycles, we obviously need information on election dates. In parliamentary democracies, elections of the legislature and the executive coincide. In presidential democracies, the executive is elected separately, but the legislature is almost always elected in the same year (in our sample, only about 10 presidential elections do not coincide with elections of the legislature). Nevertheless, in presidential regimes, there are also many "midterm" legislative elections in between the years of simultaneous presidential and legislative elections. Our prior is that the incentives created by these midterm elections are weaker than those generated in years when both the president and the legislature are elected. Indeed, this is what the data suggest: when we estimate electoral-cycle models for our different policy instruments, we never find midterm elections to be significant determinants of policy. In the following, we therefore limit our attention to the years of presidential elections.[12] That is, in all regimes, we code the year in which the executive is elected. The resulting variable ($ELEX$) is thus equal to 1 in the years of presidential elections in presidential countries and in the years of legislative elections (for the lower house) in parliamentary countries; in all other years, it is equal to $\emptyset$. To study fiscal policy behavior both before and after elections, we also use the one-year lags of the executive election dates ($LELEX$).

A prospective econometric problem with this approach is that some election dates may not be exogenous. This is less important in presidential regimes, where elections are typically held on a fixed schedule with, say, four or six years between elections. The concern is greater for parliamentary democracies, where the election date often reflects tactical choices by incumbents or government crises. Specifically, endogenous election dates may be correlated with the economic cycle, with incumbent governments calling early elections when the economy is doing well, or government crises (and new elections) erupting when it is doing badly. This may bias our estimates of electoral cycles, as our policy instruments are expressed as percentages of GDP. But this prospective problem is addressed by our inclusion of income shocks ($YGAP$) among the controls, both alone and interacted with the constitutional indicators. These variables should account for any regime-specific correlation between the policy variable of interest and the election date induced by the economic cycle. This, in turn, should reduce any simultaneity bias that may result from an error term correlated with election dates.

We start out the next subsection by constraining the coefficients of the electoral dummy variables to be the same for all countries, irrespective of their constitution, and to characterize the nature of unconditional electoral cycles in fiscal policy. We then allow their coefficients to differ with the electoral rule, thereby contrasting majoritarian and proportional elections. Subsequently, we study electoral cycles, conditional on the form of government, contrasting presidential and parliamentary countries. A final subsection digs deeper for the roots of the results by disaggregating the electoral variables into a full four-way classification of constitutional groups.

---

12. We have another, more pragmatic reason for leaving out the midterm elections, namely that we want to study both preelection and postelection years. In some countries, this poses problems because of the crowding that results. If presidential elections are held every four years and legislative elections every second year, for example, each year would then either be an election year, or a postelection year.

8.5.1 Unconditional Electoral Cycles

We start with the results when all constitutional groups are constrained to respond to election dates in the same way. As mentioned above, we report the results for elections to the executive (the *ELEX* and *LELEX* indicators). Our broadest sample includes more than 500 executive elections, but that number is somewhat reduced, depending on data availability for the policy variables under consideration (especially welfare state spending) and whether we restrict our sample to better democracies. The results corresponding to legislative elections are very similar to those presented below. As already mentioned, this similarity is likely to reflect the coincidence of these two functions of elections in all parliamentary regimes, the coincidence of electoral dates for the executive and legislature in many presidential regimes, and the lesser importance of midterm elections compared to those in which the executive is elected.

Table 8.7 shows the results for all fiscal policy variables studied in this chapter: overall spending (*CGEXP*), overall revenue (*CGREV*), budget surplus (*SPL*), and welfare spending (*SSW*). For each policy variable, we report the results from two different samples corresponding to our most and least generous definitions of democracy (*POLITY_GT* less than 3.7 and 1.1, respectively; see chapter 4).

A number of regularities in the results stand out. First, there is no significant effect on overall spending in the election year. But the estimated coefficient of lagged elections (*LELEX*) on spending is about −0.3 in both samples (columns 1–2); it is statistically significant in the broad sample but not in the sample of better democracies. Thus on average, spending is reduced by 0.3% of GDP in the year after elections. It appears that re-elected incumbent executives procrastinate over painful cuts in spending until the year after an election; alternatively, newly elected executives carry out necessary fiscal adjustments early on in their term. Second, taxes are cut by about 0.4% of GDP on average during an election year. Revenues are also raised after elections, adding further evidence that painful adjustments are postponed until after elections are over, but a significant postelection tax hike is present only in the better democracies (columns 3–4). Third, budget surpluses improve in years immediately after elections by about the same order of magnitude. Surpluses also deteriorate in the election year, but this preelection effect is small and not statistically significant (columns 5–6). Finally, no electoral cycle is evident in social security and welfare spending

Table 8.7
Electoral cycles in fiscal policy: Executive elections

	(1)	(2)	(3)	(4)	(5)	(6)	(7)	(8)
Dependent variable	CGEXP	CGEXP	CGREV	CGREV	SPL	SPL	SSW	SSW
ELEX	−0.01	0.03	−0.40	−0.40	−0.19	−0.16	0.07	0.07
	(0.16)	(0.18)	(0.14)***	(0.16)**	(0.14)	(0.16)	(0.06)	(0.07)
LELEX	−0.31	−0.26	0.20	0.29	0.38	0.38	0.05	0.06
	(0.16)**	(0.18)	(0.14)	(0.16)*	(0.14)***	(0.15)**	(0.06)	(0.07)
Sample	Broad	Narrow	Broad	Narrow	Broad	Narrow	Broad	Narrow
Number of observations	1,521	1,248	1,472	1,210	1,495	1,217	931	785
Number of countries	60	55	59	55	60	55	56	49
Adjusted R^2	0.83	0.84	0.83	0.84	0.58	0.61	0.80	0.81

Note: Standard errors in parentheses. All regressions include fixed country and year effects and the following covariates: *LYP, TRADE, PROP1564, PROP65, YGAP* (alone and interacted with *MAJ* and *PRES*), and lagged dependent variable (alone and interacted with *PRES* and *MAJ*). Narrow sample corresponds to countries and years where *POLITY_GT* is less than 1.1. "Adjusted R^2" refers to within-R^2.
* significant at 10%; ** significant at 5%; *** significant at 1%.

(columns 7–8). Contrary to the findings of earlier studies, we find no systematic evidence of worse democracies' having larger electoral cycles.

These findings are broadly in line with our priors and the predictions of the literature on electoral cycles. According to existing models, both opportunistic and rent-seeking incumbents want to appear competent in the eyes of imperfectly informed voters just before the elections, and they do this by manipulating policy in the election year. Government revenues do indeed fall in an election year, as predicted by both opportunistic and agency models of cycles. But government spending does not change in an average election year; the data are thus silent on the point at which the two models deliver different predictions. Instead, spending cuts are postponed until after elections. The latter effect seems to dominate the government budget balance, since the budget surplus also improves after elections. One interpretation of these findings is that tax revenue is easier to manipulate in a discretionary way, whereas aggregate government spending is more rigid, so that its timing is harder to fine-tune; when unpleasant spending cuts are perceived to be necessary, politicians procrastinate and do not impose them until after elections.[13] Another possible explanation is that these unconditional results conceal systematic differences across different political systems. We now turn to this possibility.

8.5.2 Proportional versus Majoritarian Democracies

Are electoral cycles similar under proportional and majoritarian elections? To answer this question, we split the two earlier indicator variables for election years (current and lagged) into four, two for proportional and two for majoritarian electoral systems. For example, the variable EL_MAJ is defined as $MAJ * ELEX$, and EL_PRO is defined as $(1 - MAJ) * ELEX$, with two new variables created from the lagged election indicators as well. Table 8.8 reports the results when we use these new indicators to estimate the same regression

---

13. The finding that tax cuts are enacted in election years is also in line with the empirical research quoted earlier in this section. But the existing literature typically estimates the coefficient only of a single election dummy variable and does not distinguish between preelection and postelection cycles (or imposes the restriction that the coefficients on election and postelection years be the same but with opposite signs). Thus to the best of our knowledge, the finding that painful fiscal adjustments tend to be delayed until after an election is new.

Table 8.8
Electoral cycles in fiscal policy: Alternative electoral rules

Dependent variable	(1) CGEXP	(2) CGEXP	(3) CGREV	(4) CGREV	(5) SPL	(6) SPL	(7) SSW	(8) SSW
EL_MAJ	-0.40	-0.42	-0.57	-0.52	-0.20	-0.15	-0.11	-0.17
	(0.28)	(0.31)	(0.24)**	(0.27)*	(0.25)	(0.27)	(0.10)	(0.11)
EL_PRO	0.20	0.27	-0.30	-0.33	-0.18	-0.16	0.17	0.21
	(0.20)	(0.22)	(0.18)*	(0.20)*	(0.18)	(0.19)	(0.08)**	(0.08)**
LEL_MAJ	-0.21	-0.15	0.14	0.28	0.27	0.37	-0.05	-0.07
	(0.28)	(0.31)	(0.24)	(0.27)	(0.25)	(0.26)	(0.10)	(0.11)
LEL_PRO	-0.36	-0.32	0.23	0.29	0.44	0.40	0.11	0.14
	(0.20)*	(0.22)	(0.17)	(0.20)	(0.18)**	(0.19)**	(0.08)	(0.09)
F: MAJ = PRO	3.05*	3.19*	0.80	0.35	0.00	0.00	4.98**	6.88***
F: LMAJ = LPRO	0.20	0.21	0.09	0.00	0.33	0.01	1.62	2.13
Sample	Broad	Narrow	Broad	Narrow	Broad	Narrow	Broad	Narrow
Number of observations	1,521	1,248	1,472	1,210	1,495	1,217	931	785
Number of countries	60	55	59	55	60	55	56	49
Adjusted R^2	0.83	0.84	0.83	0.84	0.58	0.61	0.80	0.81

Note: Standard errors in parentheses. All regressions include fixed country and year effects and the following covariates: *LYP, TRADE, PROP1564, PROP65, YGAP* (alone and interacted with *MAJ* and *PRES*), and lagged dependent variable (alone and interacted with *MAJ* and *PRES*). F: *MAJ = PRO* and F: *LMAJ = LPRO* refer to the test statistics for equal coefficients on *EL_MAJ* and *EL_PRO*, and *LEL_MAJ* and *LEL_PRO*, respectively. Narrow sample corresponds to countries and years where *POLITY_GT* is less than 1.1. "Adjusted R^2" refers to within-R^2.

* significant at 10%; ** significant at 5%; *** significant at 1%.

package as in section 8.5.1. The table also reports the F-statistic for a test of the hypothesis that the coefficients on the current (lagged) election indicators are equal across electoral rules.

Different electoral rules do indeed seem to induce quite different electoral cycles. Starting with the aggregate variables, we find that the election year tax cuts identified in section 8.5.1 seem to be common to both proportional and majoritarian elections (columns 3–4). But the estimated tax cuts in majoritarian countries are more aggressive, amounting to about 0.6% of GDP. In proportional countries, the tax cuts are smaller and not as precisely estimated. But we cannot reject the hypothesis that the policy shifts are the same in majoritarian and proportional countries.

Majoritarian countries cut spending during election years, though the estimated coefficients for the spending cuts (columns 1–2) are smaller and less precisely estimated than those of the tax cuts. In columns 1 and 2, an election has no effect on spending in proportional countries (if anything, spending goes up), and the difference between majoritarian and proportional countries is (marginally) significant. The postelection cycle with spending and deficit cuts estimated in section 8.5.1 is not perceptibly different across electoral rules, even though the coefficients are more precisely estimated (and only reach statistical significance) in proportional countries (columns 5–6).

The results for welfare state spending (columns 7–8) are starker. Proportional elections are associated with hikes in welfare state spending: transfers increase by 0.2% of GDP in election years and by almost as much in postelection years. If anything, this component of spending decreases under majoritarian elections, and the difference across electoral rules is highly significant for the preelection cycle. These results contrast sharply with the cycle in aggregate fiscal variables.

How can these findings be interpreted? On the one hand, majoritarian elections do induce more pronounced cycles in aggregate fiscal policy compared to proportional elections. This is in line with the general idea discussed in chapter 2 that electoral accountability and incentives to perform well are stronger under plurality rule than under PR. Specifically, the preelection tax cum spending cuts in majoritarian countries are consistent with agency models of political cycles, such as Besley and Case 1995 and Persson and Tabellini 2000a. Interestingly, our results for majoritarian countries are similar to Besley and Case's (1995) findings of preelection tax and spending cuts in U.S.-state executive elections. If anything, the preelection cycle estimated in proportional countries is consistent with an opportunistic/traditional political business cycle, à la Rogoff (1990). On the other hand, expansions in welfare state spending in proximity to elections are observed only in proportional countries. This finding is thus consistent with the theoretical hypothesis in chapter 2 that proportional electoral rules induce politicians to seek support among broad coalitions of voters, whereas majoritarian electoral rules instead induce them to target spending to smaller (geographic) groups, once we assume that these incentives are particularly strong around elections.

Overall, the results in this section correspond well with another general idea from comparative politics research in political science (also mentioned in the introductory chapter), namely, that majoritarian elections are mainly a vehicle for promoting accountability, whereas proportional elections are mainly a vehicle for promoting representation.

8.5.3 Parliamentary versus Presidential Democracies

We turn next to differences in electoral cycles among democracies with different forms of government. In analogy with the approach in section 8.5.2, we create four different indicator variables, interacting election dates with regime indicators: $EL\_PRE = PRES * ELEX$, $EL\_PAR = (1 - PRES) * ELEX$, and analogously for the lagged election dates. Using these new indicators in the estimations for our four fiscal instruments generates the results displayed in table 8.9.

The results of these estimations strongly suggest that the postelection cycle in overall government spending, taxes, and budget surplus identified above is predominantly due to the presidential countries. Governments in presidential regimes cut spending considerably just after an election, by about 0.8% of GDP. They also postpone tax hikes by the same magnitudes, with correspondingly large effects on the budget surplus, which improves by about 0.75% of GDP after a typical presidential election. Some postelection spending and deficit adjustments also appear to take place in parliamentary regimes, but the effects of these are smaller and not statistically significant. The postelection differences between the two regime types are strongest (and highly significant) for taxes and overall spending.

Table 8.9
Electoral cycles in fiscal policy: Alternative forms of government

Dependent variable	(1) CGEXP	(2) CGEXP	(3) CGREV	(4) CGREV	(5) SPL	(6) SPL	(7) SSW	(8) SSW
EL_PRE	-0.23	-0.17	-0.26	-0.03	-0.21	-0.09	0.07	0.08
	(0.32)	(0.43)	(0.28)	(0.37)	(0.28)	(0.36)	(0.13)	(0.16)
EL_PAR	0.08	0.08	-0.45	-0.48	-0.18	-0.18	0.07	0.07
	(0.19)	(0.20)	(0.16)***	(0.18)***	(0.17)	(0.17)	(0.07)	(0.08)
LEL_PRE	-0.76	-0.93	0.53	1.01	0.69	0.82	-0.10	-0.17
	(0.32)**	(0.41)**	(0.28)*	(0.36)***	(0.28)**	(0.35)**	(0.12)	(0.16)
LEL_PAR	-0.14	-0.10	0.08	0.12	0.27	0.28	0.10	0.12
	(0.19)	(0.20)	(0.16)	(0.17)	(0.17)	(0.17)	(0.07)	(0.08)
F: PRE = PAR	0.69	0.27	0.37	1.19	0.01	0.06	0.00	0.00
F: LPRE = LPAR	2.75*	3.21*	1.88	4.84**	1.69	1.88	1.90	2.72*
Sample	Broad	Narrow	Broad	Narrow	Broad	Narrow	Broad	Narrow
Number of observations	1,521	1,248	1,472	1,210	1,495	1,217	931	785
Number of countries	60	55	59	55	60	55	56	49
Adjusted R^2	0.83	0.84	0.83	0.84	0.58	0.61	0.80	0.81

Note: Standard errors in parentheses. All regressions include fixed country and year effects and the following covariates: *LYP, TRADE, PROP1564, PROP65, YGAP* (alone and interacted with *MAJ* and *PRES*), and lagged dependent variable (alone and interacted with *MAJ* and *PRES*). F: *PRE = PAR* and F: *LPRE = LPAR* refer to the test statistics for equal coefficients on *EL_PRE* and *EL_PAR*, and *LEL_PRE* and *LEL_PAR*, respectively. Narrow sample corresponds to countries and years where *POLITY_GT* is less than 1.1. "Adjusted R^2" refers to within-R^2.

* significant at 10%; ** significant at 5%; *** significant at 1%.

As already suggested by the division according to electoral rules, systematic preelection tax cuts are common for all countries, regardless of regime type. They are stronger and more precisely estimated in the parliamentary regimes, however, for which the estimates suggest tax cuts of about 0.5% of GDP in an average election year. The results for welfare state spending do not indicate pronounced effects anywhere, except perhaps among the better democracies, in which parliamentary governments raise this component of spending after elections, and presidential governments seem to cut it after elections, along with aggregate spending.

The postelection cycles in presidential countries are intriguing, and existing theory does not suggest a straightforward explanation for them. One difference between the two regimes is that the election dates in presidential regimes are generally fixed, whereas they are subject to choice in most parliamentary countries (Norway and Sweden are among the few exceptions). As mentioned above, however, we deal with the potential endogeneity problem by including output gaps in our econometric specification. The different electoral cycles in the two regimes are thus not likely to be a statistical artifact.

The different rules for legislative bargaining discussed in chapter 2 may provide an interpretation of the postelection cycle. Presidential regimes tend to have more decision makers with proposal and veto rights than parliamentary regimes; for instance, in many presidential countries, both the president and the legislature must approve the budget. The possibility of fiscal deadlock might accordingly be more serious, particularly in the case of divided government (i.e., when the president and congress belong to different parties or when the congress does not have a well-defined majority party). Each decision maker may be able to veto painful adjustments before elections, but none may have the strength to pass deliberate fiscal expansions or tax cuts. In parliamentary democracies, in contrast, the same legislative majority typically also controls the executive and approves the budget in the parliament and is thus better able to fine-tune fiscal policy to its electoral concerns.[14] Testing this interpretation would

---

14. This reasoning is similar to the idea in the literature on U.S. state fiscal policy that legislative institutions, such as a governor's line item veto, have more bite on taxes, spending, and deficits in situations of divided government, an idea that has received some empirical support. See Besley and Case 2002 for an extensive survey of this literature.

require careful data collection and coding of the partisan identity of presidents and legislative majorities.

But this is not the only plausible interpretation. Another possibility, also consistent with other results in this chapter, is that presidential countries are more likely to face binding government borrowing constraints. In section 8.4, we saw that presidential countries tend to have an acyclical or procyclical, rather than a countercyclical, fiscal policy. If governments in presidential countries do face tighter borrowing constraints, they may also have to undertake more painful fiscal adjustments than parliamentary democracies. It might be optimal to postpone such painful adjustments until after elections. Indeed, empirical research by Frieden and Stein (2001) has found robust evidence that exchange rate devaluations tend to be postponed until after presidential elections in many Latin American countries (among which presidential regimes are overrepresented). The results in the next section offer other indirect evidence in favor of this interpretation.

8.5.4   A Four-Way Constitutional Split

So far, we have chosen to look for system-dependent electoral cycles in parsimonious specifications in which we condition only on one constitutional difference at a time. Although the tests for different electoral cycles in policy are valid under the null hypothesis of no differences, the reader may legitimately ask whether the specifications in the two preceding subsections can be true at the same time to the extent that we find differences across constitutional features. The answer is probably in the negative: even under our implicit assumption that any constitutional differences are additive, the estimates of constitution-dependent cycles will still be biased if the frequency of the omitted constitutional feature, say, form of government, differs across the included feature, say, electoral rule. The likely culprit here is that our sample includes few elections in presidential countries with majoritarian electoral rules. For a total of 503 non-midterm election dates in our panel, only 24 are thus associated with presidential-majoritarian constitutional features, whereas the other three types are much better represented (for presidential countries with proportional elections, we have 131 elections, and for parliamentary-majoritarian and parliamentary-proportional, we have 135 and 213 elections, respectively). This means that our estimates above of the cycle under majoritarian elections may be biased in the direction of the cycle found for parliamentary countries (if different from the presidential cycle). Conversely, estimates of the cycle in presidential countries may be biased in the direction of the cycle found for proportional elections (if different from the majoritarian cycle).

To address this issue and further explain the source of our results, we condition the electoral-cycle estimates on four separate constitutional groups (labeled EL_MAJPRE, and so on, in the obvious notation). Table 8.10 shows the estimates of pre- and postelection cycles in these four groups.

Key findings in table 8.8 are the unique preelection spending cuts and stronger preelection tax cuts under majoritarian elections. Are these driven by the higher frequency of parliamentary countries and the regime differences found in table 8.9, as the above discussion suggests might be the case? The results in table 8.10 indicate the answer to be no (see the upper part of columns 1–4). The coefficients show that election year spending and tax cuts occur in both the presidential (called EL_MAJPRE) and the parliamentary (called EL_MAJPAR) subgroups of majoritarian countries. Moreover, the tax cuts are larger among the majoritarian-presidential democracies for all specifications. A more balanced sample (with more presidential countries) would thus have produced even larger estimates (in absolute value) in table 8.8.

Another key result in table 8.8 is the finding that electoral cycles in welfare state spending are uniquely associated with proportional electoral rules. The estimates in table 8.10 (columns 7–8) show that the results for the preelection cycle reflect hikes in welfare state spending in the parliamentary and presidential subgroups alike. But postelection hikes in welfare state spending are found exclusively among proportional-parliamentary countries, a group that includes many of the European welfare states.

The key finding in table 8.9 is the uniqueness of postelection fiscal adjustment to presidential democracies. The results in table 8.10 (the lower part of columns 1–6) do indeed suggest that the results are driven by the higher frequency of proportional-presidential than of majoritarian-presidential democracies in our sample. Although the postelection fiscal adjustments are made in the same direction in both these groups, they are always larger in the proportional-presidential subgroup. Since this group is predominant in Latin America, the results give some indirect support for an interpretation

Table 8.10
Electoral cycles in fiscal policy: Alternative constitutional groups

Dependent variable	(1) CGEXP	(2) CGEXP	(3) CGREV	(4) CGREV	(5) SPL	(6) SPL	(7) SSW	(8) SSW
EL_MAJPRE	-1.04	-0.82	-1.11	-0.73	0.19	0.22	0.00	-0.08
	(0.70)	(0.80)	(0.59)*	(0.68)	(0.61)	(0.68)	(0.26)	(0.28)
EL_PROPRE	0.00	0.10	-0.00	0.26	-0.33	-0.21	0.10	0.15
	(0.36)	(0.50)	(0.32)	(0.45)	(0.31)	(0.43)	(0.15)	(0.19)
EL_MAJPAR	-0.27	-0.34	-0.48	-0.50	-0.28	-0.23	-0.13	-0.18
	(0.31)	(0.33)	(0.26)*	(0.29)*	(0.27)	(0.29)	(0.11)	(0.12)
EL_PROPAR	0.30	0.31	-0.44	-0.48	-0.12	-0.16	0.20	0.22
	(0.24)	(0.25)	(0.21)**	(0.22)**	(0.22)	(0.22)	(0.09)**	(0.09)**
LEL_MAJPRE	-0.32	-0.27	0.27	0.47	0.50	0.82	-0.09	-0.07
	(0.71)	(0.78)	(0.59)	(0.68)	(0.63)	(0.67)	(0.27)	(0.28)
LEL_PROPRE	-0.87	-1.22	0.61	1.24	0.74	0.83	-0.09	-0.21
	(0.36)**	(0.50)**	(0.32)*	(0.44)***	(0.31)**	(0.43)*	(0.14)	(0.19)
LEL_MAJPAR	-0.18	-0.12	0.11	0.23	0.22	0.28	-0.03	-0.07
	(0.31)	(0.34)	(0.26)	(0.29)	(0.27)	(0.29)	(0.11)	(0.12)
LEL_PROPAR	-0.12	-0.09	0.06	0.05	0.31	0.28	0.19	0.22
	(0.24)	(0.25)	(0.21)	(0.22)	(0.21)	(0.21)	(0.09)**	(0.09)**
Sample	Broad	Narrow	Broad	Narrow	Broad	Narrow	Broad	Narrow
Number of observations	1,521	1,248	1,472	1,210	1,493	1,215	931	785
Number of countries	60	55	59	55	60	55	56	49
Adjusted R^2	0.83	0.85	0.83	0.84	0.58	0.61	0.80	0.81

Note: Standard errors in parentheses. All regressions include fixed country and year effects and the following covariates: *LYP, TRADE, PROP1564, PROP65, YGAP* (alone and interacted with *MAJ* and *PRES*), and lagged dependent variable (alone and interacted with *PRES* and *MAJ*). Narrow sample corresponds to countries and years where *POLITY_GT* is less than 1.1. "Adjusted R^2" refers to within-R^2.
* significant at 10%; ** significant at 5%; *** significant at 1%.

in terms of borrowing constraints, such as the one offered at the end of section 8.5.3.

8.5.5 Summary

We have uncovered strong constitutional effects on the presence and nature of electoral cycles in fiscal policy. True, governments in all countries appear to cut taxes in election years. But only presidential regimes postpone unpopular fiscal policy adjustments until after elections. Only governments in majoritarian countries cut spending during election years. And only proportional democracies raise welfare spending before elections, with further commitments for post-election years.

8.6 Concluding Remarks

In chapter 6, we exploited the variation in fiscal policy across *countries* to draw inferences about constitutional effects. In that chapter, we found presidential and majoritarian systems to have smaller governments, as compared to parliamentary and proportional systems; moreover, majoritarian elections were found to induce smaller welfare states and budget deficits than proportional elections. This chapter has instead exploited the variation in fiscal policy across *time*. Our findings here shed further light on our earlier conclusions and the mechanisms through which a country's constitution might shape its fiscal policy.

Proportional-parliamentary democracies differ from other constitutional groups in several respects. First, fiscal policy is much more persistent in this group than in the others. Second, this is the only group of countries in which we find a ratchet effect on spending: downturns lead to a lasting expansion of outlays and welfare spending in proportion to GDP that is not reversed during upturns. Third, in this group of countries, welfare state programs expand more in the proximity of elections than in other years. Fourth, the difference in the size of government between this group and the others grew particularly large in the period up to the early 1980s (the early 1990s in the case of welfare spending), in response to some unobserved events that led to a generalized increase of government outlays everywhere. These features of proportional-parliamentary systems all contribute to an explanation of why such systems have larger governments than other constitutional groups in the 1990s.

Presidential regimes also stand out from parliamentary regimes in some important respects. Procyclical responses of fiscal policy and procrastination with regard to painful fiscal adjustments are peculiar to this group, A possible explanation for these characteristics is that presidential regimes are more likely than parliamentary regimes to face tight borrowing constraints. Fiscal policy is also less persistent among presidential countries than among parliamentary countries. Countries with majoritarian elections share some of these features, although they do not have them to the same extent that presidential countries do; majoritarian countries are also unique in cutting not only taxes, but also overall spending, during election years.

In many ways, the findings in this chapter are more preliminary than those reported in chapter 6 (and chapter 7). Much more remains to be done to exploit the observed variation in the data. The dynamic interaction between fiscal policy and the business cycle could be more carefully studied, for example, by allowing for a (contemporaneous or delayed) impact of policy on the state of the economy, as in a panel Vector Auto Regression. The findings on electoral cycles in this chapter suggest that it may be worth it to dig deeper into the institutional details of such cycles by studying, for example, the effect of time limits for presidential terms or the specific rules for breaking up the government and calling new elections in parliamentary regimes. Interesting sources of time variation in the data that might interact with the constitution have not been exploited in this chapter, such as swings of the executive from the left to the right or changes in the quality of a democracy. For empirical efforts in the directions we are suggesting to be fruitful, existing theory needs to be extended so as to generate more precise empirical predictions. We leave it to future research to pursue these interesting issues.

9   What Have We Learned?

It is time to take stock of our findings. We start by summarizing the empirical results uncovered in chapters 6 through 8. The summary provokes a discussion of what lessons one may learn from these results, first concerning the electoral rule, then for the form of government. Which theoretical ideas are supported by the data? Which ought to be reformulated? What are the main puzzles? On the basis of this discussion, we then close the chapter and the book by outlining some directions for future research.

9.1   Theoretical Priors and Empirical Results

In chapter 2, we recapitulated the priors from existing theory in a list of questions to be posed to the data. That list becomes a useful checklist when accounting for the results of our empirical investigation. The columns in table 9.1 headed "Theory" thus reproduce the contents of table 2.1 and summarize the predicted constitutional effects of changing the electoral rule (in a randomly drawn country) from proportional to majoritarian or the form of government from parliamentary to presidential. The columns headed "Data" show a bold attempt to sum up succinctly our empirical findings. In those columns, a zero means that no significant constitutional effect was found, whereas a plus sign or a minus sign indicates the qualitative direction of a statistically significant effect. Naturally, distilling the many dimensions and edges of our quantitative findings into this simple scheme makes it necessary to cut some corners. But as the theory provides only qualitative predictions, the table provides a useful perspective on the mapping from priors to posteriors that is suggested by the data.

Table 9.1
Constitutions and economic policy: Questions and findings

Policy outcome	Electoral rules Majoritarian vs. proportional		Form of government Presidential vs. parliamentary	
	Theory	Data	Theory	Data
Overall size of government	$-/?$	$-$	$-$	$-$
Composition: Broad versus narrow programs	$-$	$-$	$-$	$0/-$
Rent extraction	$+/-$	$+/-$	$-$	0
Government deficits	$-/?$	$-$	$?$	0
Structural policy / Economic performance	$?$	$+/-$	$?$	$-$
Adjustment to shocks	$?$	$0/-$	$?$	$-$
Electoral cycles	$+/?$	$+/-$	$?$	$+/-$

Note: A plus (minus) sign in a Theory column indicates that a constitutional reform, replacing the feature on the right at the top of the column with the feature on the left will induce a greater (smaller) degree or a higher (lower) level of the policy outcome for that row. A question mark indicates an unclear theoretical prior about the sign of the constitutional effect. The sign in the Data column indicates the direction of the empirically estimated effect of such a reform (a 0 indicates an inconclusive empirical result). See the discussion of this table in section 9.1 for more specific interpretations of the symbols.

9.1.1 Electoral Rules

One of the central findings in this book is the strong constitutional effect of electoral rules on fiscal policy. Existing theoretical arguments, emphasizing different aspects of electoral rules, predict that majoritarian elections induce smaller welfare states than proportional elections; some, but not all, theories also predict smaller governments and smaller deficits in countries with majoritarian election rules. In the data, we find that welfare states are indeed smaller in majoritarian countries; so are overall government spending and deficits, which sharpens our fuzzy theoretical priors. According to the cross-sectional evidence presented in chapter 6, a switch from proportional to majoritarian elections reduces overall government spending by almost 5% of GDP, welfare spending by 2–3% of GDP, and budget deficits by about 2% of GDP. Advocates in the United Kingdom of the opposite switch, from majoritarian to proportional, should take careful note of these findings. The electoral rule emerges from this research as one of the primary determinants of fiscal policy in modern democracies. According to our results, the proposed electoral reform in the United Kingdom would increase its public sector to a size more similar to that in continental Europe.

A related finding in chapter 8 concerns the response of spending to common unobserved events: the worldwide growth of welfare state spending and total government spending in the 1970s and 1980s was much more pronounced in proportional than in majoritarian countries. The cumulative effect of the different growth profiles amounts to almost 5% of GDP for total government spending and to about 2% of GDP for welfare spending, numbers remarkably similar to the cross-sectional effect. The panel data analysis does not point to a large impact of electoral rules on the cyclical reaction of fiscal policy or on its degree of persistence, but for these effects, we did not have any meaningful theoretical priors.

Some theoretical models also suggest a stronger electoral cycle under majoritarian elections, as politicians face sharper individual incentives to please their constituencies than under proportional elections. In chapter 8, we do find that electoral cycles vary with the electoral rule in a subtle pattern. The findings do not contradict our theoretical priors, but they contain some unexpected elements. On the one hand, majoritarian countries alone cut not only taxes, but also spending, ahead of elections, by as much as 0.5% of GDP. An interpretation of this finding is that incumbent governments under majoritarian rule want to appear less wasteful in the eyes of voters, as suggested by agency theories of politics. On the other hand, proportional countries alone expand welfare programs in election years, by something like 0.2% of GDP (about 2.5% of program size in the average country in our sample). A possible interpretation is that incumbent governments under proportional rule have strong incentives to seek reelection support from broad coalitions of voters and that these incentives are at their peak just before elections. As we observe an additional expansion of these programs in the years immediately following elections, some garnering of votes may take the form of promises in electoral platforms (subsequently honored), rather than expansions before elections.

In the case of political rents and corruption, we expected the fine details of electoral rules to influence outcomes, but not necessarily the coarse distinction between majoritarian and proportional rule. Our empirical findings in chapter 7 are in line with the theoretical predictions. Direct individual accountability via individual ballots under plurality rule reduces both corruption and government ineffectiveness, as expected. Small electoral districts do the opposite, in line with the idea that barriers to entry are higher in single-member districts. Both effects are statistically robust and quantitatively significant. Since these two dimensions of the electoral rule covary, the net effect of a comprehensive reform toward majoritarian elections on rent extraction is ambiguous, even though the effect of individual accountability seems to (weakly) prevail in the data.

We did not have much of a theoretical prior concerning growth-promoting policies and productivity. The empirically estimated constitutional effects in chapter 7 are similar to those for rent extraction. Both larger electoral districts and more direct individual accountability promote higher productivity through policies that better protect private property rights. But the crude classification into majoritarian versus proportional elections has no robust effect on these variables. Although there is some evidence of a direct negative effect of majoritarian elections on labor productivity, this constitutional effect is not robust to selection bias.

These findings support a general idea in the political-science literature on comparative politics: the design of electoral rules entails a trade-off between accountability and representation. Aspects of this general idea also appear in recent theoretical studies in political economics. Majoritarian elections and, in particular, plurality rule make electoral outcomes more sensitive to marginal changes in the distribution of votes. On the one hand, this creates stronger incentives for politicians not to use their office for private gain (reduces rents and corruption). On the other hand, marginal groups of voters may be targeted in electoral platforms or overrepresented in the assembly, so that narrow programs benefiting these voters may crowd out broad programs benefiting larger groups of citizens, such as welfare state spending and general public goods. The general idea of a trade-off between accountability and representation is both intuitive and theoretically robust. Now we can add that the trade-off shows up in observed policies, given our empirical findings on political rents, the character of electoral cycles, and the size of broad welfare state programs.

But perhaps the terms of this trade-off can be made more favorable by specific reforms. A lesson suggested by our results is that any real-world electoral reform should pay attention to the finer details of the electoral system. The accountability effects of majoritarian systems seem to be directly related to ballot structures and plurality rule, as well as to the size of electoral districts. Voting over individuals in two- or three-member districts, as in Chile and Mauritius, might be a way of reaping the benefits of plurality rule and individual accountability without erecting too-high barriers for entry in the electoral process. Such hybrid systems might present an interesting alternative to the mixed-member systems introduced by a number of countries in the 1990s (cf. chapter 4).

Another theoretical idea, indirectly supported by our evidence, is that majoritarian elections may help resolve the common-pool problem in fiscal policy. A robust finding in the comparative politics literature cited in chapter 2 is that PR promotes coalition governments. The theoretical literature on political economics has suggested that such governments have a hard time controlling government spending and budget deficits, because of inefficient bargaining inside the coalition. The idea may not be as fully fleshed out in formal terms as the accountability/representation trade-off, but it does suggest that proportional electoral rule induces both larger government spending and larger budget deficits. This is precisely what we uncover in the data, with the large and robust constitutional effects estimated in chapter 6.

Another idea about coalition governments is that they are prone to a status quo bias, because they have several veto players. Hence, their reaction to adverse economic shocks is more likely to be inefficient than the response of single-party governments. The findings in chapter 8 on the cyclical response of fiscal policy lend some indirect support to this idea. According to the data, governments elected under majoritarian rule seem to react to cyclical downturns (consistent with Keynesian stabilization policies) by cutting taxes. Governments elected under proportional rule, on the other hand, are more likely to let spending rise (as a percentage of GDP) during downturns but are unable to scale it down during upturns: this is the ratchet effect uncovered in chapter 8.

9.1.2 Forms of Government

The theory of policy choices under different forms of government is less developed than that on electoral rules. But a central theoretical prediction is that presidential countries are less plagued by political rent extraction (corruption) than parliamentary countries, at the expense of public-goods provision and smaller transfers to broad population groups. Another strong prediction is a smaller overall size of government in presidential regimes. No clear-cut predictions are available for the other outcomes listed in table 9.1 (the budget deficit, the dynamic and cyclical response of policy, electoral cycles, and structural policy and economic performance).

With regard to the size of government, the data strongly support the predictions. According to the cross-sectional estimates in chapter 6, presidentialism reduces the overall size of government at least as much as majoritarian elections, by about 5% of GDP. The interaction effects uncovered by our panel data analysis in chapter 8 suggest even larger differences. Indeed, much of the difference in the size of government across regimes can be traced back to a less rapid growth of government in presidential regimes during the 1970s and 1980s. Compared to that in parliamentary regimes, government spending in presidential democracies is also much less persistent, with a more dampened response to common unobserved events. Moreover, the ratchet effect on government spending in response to cyclical fluctuations that we observe in parliamentary-proportional democracies is certainly not a feature of presidential democracies.

Unconditionally, presidential democracies do have lower welfare spending than parliamentary democracies, in line with our prior, as well as smaller deficits. But here the constitutional effects estimated in chapter 6 are less robust, and it is difficult to identify the constitutional effect separately from that of other policy determinants: smaller welfare spending can be attributed to younger populations, and smaller budget deficits could result from tighter borrowing constraints in more unstable and crisis-prone societies, rather than from institutionally induced policy preferences.

An electoral fiscal policy cycle in presidential countries is evident from our results in chapter 8. It takes a peculiar, postelectoral form, however, quite different from the cycle observed in parliamentary democracies: spending cuts and fiscal contractions by as much as 1% of GDP are postponed until an incumbent president has survived an election or a newly elected president has been installed.

According to the empirical results of chapter 7, and contrary to the predictions of theory, perceptions of corruption and government ineffectiveness are not generally higher under parliamentary forms of government than under presidential forms. Moreover, presidential regimes are associated with significantly worse economic performance, because of their worse structural policies, in which the legal infrastructure is less respectful of property rights and less likely to enforce government contracts than that in parliamentary regimes. This effect is quantitatively significant: our estimates in chapter 7 suggest that adoption of a presidential regime in Spain would (in the long run) eliminate the country's lead over Greece in structural policy and productivity. Both of these effects seem to interact with the quality of democratic institutions, however: a negative effect of presidentialism on corruption seems to be present among better democracies, whereas the negative effect of presidentialism on productivity and growth-promoting policies appears to be stronger among worse democracies.

The theory discussed in chapter 2 suggests an analogy between the constitutional choices associated with electoral rules and forms of government. Although the reasons in each case are somewhat different, both imply a trade-off between accountability and representation. For the form of government, this trade-off is not apparent in the data, however. We obtain robust support for one prediction (presidential regimes have smaller governments than parliamentary regimes), but our results for the central predictions regarding rent extraction and welfare programs are much more fragile.

A possible reason for this inconsistency is that theory relies on more than one feature that are not well captured empirically by a single binary classification. In the theory surveyed in chapter 2, a presidential democracy has two features: the executive is not accountable to the legislature through a confidence requirement, and institutional checks and balances induce effective separation of powers between the executive and the legislature or among different congressional committees. Our empirical classification is based on the first dimension (lack of a confidence requirement on the executive), neglecting the separation-of-powers aspect.

As noted several times in the book, presidential regimes are over-represented in Latin America and among more dubious (or at least younger) democracies. Thus they are less likely to have effective checks and balances, not only because of their imperfect political institutions, but also because the media in those democracies are less likely to be independent and the respect for democratic traditions less deeply entrenched. Presidential states typically have stronger executives than parliamentary states. If bad democracies have fewer checks and balances, the resulting concentration of political power could lead to harmful policies. On the other side of the coin, a good democracy may be needed for a presidential regime to restrain the abuse of political power. Our preliminary result in chapter 7 that presidentialism possibly restrains corruption among the best democracies while it particularly harms economic performance among the worst democracies gives some indirect support to this interpretation. It also suggests that presidentialism could lead to overall better policies in consolidated and solid democracies, but not in more precarious democratic situations. A more direct way to address this interpretation is to collect more data, along the lines suggested in chapter 4, trying to document the dispersion in the separation of powers across countries. This observation takes us right into the agenda for future research discussed in the next and final section.

9.2   What Next?

The comparison between theoretical priors and empirical findings in table 9.1 is certainly encouraging. Several of the empirical regularities discovered in the book are in line with the first wave of theory. The constitutional effects on fiscal policy and political rents found in the data match up strikingly well with theory, particularly for the electoral rule.

But in many ways, the state of our knowledge is still very preliminary. The theoretical models motivating our empirical investigation are only a first step. And the constitutional effects uncovered in this book concern reduced forms in the data—from constitutional rules to policy outcomes. A first-order priority in the next wave of research, both theoretical and empirical, should be to gain a better understanding of the detailed mechanisms through which a country's constitution influences its policy. Making progress on this task would also help build a stronger bridge between existing research in economics and political science.

Consider the electoral rule, for example. Existing theories formulated by economists have mainly focused on how the electoral rules shape electoral competition or electoral accountability (mainly in a two-party system) and how this, in turn, affects policy outcomes. This way of formulating the comparative politics problem neglects the links from the electoral system to party structure, from party structure to government formation and legislative bargaining, and from these political outcomes to policy formation. As mentioned in chapters 1 and 2, political scientists have studied each of these links as a separate phenomenon. Understanding the relative importance of the direct effects, via policymaking incentives for given political outcomes, and the indirect effects, via altered political outcomes, requires a more encompassing approach.

Bridging the gap between the economics and political science research on electoral rules constitutes an important, interesting, and very open agenda. In theoretical research, that agenda entails addressing the difficult issues of legislative bargaining under different electoral rules, perhaps with an endogenous number of political parties. In empirical research, it entails studying how observed policy outcomes correlate with observed political outcomes—party structures, types of government, legislative majorities—and how those outcomes, in turn, are associated with alternative electoral rules.

Although data on such political outcomes are readily available for a small group of developed democracies, this is not the case for most of the other countries in our two data sets. Further empirical work thus requires a nontrivial investment in data collection, particularly to obtain political outcome data going back in time. New data collection is also necessary to exploit the time variation associated with electoral reform for more secure causal inference. Although the broad features of electoral systems are very stable, countries tinker much more with the finer details: district magnitudes, ballot structures, thresholds for representation, the openness of party lists, etc. Once more, it is necessary to invest considerable time and effort to document all such piecemeal reforms for, say, 60 countries over 40 years.

The future research agenda on alternative forms of government is even more open. Little is known in theory about how alternative rules for government formation or dissolution, or alternative rules for the functioning of legislatures, shape economic policy outcomes. Even less is known about the empirical association of these detailed institutional features and observed economic policies. At the end of section 9.1, we mentioned that our empirical measures are incomplete in the separation-of-powers dimension and that this makes them less suitable for the testing of certain predictions.

Existing theory of policymaking and comparative politics is restrictive also in a different dimension: it is generally confined to *static* models of economics and politics. The lack of dynamics becomes a glaring omission when we try to interpret the empirical puzzles associated with time patterns in observed policy. To understand how fiscal policy responds to economic fluctuations, why fiscal adjustments are delayed, and why some political systems are more likely to pile up government debt or face tight borrowing constraints, we obviously need dynamic models. In particular, we need models that assign an important role to state variables, such as government debt, and models that include links between current policy decisions and future status quo points.

On the policy side, we have concentrated on fiscal policy and rent extraction. We have also scratched the surface of the policies most likely to promote economic growth. But much more could be done to gain a better understanding of how constitutional features shape economic performance through public policy. It would then be interesting and feasible to study other policy instruments, such as the structure of taxation, microregulatory policies, more detailed measures of trade policy, and perhaps environmental policy, with the methods illustrated in this book.

On the constitutional side, we have concentrated on electoral rules and forms of government. In the process, however, we have also discovered interesting effects of other fundamental constitutional features, such as federal structure and quality of democratic institutions. The quality and age of democracies seem to interact with the electoral rule and form of government in shaping various aspects of economic policies. These findings further strengthen our belief that several aspects of a country's constitution help shape its economic policy. Our data indicate important and subtle complementarities between political rights, democratic traditions, details of the electoral rule, and the form of government.

All in all, exploring further the constitutional effects on economic policy and performance is a worthwhile but challenging task that requires an iteration through rigorous theory, careful collection of data, and solid statistical work. Progress on this task will advance the research frontier in economics as well as political science.

Data Appendix

The two data sets used in the book and including the variables defined below are available at our home pages: ⟨http://www.iies.su.se/~perssont/⟩ and ⟨http://www.uni-bocconi.it/tabellini⟩.

AFRICA: regional dummy variable, equal to 1 if a country is in Africa, 0 otherwise.

AGE: age of democracy, defined as $AGE = (2000 - DEM\_AGE)/200$ and varying between 0 and 1, with the United States being the oldest democracy (value of 1). Source: see *POLITY*.

ASIAE: regional dummy variable, equal to 1 if a country is in East Asia, 0 otherwise.

AUTOC: indicator of institutionalized autocracy, derived from codings of the competitiveness of political participation, the regulation of participation, the openness and competitiveness of executive recruitment, and constraints on the chief executive. Source: Polity IV Project ⟨http://www.cidcm.umd.edu/inscr/polity/index.htm⟩.

AVELF: index of ethnolinguistic fractionalization, approximating the level of lack of ethnic and linguistic cohesion within a country, ranging from 0 (homogeneous) to 1 (strongly fractionalized) and averaging five different indexes. Source: La Porta et al. 1999. For central and eastern Europe countries computations follow Mauro 1995, with data from Quain 1999.

CATHO80: percentage of a country's population belonging to the Roman Catholic religion in 1980. Source: La Porta et al. 1998.

CCG_NET_0: consolidated central government net domestic debt as a percentage of gross national disposable income in the first year for which a value of *SPL* is available. Consolidated central government (CCG) is defined as budgetary central government plus extrabudgetary central government plus social security agencies. The definition of central government is equivalent to that of general government minus local and regional governments. Source: World Savings Database.

CGEXP: central government expenditures as a percentage of GDP, constructed using the item Government Finance–Expenditures in the IFS, divided by GDP at current prices and multiplied by 100. Sources: IMF-IFS CD-ROM and *IMF-IFS Yearbook*.

CGREV: central government revenues as a percentage of GDP, constructed using the item Government Finance–Revenues in the IFS, divided by GDP at current prices and multiplied by 100. Sources: IMF-IFS CD-ROM and *IMF-IFS Yearbook*.

CLIST: dummy variable for closed party lists. Sources: see *LIST* and *SEATS*.

COL_ESP: dummy variable, equal to 1 if the country is a former colony of Spain or Portugal, 0 otherwise. Source: Wacziarg 1996.

COL_ESPA: Spanish colonial origin, discounted by the number of years since independence (*T_INDEP*), and defined as $COL\_ESPA = COL\_ESP * (250 - T\_INDEP)/250$. Source: Wacziarg 1996.

COL_OTH: dummy variable, equal to 1 if the country is a former colony of a country other than Spain, Portugal, or the United Kingdom, 0 otherwise. Source: Wacziarg 1996.

COL_OTHA: defined as $COL\_OTH * (250 - T\_INDEP)/250$. See also *COL_ESPA*. Source: Wacziarg 1996.

COL_UK: dummy variable, equal to 1 if the country is a former U.K. colony, 0 otherwise. Source: Wacziarg 1996.

COL_UKA: defined as $COL\_UKA = COL\_UK * (250 - T\_INDEP)/250$. See also *COL_ESPA*. Source: Wacziarg 1996.

CON2150: dummy variable for the period in which a country's current constitutional features originated, equal to 1 if either *YEARELE* or *YEARREG* falls in the period between 1921 and 1950, 0 otherwise.
Source: see *YEARREG* and *YEARELE*.

CON5180: dummy variable for the period in which a country's current constitutional features originated, equal to 1 if either *YEARELE* or *YEARREG* falls in the period between 1951 and 1980, 0 otherwise.
Source: see *YEARREG* and *YEARELE*.

CON81: dummy variable for the period in which a country's current constitutional features originated, equal to 1 if either *YEARELE* or *YEARREG* falls in the period after 1981, 0 otherwise. Source: see *YEARREG* and *YEARELE*.

CONFU: dummy variable for the religious tradition in a country, equal to 1 if the majority of the country's population is Confucian/Buddhist/Zen, 0 otherwise. Sources: Wacziarg 1996, CIA 2000.

CPI9500: corruption perception index, measuring perceptions of abuse of power by public officials. Average, over 1995–2000, of the CPI, which ranges from 0 to 10, with higher values denoting more corruption. Sources: Transparency International ⟨www.transparency.de⟩ and Internet Center for Corruption Research ⟨www.gwdg.de/~uwvw⟩.

DCGEXP: first difference of *CGEXP*. Source: see *CGEXP*.

DEM_AGE: first year of democratic rule in a country, corresponding to the first year of a string of positive yearly values of the variable *POLITY* for that country that continues uninterrupted until the end of the sample, given that the country was also an independent nation during the entire time period. Does not count foreign occupation during World War II as an interruption of democracy. Source: see *POLITY*.

DEMOC: institutionalized democracy index, derived from codings of the competitiveness of political participation, the regulation of participation, the openness and competitiveness of executive recruitment, and constraints on the chief executive. Source: Polity IV Project ⟨http://www.cidcm.umd.edu/ inscr/polity/index.htm⟩.

DISTRICTS: number of electoral districts in a country (including the number of primary as well as secondary and tertiary, if applicable). Sources: Quain 1999, Kurian 1998, and national sources.

DSPL: first difference of *SPL*. Source: see *SPL*.

DSSW: first difference of *SSW*. Source: see *SSW*.

EDUGER: total enrollment in primary and secondary education in a country, as a percentage of the relevant age group in the country's population. Computed by dividing the number of pupils (or students) enrolled in a given level of education (regardless of age) by the population of the age group that officially corresponds to the given level of education and multiplying the result by 100. *Source:* UNESCO–Education Indicator–Category Participation, available at ⟨www.unesco.org⟩.

ELEX: dummy variable for elections of a country's executive, equal to 1 in a year when the executive is elected, and 0 otherwise. Takes into consideration both presidential elections and legislative elections. Sources: ⟨http:// www.ifes.org/eguide/elecguide.htm⟩ plus other national sources.

ELLEG: dummy variable for legislative elections in a country, equal to 1 in the year the legislature is elected, independent of the form of government, and 0 otherwise. Sources: ⟨http://www.ifes.org/eguide/elecguide.htm⟩ plus other national sources.

$EL\_MAJ = MAJ * ELEX$. Sources: see *ELEX* and *MAJ*.

$EL\_MAJPAR = (1 - PRES) * MAJ * ELEX$. Sources: see *ELEX*, *PRES*, and *MAJ*.

$EL\_MAJPRE = PRES * MAJ * ELEX$. Sources: see *ELEX*, *PRES*, and *MAJ*.

$EL\_PAR = (1 - PRES) * ELEX$. Sources: see *ELEX* and *PRES*.

$EL\_PRE = PRES * ELEX$. Sources: see *ELEX* and *PRES*.

$EL\_PRO = (1 - MAJ) * ELEX$. Sources: see *ELEX* and *MAJ*.

$EL\_PROPAR = (1 - PRES) * (1 - MAJ) * ELEX$. Sources: see *ELEX*, *PRES*, and *MAJ*.

$EL\_PROPRE = PRES * (1 - MAJ) * ELEX$. Sources: see *ELEX*, *PRES*, and *MAJ*.

ENGFRAC: fraction of a country's population that speaks English as a native language. Source: Hall and Jones 1999.

EURFRAC: fraction of a country's population that speaks one of the major languages of western Europe: English, French, German, Portuguese, or Spanish. Source: Hall and Jones 1999.

FEDERAL: dummy variable, equal to 1 if a country has a federal political structure, 0 otherwise. Source: Adserà, Boix, and Paine 2001.

FRANKROM: natural log of the Frankel-Romer forecasted trade share, derived from a gravity model of international trade that takes into account only country population and geographical features. Source: Hall and Jones 1999.

GADP: index of a government's antidiversion policies, measured in 1986–1995. An equal-weighted average of five categories: (1) law and order, (2) bureaucratic quality, (3) corruption, (4) risk of expropriation, and (5) government repudiation of contracts (each of these items has higher values for governments with more effective policies toward supporting production); ranges from 0 to 1. Source: Hall and Jones 1999.

GASTIL: average of indexes for civil liberties and political rights, where each index is measured on a 1-to-7 scale with 1 representing the highest degree of freedom and 7 the lowest. Countries whose combined averages for political rights and civil liberties fall between 1.0 and 2.5 are designated "free," those whose averages fall between 3.0 and 5.5 are designated "partly free," and those whose averages fall between 5.5 and 7.0 "not free." Source: Freedom House, "Annual Survey of Freedom Country Ratings."

GDP: gross domestic product at current price. Sources: IMF-IFS CD-ROM and *IMF-IFS Yearbook.*

GINI_8090: Gini index of income distribution, computed as the average of two data points: the observation closest to 1980 and the observation closest to 1990. When data for only one of the two years are available, only that year is included. Source: Deininger and Squire 1996.

GOVEF: point estimate of "government effectiveness," the third cluster of the Kaufmann et al. (1999) governance indicators. Combines perceptions of the quality of public service provision, the quality of the bureaucracy, the competence of civil servants, the independence of the civil service from political pressures, and the credibility of the government's commitment to policies into a single grouping. Ranges from around 0 to around 10 (lower values correspond to better outcomes). Source: Kaufmann et al. (1999), available at ⟨http://www.worldbank.org/wbi/gac⟩.

GRAFT: point estimate of "Graft," the sixth cluster of Kaufmann et al.'s (1999) governance indicators, focusing on perceptions of corruption. Ranges from around 0 to around 10 (lower values correspond to better outcome). Source: Kaufmann et al. 1999, available at ⟨www.worldbank.org/wbi/gac⟩.

LAAM: regional dummy variable, equal to 1 if a country is in Latin America, Central America, or the Caribbean, 0 otherwise.

LAT01: rescaled variable for latitude, defined as the absolute value of *LATITUDE* divided by 90 and taking values between 0 and 1. Source: Hall and Jones 1999.

LATITUDE: distance from the equator (in degrees), ranging between −90° to 90°. Source: Hall and Jones 1999.

LCGEXP: one-year lag of *CGEXP*. Sources: see *CGEXP*.

LCGREV: one-year lag of *CGREV*. Sources: see *CGREV*.

LEGOR_FR, LEGOR_GE, LEGOR_SC, LEGOR_SO, LEGOR_UK: dummy variables for the origin of the legal system in a country, classifying a country's legal system as having its origin in French civil law (FR), German civil law (GE), Scandinavian law (SC), Socialist law (SO), or Anglo-Saxon common law (UK). Source: La Porta et al. 1998.

LELEX: one-year lag of *ELEX*. Sources: see *ELEX*.

LEL_MAJ: one-year lag of *EL_MAJ* Sources: see *ELEX* and *MAJ*.

LEL_MAJPAR: one-year lag of *EL_MAJPAR*. Sources: see *ELEX*, *PRES*, and *MAJ*.

LEL_MAJPRE: one-year lag of *EL_MAJPRE*. Sources: see *ELEX*, *PRES*, and *MAJ*.

LEL_PAR: one-year lag of *EL_PAR*. Sources: see *ELEX* and *PRES*.

LEL_PRE: one-year lag of *EL_PRE*. Sources: see *ELEX* and *PRES*.

LEL_PRO: one-year lag of *EL_PRO*. Sources: see *ELEX* and *MAJ*.

LEL_PROPAR: one-year lag of *EL_PROPAR*. Sources: see *ELEX*, *PRES*, and *MAJ*.

LEL_PROPRE: one-year lag of *EL_PROPRE*. Sources: see *ELEX*, *PRES*, and *MAJ*.

LIST: number of lower-house legislators elected through party list systems (see chapter 4 for further discussion and clarification). Sources: Cox 1997, International Institute for Democracy and Electoral Assistance 1997, Quain 1999, and Kurian 1998 and national sources.

LOGA: natural logarithm of total factor productivity, measured in 1988. Source: Hall and Jones 1999.

LOGYL: natural logarithm of output per worker, measured in 1988. Source: Hall and Jones 1999.

LPOP: natural logarithm of total population (in millions). Source: World Bank 2000.

LSPL: one-year lag of *SPL*. Sources: see *SPL*.

LSSW: one-year lag of *SSW*. Sources: See *SSW*.

LYP: natural logarithm of real GDP per capita in constant dollars (chain index) expressed in international prices, base year 1985. Data through 1992 are taken from Penn World table 5.6 (from the variable named RGDPC); data for 1993–1998 are computed from data from the World Development Indicators. These later observations are computed on the basis of the latest observation available from the Penn Word tables and the growth rates of GDP per capita in the subsequent years computed from the series of GDP at market prices (in constant 1995 U.S. dollars) and population, from the World

Development Indicators. Sources: Penn World tables, mark 5.6, available at ⟨http://datacentre2.chass.utoronto.ca/pwt/docs/topic.html⟩, World Bank, World Development Indicators, available at ⟨www.worldbank.org⟩.

MAGN: inverse of district magnitude, defined as *DISTRICTS* divided by *SEATS*. Sources: see *DISTRICTS* and *SEATS*.

MAJ: dummy variable for electoral systems, equal to 1 if all the lower house in a country is elected under plurality rule, 0 otherwise. Only legislative elections (lower house) are considered (see chapter 4 for further clarification). Sources: Cox 1997, International Institute for Democracy and Electoral Assistance 1997, Quain 1999, Kurian 1998, and national sources.

*MAJ_BAD = MAJ * GASTIL.* Sources: see *MAJ* and *GASTIL.*

*MAJ_GIN = MAJ * GINI_8090.* Sources: see *MAJ* and *GINI_8090.*

*MAJ_OLD = MAJ * AGE.* Sources: see *MAJ* and *AGE.*

*MAJPAR = MAJ * (1 − PRES).* Sources: see *MAJ* and *PRES.*

*MAJPRES = MAJ * PRES.* Sources: see *MAJ* and *PRES.*

MINING_GDP: share of mining sector divided by GDP. Source: UN National accounts.

MIXED: dummy variable for electoral systems, equal to 1 if the electoral formula for electing the lower house in a country is neither strict plurality rule nor strict proportionality, 0 otherwise. Semiproportional (or mixed) electoral rule identifies those electoral systems characterized by both proportional and first-past-the-post representation for allocating seats (for example Bolivia, Germany, and Italy after the reform of 1993). The share of the total number of seats allocated under the proportional rule can be greater or smaller than the complementary plurality-allocated share. Only legislative elections considered. Sources: Cox 1997, International Institute for Democracy and Electoral Assistance 1997, Quain 1999, and Kurian 1998 and national sources.

NEGYG: negative values of *YGAP*, 0 if *YGAP* is positive. Source: see *YGAP.*

OECD: dummy variable, equal to 1 for all countries that were members of OECD before 1993, 0 otherwise (except for Turkey, coded as 0 even though an OECD member before the 1990s).

OIL: price of oil in U.S. dollars. Source: Datastream.

OIL_EX: OIL times a dummy variable equal to 1 if the net exports of oil are positive, 0 otherwise. Source: See *OIL.*

OIL_IM: OIL times a dummy variable equal to 1 if the net exports of oil are negative, 0 otherwise. Source: See *OIL.*

PIND: computed as $1 - \frac{LIST}{SEATS}$. Sources: see *LIST* and *SEATS.*

PINDO: computed as $1 - \frac{LIST \times CLIST}{SEATS}$. Sources: see *LIST* and *SEATS.*

POLITY: score for democracy, computed by subtracting the *AUTOC* score from the *DEMOC* score and ranging from +10 (strongly democratic) to −10 (strongly autocratic). Source: Polity IV Project ⟨http://www.cidcm. umd.edu/inscr/polity/index.htm⟩.

POLITY_GT: interpolated version of *POLITY*, rescaled to have the same units as *GASTIL* (i.e., higher values denote worse democracies). Computed as the forecasted value obtained by regressing the rescaled values of *POLITY* on *GASTIL*. Sources: see *POLITY* and *GASTIL*.

POSYG: positive values of *YGAP*, 0 if *YGAP* is negative. Source: see *YGAP*.

PRES: dummy variable for forms of government, equal to 1 in presidential regimes, 0 otherwise. Only regimes in which the confidence of the assembly is not necessary for the executive to stay in power (even if an elected president is not chief executive, or if there is no elected president) are included among presidential regimes. Most semipresidential and premier-presidential systems are classified as parliamentary (see chapter 4 for further discussion and clarification). Sources: Shugart and Carey 1992 and national sources.

PRES_BAD = *PRES* ∗ *GASTIL*. Sources: see *PRES* and *GASTIL*.

PRES_GIN = *PRES* ∗ *GINI_8090*. Sources: see *PRES* and *GINI_8090*.

PRES_OLD = *PRES* ∗ *AGE*. Sources: see *PRES* and *POLITY*.

PROP1564: percentage of a country's population between 15 and 64 years old in the total population. Source: World Development Indicators CD-Rom 1999.

PROP65: percentage of the population over the age of 65 in the total population. Source: World Development Indicators CD-ROM 1999.

PROPAR = (1 − *MAJ*) ∗ (1 − *PRES*). Sources: see *MAJ* and *PRES*.

PROPRES = (1 − *MAJ*) ∗ *PRES*. Sources: see *MAJ* and *PRES*.

PROT80: percentage of the population in a country professing the Protestant religion in 1980. Source: La Porta et al. 1998.

SDM: district magnitude, computed as a weighted average, where the weight on each district magnitude in a country is the share of legislators running in districts of that magnitude. Relative to the original variable in Seddon et al. 2001, this variable is divided by 100 so that it takes on values comparable to those of *MAGN*. Source: Seddon et al. 2001.

SEATS: number of seats in lower or single chamber for the latest legislature of a country. Also related to the number of districts in which primary elections are held. Source: International Institute for Democracy and Electoral Assistance 1997, Quain 1999, Kurian 1998, and national sources.

SPL: central government budget surplus (if positive) or deficit (if negative) as a percentage of GDP, constructed using the item Government Finance–Deficit and Surplus in the IFS, divided by GDP at current prices and multiplied by 100. Source: IMF-IFS CD-ROM and *IMF-IFS Yearbook*.

SPROPN: share of legislators in a country elected in national (secondary or tertiary) districts rather than subnational (primary) electoral districts. Source: Seddon et al. 2001.

SSW: central government expenditures consolidated on social services and welfare as a percentage of GDP (as reported in the *IMF-GFS Yearbook*) divided by GDP and multiplied by 100. Sources: *IMF-GFS Yearbook* 2000 and IMF-IFS CD-ROM.

T_INDEP: number of years of independence for a country, ranging from 0 to 250 (the latter value is used for all noncolonized countries). Source: Wacziarg 1996.

TRADE: sum of exports and imports of goods and services measured as a share of GDP. Source: World Bank 2000.

YEARELE: year in which the current electoral rule in a country, as coded by *MAJ,* was first introduced, or the first year of democratic rule, whichever came later. Sources: national constitutional documents.

YEARREG: year in which the current form of government in a country, as coded by *PRES,* was first introduced, or the first year of democratic rule, whichever came later. Sources: national constitutional documents.

YRSOPEN: index for openness to international trade in a country, compiled by Sachs and Werner (1995), measuring the fraction of years during 1950–1994 that the economy in the country has been open. Ranges between 0 and 1. Source: Hall and Jones 1999.

YGAP: deviation of aggregate output from its trend value in percent, computed as the difference between the natural logarithm of real GDP in a country and its country-specific trend (obtained using the Hodrick-Prescott filter). Source for real GDP: World Bank 2000.

References

Acemoglu, D., P. Aghion, and F. Zilibotti. 2002. "Distance to Frontier, Selection and Economic Growth." Institute for International Economic Studies, Stockholm University. Mimeographed.

Acemoglu, D., S. Johnson, and J. Robinson. 2001. "The Colonial Origins of Comparative Development: An Empirical Investigation." *American Economic Review* 91, 1369–1401.

Ades, A., and R. di Tella. 1999. "Rents, Competition and Corruption." *American Economic Review* 89, 982–993.

Adserà, A., C. Boix, and M. Payne. 2001. "Are You Being Served? Political Accountability and Quality of Government." Working paper no. 438, Research Department, Inter-American Development Bank, Washington, D.C.

Alesina, A., and A. Drazen. 1991. "Why Are Stabilizations Delayed?" *American Economic Review* 81, 1170–1188.

Alesina, A., S. Ozler, N. Roubini, and P. Swagel. 1996. "Political Instability and Economic Growth." *Journal of Economic Growth* 1, 189–212.

Alesina, A., and R. Perotti. 1995. "The Political Economy of Budget Deficits." *IMF Staff Papers* (March), 1–37.

Alesina, A., N. Roubini, and G. Cohen. 1997. *Political Cycles and the Macroeconomy.* Cambridge: MIT Press.

Alesina, A., and G. Tabellini. 1990. "A Positive Theory of Fiscal Deficits and Government Debt." *Review of Economic Studies* 57, 403–414.

Alesina, A., and R. Wacziarg. 1998. "Openness, Country Size and Government." *Journal of Public Economics* 69, 305–321.

Alt, J., and R. Lowry. 1994. "Divided Government, Fiscal Institutions and Budget Deficits: Evidence from the States." *American Political Science Review* 88, 811–828.

Angrist, J., and A. Krueger. 1999. "Empirical Strategies in Labor Economics." In *Handbook of Labor Economics*, ed. O. Ashenfelter and D. Card., vol. 3A, 1277–1398. Amsterdam: North-Holland.

Angrist, J., and A. Krueger. 2001. "Instrumental Variables and the Search for Identification: From Supply and Demand to Natural Experiments." *Journal of Economic Perspectives* 15, 69–85.

Arellano, S., and M. Bond. 1991. "Some Tests of Specification for Panel Data: Monte Carlo Evidence and an Application to Employment Equations." *Review of Economic Studies* 58, 277–297.

Austen-Smith, D. 2000. "Redistributing Income under Proportional Representation." *Journal of Political Economy* 108, 1235–1269.

Baltagi, B. 1995. *Econometric Analysis of Panel Data*. Chichester, England: Wiley.

Barro, R. 1996. "Democracy and Growth." *Journal of Economic Growth* 1, 1–28.

Besley, T., and A. Case. 1995. "Does Political Accountability Affect Economic Policy Choices? Evidence from Gubernatorial Term Limits." *Quarterly Journal of Economics* 110, 769–798.

Besley, T., and A. Case. 2002. "Political Institutions and Policy Choices: Evidence from the United States." *Journal of Economic Literature*. Forthcoming.

Blais, A., and L. Massicotte. 1996. "Electoral Systems." In *Comparing Democracies: Elections and Voting in Global Perspective*, ed. L. LeDuc, R. Niemei, and P. Norris, 48–82. Thousand Oaks, Calif.: Sage.

Blanchard, O., and J. Wolfers. 2000. "The Role of Shocks and Institutions in the Rise of European Unemployment: The Aggregate Evidence. 1999 Harry Johnson Lecture." *Economic Journal* 100, C1–C33.

Block, S. 2000. "Political Business Cycles, Democratization and Economic Reform: The Case of Africa." Working paper, Fletcher School, Tufts University, Medford, Mass.

Boix, C. 1999. "Setting the Rules of the Game: The Choice of Electoral Systems in Advanced Democracies." *American Political Science Review* 93, 609–624.

Bollen, K. 1990. "Political Democracy: Conceptual and Measurement Traps." *Studies in Corporative International Development* 25, 7–24.

Brennan, G., and J. M. Buchanan. 1980. *The Power to Tax: Analytical Foundations of a Fiscal Constitution*. Cambridge: Cambridge University Press.

Buchanan, J. M., and G. Tullock. 1962. *The Calculus of Consent: Logical Foundation of Constitutional Democracy*. Ann Arbor: University of Michigan Press.

Cameron, D. R. 1978. "The Expansion of the Public Economy: A Comparative Analysis." *American Political Science Review* 72, 1203–1261.

Carey, J., and M. Shugart. 1995. "Incentives to Cultivate a Personal Vote: A Rank Ordering of Electoral Formulas." *Electoral Studies* 14, 417–439.

Castles, F. 1998. *Comparative Public Policy: Patterns of Postwar Transformation*. Cheltenham, England: Edward Elgar.

Colomer, J. 2001. *Political Institutions, Democracy and Social Choice*. Oxford: Oxford University Press.

CIA (Central Intelligence Agency). 2000. *The World Factbook*. Washington, D.C.

Cox, G. 1997. *Making Votes Count*. Cambridge: Cambridge University Press.

Deininger, K., and L. Squire. 1996. "Measuring Income Inequality: A New Database." *World Bank Economic Review* 10, 565–591.

Diermeier, D., H. Eraslan, and A. Merlo. 2000. "A Structural Model of Government Formation." *Econometrica*. Forthcoming.

Diermeier, D., and T. Feddersen. 1998. "Cohesion in Legislatures and the Vote of Confidence Procedure." *American Political Science Review* 92, 611–621.

Döring, H., ed. 1995. *Parliaments and Majority Rule in Western Europe*. Frankfurt: Campus Verlag.

Downes, A. 2000. "Federalism and Ethnic Conflict." University of Chicago. Mimeographed.

Drazen, A. 2000a. *Political Economy in Macroeconomics*. Princeton: Princeton University Press.

Drazen, A. 2000b. "The Political Business Cycle after 25 Years." In *NBER Macroeconomics Annual 2000*, ed. B. Bernanke and K. Rogoff, 75–138. Cambridge: MIT Press.

Duverger, M. 1980. "A New Political-System Model: Semi-Presidential Government." *European Journal of Political Research* 8, 165–187.

Easterly, W. 2002. "The Middle-Class Consensus and Economic Development." The World Bank, Washington, D.C. Mimeographed.

Easterly, W., and R. Levine. 2002. "Tropics, Germs and Crops: How Endowments Influence Economic Development." Working paper no. 9106, National Bureau of Economic Research, Cambridge, Mass.

Eckstein, H., and T. Gurr. 1975. *Patterns of Authority: A Structural Basis for Political Inquiry*. New York: Wiley Interscience.

Elster, J., and R. Slagstad, eds. 1988. *Constitutionalism and Democracy*. Cambridge: Cambridge University Press.

Engerman, S., and K. Sokoloff. 2000. "History Lessons: Institutions, Factor Endowments and Paths of Development in the New World." *Journal of Economic Perspectives* 14, 217–232.

Ferejohn, J. 1986. "Incumbent Performance and Electoral Control." *Public Choice* 50, 5–25.

Fisman, R., and R. Gatti. 1999. "Decentralization and Corruption: Cross-Country and Cross-State Evidence." The World Bank, Washington, D.C. Mimeographed.

Frankel, J. A., and D. Romer. 1996. "Trade and Growth: An Empirical Investigation." Working paper no. 5476, National Bureau of Economic Research, Cambridge, Mass.

Franzese, R. 2002. *Macroeconomic Policies of Developed Democracies*. Cambridge: Cambridge University Press. Forthcoming.

Frieden, J., and E. Stein, eds. 2001. *The Currency Game—Exchange Rate Politics in Latin America*. Washington, D.C.: Inter-America Development Bank.

Gavin, M., and R. Perotti. 1997. "Fiscal Policy in Latin America." In *NBER Macroeconomics Annual 1997*, ed. B. Bernanke and J. Rotemberg, 11–72. Cambridge: MIT Press.

Gonzalez, M. 1999. "Political Budget Cycles and Democracy: A Multi-Country Analysis." Princeton University, Princeton, N.J. Mimeographed.

Goode, R. 1984. *Government Finance in Developing Countries*. Washington, D.C.: Brookings.

Green, W. 2000. *Econometric Analysis*. New York: McMillan.

Grilli, V., Masciandaro, D., and G. Tabellini. 1991. "Political and Monetary Institutions and Public Financial Policies in the Industrial Countries." *Economic Policy* 13, 342–392.

Grofman, B., and A. Lijphart, eds. 1986. *Electoral Laws and Their Political Consequences*. New York: Agathon.

Grossman, G., and E. Helpman. 2001. *Special Interest Politics*. Cambridge: MIT Press.

Gunnemark, E. 1991. *Countries, Peoples and Their Languages: The Geolinguistic Handbook*. Gothenburg, Sweden: Geolingua.

Hall, R., and C. Jones. 1997. "Levels of Economic Activities across Countries." *American Economic Review Papers and Proceedings* 87, 173–177.

Hall, R., and C. Jones. 1999. "Why Do Some Countries Produce So Much More Output per Worker than Others?" *Quarterly Journal of Economics* 114, 83–116.

Hallerberg, M., and J. von Hagen. 1998. "Electoral Institutions and the Budget Process." In *Democracy, Decentralization and Deficits in Latin America*, ed. K. Fukasaku and R. Hausmann, 65–94. Paris: Organisation for Economic Cooperation and Development.

Hallerberg, M., and J. von Hagen. 1999. "Electoral Institutions, Cabinet Negotiations, and Budget Deficits in the European Union." In *Fiscal Institutions and Fiscal Performance*, ed. J. Poterba and J. von Hagen, 209–232. Chicago: University of Chicago Press.

Heckman, J. J. 1974. "Shadow Wages, Market Wages and Labor Supply." *Econometrica* 42, 679–693.

Heckman, J. J. 1976a. "The Common Structure of Statistical Models of Truncation, Sample Selection and Limited Dependent Variables and a Simple Estimator for Such Models." *Annals of Economic and Social Measurement* 5, 475–492.

Heckman, J. J. 1976b. "Simultaneous Equations Models with Continuous and Discrete Endogenous Variables and Structural Shifts." In *Studies in Non-Linear Estimation*, ed. S. Goldfeld and R. Quandt. Cambridge, MA: Ballinger.

Heckman, J. J. 1979. "Sample Selection Bias as a Specification Error." *Econometrica* 47, 153–161.

Heckman, J. J., J. R. Lalonde, and J. Smith. 1999. "The Economics and Econometrics of Active Labor Market Programs." In *Handbook of Labor Economics*, ed. O. Ashenfelter and D. Card, vol. 3A, 1865–2095. Amsterdam: North-Holland.

Hsiao, C. 1986. *Analysis of Panel Data*. Cambridge: Cambridge University Press.

Huber, E., C. Ragin, and J. Stephens. 1993. "Social Democracy, Christian Democracy and the Welfare State." *American Journal of Sociology* 99, 711–749.

Huber, J. 1996. "The Vote of Confidence in Parliamentary Democracies." *American Political Science Review* 90, 269–282.

Hunter, B., ed. 1992. *Ethnologue: Languages of the World*. 12th ed. Gothenburg, Sweden: Länstryckeriet.

Huntington, S. 1991. *The Third Wave Democratization in the Late Twentieth Century*. Norman: University of Oklahoma Press.

Ichino, A. 2002. "The Problem of Causality in the Analysis of Educational Choices and Labor Market Outcomes." Lecture notes, European University Institute, Firenze, Italy.

International Institute for Democracy and Electoral Assistance. 1997. *Handbook of Electoral System Design*. Stockholm: Author.

Kaufmann, D., and A. Kraay. 2002. "Growth without Governance." The World Bank, Washington, D.C. Mimeographed.

Kaufmann, D., A. Kraay, and P. Zoido-Lobatón. 1999. "Aggregating Governance Indicators." Working paper no. 2195, The World Bank, Washington, D.C.

King, G., and L. Zeng. 2001. "How Factual Is Your Counterfactual?" Harvard University, Cambridge, Mass. Mimeographed.

Knack, S., and P. Keefer. 1995. "Institutions and Economic Performance: Cross-Country Tests Using Alternative Institutional Measures." *Economics and Politics* 7, 207–227.

Kontopoulos, Y., and R. Perotti. 1999. "Government Fragmentation and Fiscal Policy Outcomes: Evidence from the OECD Countries." In *Fiscal Institutions and Fiscal Preference*, ed. J. Poterba and J. von Hagen, 81–102. Chicago: University of Chicago Press.

Kurian, G., ed. 1998. *World Encyclopedia of Parliaments and Legislatures*. Chicago: Fitzroy Dearborn.

Lambsdorff, J. G. 1998. "Corruption in Comparative Perception." In *The Economics of Corruption*, ed. A. K. Jain, 81–109. Boston: Kluwer Academic.

Landes, W. 1968. "The Economics of Fair Employment Laws." *Journal of Political Economy* 76, 507–552.

La Porta, R., F. Lopez-De-Silanes, A. Shleifer, and R. Vishny. 1998. "Law and Finance." *Journal of Political Economy* 106, 1113–1155.

La Porta, R., F. Lopez-De-Silanes, A. Shleifer, and R. Vishny. 1999. "The Quality of Government." *Journal of Law, Economics and Organization* 15, 222–279.

Lijphart, A. 1984a. *Democracies*. New Haven: Yale University Press.

Lijphart, A. 1984b. "Advances in the Comparative Study of Electoral Systems." *World Politics* 36, 424–436.

Lijphart, A. 1990. "The Political Consequences of Electoral Laws 1945–85." *American Political Science Review* 84, 481–496.

Lijphart, A. 1994. *Electoral Systems and Party Systems*. Oxford: Oxford University Press.

Lijphart, A. 1999. *Patterns of Democracy: Government Forms and Performance in Thirty-Six Countries*. New Haven: Yale University Press.

Linz, J. 1990. "The Perils of Presidentialism." *Journal of Democracy* 1, 51–69.

Lipset, S. M., and S. Rokkan. 1967. *Party Systems and Vote Alignments: Cross National Perspectives*. New York: Free Press.

Lizzeri, A., and N. Persico. 2001. "The Provision of Public Goods under Alternative Electoral Incentives." *American Economic Review* 91, 225–245.

Lowry, R., J. Alt, and K. Ferree. 1998. "Political Outcomes and Electoral Accountability in American States." *American Political Science Review* 92, 759–774.

Maddala, G. 1977. *Econometrics*. Tokyo: McGraw Hill.

Maddala, G. 1983. *Limited Dependent and Qualitative Variables in Econometrics*. Cambridge: Cambridge University Press.

Mauro, P. 1995. "Corruption and Growth." *Quarterly Journal of Economics* 110, 681–712.

Meltzer, A., and S. Richard. 1981. "A Rational Theory of the Size of Government." *Journal of Political Economy* 89, 914–927.

Milesi-Ferretti, G.-M., R. Perotti, and M. Rostagno. 2002. "Electoral Systems and the Composition of Public Spending." *Quarterly Journal of Economics* 117, 609–657.

Mokyr, J. 1990. *Lever of Riches: Technological Creativity and Economic Progress*. Oxford: Oxford University Press.

Mueller, D. 1996. *Constitutional Democracy*. Oxford: Oxford University Press.

Myerson, R. 1993. "Effectiveness of Electoral Systems for Reducing Government Corruption: A Game Theoretic Analysis." *Games and Economic Behaviour* 5, 118–132.

Myerson, R. 1999. "Theoretical Comparison of Electoral Systems. 1998 Joseph Schumpeter Lecture." *European Economic Review* 43, 671–697.

North, D. 1981. *Structure and Change in Economic History*. New York: Norton.

Olson, M. 1982. *The Rise and Decline of Nations*. New Haven: Yale University Press.

Parente, S., and E. Prescott. 2000. *Barriers to Riches*. Cambridge: MIT Press.

Persson, T., G. Roland, and G. Tabellini. 1997. "Separation of Powers and Political Accountability." *Quarterly Journal of Economics* 112, 310–327.

Persson, T., G. Roland, and G. Tabellini. 2000. "Comparative Politics and Public Finance." *Journal of Political Economy* 108, 1121–1161.

Persson, T., and G. Tabellini. 1999. "The Size and Scope of Government: Comparative Politics with Rational Politicians. 1998 Alfred Marshall Lecture." *European Economic Review* 43, 699–735.

Persson, T., and G. Tabellini. 2000a. *Political Economics: Explaining Economic Policy*. Cambridge: MIT Press.

Persson, T., and G. Tabellini. 2000b. "Political Institutions and Economic Policy Outcomes: What Are the Stylized Facts?" Institute for International Economic Studies, Stockholm University. Mimeographed.

Persson, T., and G. Tabellini. 2002. "Do Constitutions Cause Large Governments? Quasi-Experimental Evidence." *European Economic Review* 46, 908–918.

Persson, T., G. Tabellini, and F. Trebbi. 2003. "Electoral Rules and Corruption." *Journal of the European Economic Association*, forthcoming.

Pettersson-Lidbom, P. 2002. "A Test of the Rational Electoral-Cycle Hypothesis." Stockholm University. Mimeographed.

Pierson, P., ed. 2001. *The New Politics of the Welfare State*. Oxford: Oxford University Press.

Pommerehne, W. W., and B. S. Frey. 1978. "Bureaucratic Behaviour in Democracy: A Case Study." *Public Finance* 33, 98–112.

Powell Jr., G. B. 1982. *Contemporary Democracies: Participation, Stability and Violence*. Cambridge: Cambridge University Press.

Powell Jr., G. B. 1989. "Constitutional Design and Citizen Electoral Control." *Journal of Theoretical Politics* 1, 107–130.

Powell Jr., G. B. 2000. *Elections as Instruments of Democracy*. New Haven and London: Yale University Press.

Quain, A., ed. 1999. *The Political Reference Almanac*. 1999/2000 ed. Arlington, Va.: Keynote. Available online at ⟨www.polisci.com⟩.

Rae, D. 1967. *The Political Consequences of Electoral Laws*. New Haven: Yale University Press.

Rodrik, D. 1998. "Why Do More Open Economies Have Bigger Governments?" *Journal of Political Economy* 106, 997–1032.

Rogoff, K. 1990. "Equilibrium Political Budget Cycles." *American Economic Review* 80, 21–36.

Rogowski, R. 1987. "Trade and the Variety of Democratic Institutions." *International Organization* 41, 203–223.

Rokkan, S. 1970. *Citizens, Elections, Parties: Approaches to the Comparative Study of the Process of Development*. Oslo: Oslo Universitets-förlaget.

Roll, R., and J. Talbott. 2002. "Why Many Developing Countries Just Aren't." Anderson School, University of California, Los Angeles. Mimeographed.

Rosenbaum, P., and D. Rubin. 1983. "The Central Role of the Propensity Score in Observational Studies for Causal Effects." *Biometrika* 70, 41–55.

Roubini, N., and J. Sachs. 1989. "Political and Economic Determinants of Budget Deficits in the Industrial Democracies." *European Economic Review* 33, 903–933.

Ruud, P. 2000. *An Introduction to Classical Econometric Theory*. Oxford and New York: Oxford University Press.

Sachs, J., and A. Werner. 1995. "Economic Reform and the Process of Global Interpretation." *Brookings Papers on Economic Activity* 1, 1–95.

Sartori, G. 1994. *Comparative Constitutional Engineering: An Inquiry into Structures, Incentives and Outcomes*. London: Macmillan.

Scartascini, C., and M. Crain. 2001. "The Size and Composition of Government Spending in Multi-Party Systems." George Mason University, Fairfax, Va. Mimeographed.

Schuknecht, L. 1996. "Political Business Cycles in Developing Countries." *Kyklos* 49, 155–170.

Seddon, J., A. Gaviria, U. Panizza, and E. Stein. 2001. "Political Particuliarism around the World." Stanford University, Stanford, Calif. Mimeographed.

Shi, M., and J. Svensson. 2001. "Conditional Political Business Cycles: Theory and Evidence." Institute for International Economic Studies, Stockholm University. Mimeographed.

Shugart, M. 2001. "Electoral Efficiency and the Move to Mixed-Member Systems." *Electoral Studies* 20, 173–193.

Shugart, M., and J. Carey. 1992. *Presidents and Assemblies: Constitutional Design and Electoral Dynamics*. Cambridge: Cambridge University Press.

Shugart, M., and M. Wattenberg, eds. 2001. *Mixed Member Electoral Systems: The Best of Both Worlds?* Oxford: Oxford University Press.

Staiger, D., and J. Stock. 1997. "Instrumental Variables Regression with Weak Instruments." *Econometrica* 65, 557–586.

Stock, J. 1999. "Instrumental Variables in Economics and Statistics." In *International Encyclopedia for the Social and Behavioral Sciences*. Elsevier Science. Forthcoming.

Strom, K. 1990. *Minority Governments and Majority Rule*. Cambridge: Cambridge University Press.

Strömberg, D. 2002. "Optimal Campaigning in Presidential Elections: The Probability of Being Florida." Institute for International Economic Studies, Stockholm University. Mimeographed.

Swank, D. 2002. *Global Capital Political Institutions and Policy Change in Developed Welfare States*. Cambridge: Cambridge University Press.

Taagepera, R., and M. Shugart. 1989. *Seats and Votes: The Effects and Determinants of Electoral Systems*. New Haven: Yale University Press.

Tanzi, V. 1998. "Corruption and the World: Cases, Consequences, Scope and Cures." *IMF Staff Papers* 45, 559–594.

Treisman, D. 2000. "The Causes of Corruption: A Cross-National Study." *Journal of Public Economics* 76, 399–457.

Tsebelis, G. 1995. "Decision-Making in Political Systems: Veto Players in Presidentialism, Parliamentarism, Multicameralism and Multipartyism." *British Journal of Political Science* 25, 289–326.

Tsebelis, G. 1999. "Veto Players and Law Production in Parliamentary Democracies." *American Political Science Review* 93, 591–608.

Tsebelis, G. 2002. *Veto Players: How Political Institutions Work*. Princeton: Princeton University Press.

Velasco, A. 1999. "A Model of Endogenous Fiscal Deficit and Delayed Fiscal Reforms." In *Fiscal Rules and Fiscal Performance*, ed. J. Poterba and J. von Hagen. Chicago: University of Chicago Press.

Wacziarg, R. 1996. "Information to Create Colonization Dummies." Harvard University, Cambridge, Mass. Mimeographed.

Wagner, A. 1893. *Grundlegung der Politischen Oekonomie* (Foundation of Political Economy). 3rd ed. Leipzig, Germany: C.F. Winter.

Wei, S. J. 1997a. "How Taxing Is Corruption on International Investors." Working paper no. 6030, National Bureau of Economic Research, Cambridge, Mass.

Wei, S. J. 1997b. "Why Is Corruption So Much More Taxing than Tax? Arbitrariness Kills." Working paper no. 6255, National Bureau of Economic Research, Cambridge, Mass.

Wiggins, V. 2000. "Two-Stage Least Squares Regression." Available online at ⟨http://www.stata.com/support/tags/stat/irreg.html⟩.

Wooldridge, J. 2002. *Econometric Analysis of Cross Section and Panel Data*. Cambridge: MIT Press.

World Bank. 2000. *World Development Indicators*. CD-ROM. Washington, D.C.: Author.

Name Index

Subject Index